THE LAST KING IN INDIA

ROSIE LLEWELLYN-JONES

The Last King in India

Wajid 'Ali Shah, 1822–1887

HURST & COMPANY, LONDON

First published in the United Kingdom in 2014 by
C. Hurst & Co. (Publishers) Ltd.,
41 Great Russell Street, London, WC1B 3PL
© Rosie Llewellyn-Jones, 2014
All rights reserved.

Printed in India

Distributed in the United States, Canada and Latin America by
Oxford University Press, 198 Madison Avenue, New York, NY 10016,
United States of America

The right of Rosie Llewellyn-Jones to be identified as the author of this publication is asserted by her in accordance with the Copyright, Designs and Patents Act, 1988.

A Cataloguing-in-Publication data record for this book is available from the British Library.

ISBN: 978-1-84904-408-0

www.hurstpublishers.com

This book is printed on paper from registered sustainable and managed sources.

*To the memory of Stanley Menezes,
'better than the best'*

CONTENTS

Acknowledgements	ix
List of Illustrations	xi
Chronology	xiii
Glossary	xix
Introduction	1
1. 'That Energetic Old Lady'	11
2. Pageants and Pantomimes	49
3. The Sorrows of Akhtar	83
4. The House of Fairies	127
5. At Garden Reach	165
6. A Tigress Escapes from the Menagerie	205
7. A Mimic Kingdom	239
Conclusion	275
Notes	283
Bibliography	301
Index	307

ACKNOWLEDGEMENTS

Although writing is a solitary task, luckily there are people with whom I can share my ideas, my finds and my enthusiasm. A number of friends (and some email acquaintances) have been helpful, particularly in finding images, which I did not have time to search for. I would like to thank the following:

Nawab Jafar Mir Abdullah, an old friend, who has done much to keep the spirit of nawabi Lucknow alive, not least with his theatrical interpretations of the king.

Sahebzada Humayun 'Ali, a direct descendant of the king, who provided me with some images and much material on the royal burial ground near Garden Reach.

Dr Sâqib Bâburî, who has not only advised on mundane matters like the proper transliteration and meaning of Urdu and Persian words, but has also made many helpful scholarly suggestions. Like me, he shares a growing feeling that some, at least, of Wajid 'Ali Shah's literary compositions deserve to be made available to a wider audience.

Michael Brooke and his cousin Michael Douglas, descendants of Sir William Sleeman, who identified a previously unknown portrait of their ancestor, and led me to see him in a more sympathetic light.

Christopher Buyers, whose online genealogical tables of the Awadh royal family (and many other royal families) are invaluable in tracing the tangled mesh of Wajid 'Ali Shah's hundreds of wives and descendants.

ACKNOWLEDGEMENTS

Dr Sophie Gordon, curator of the Royal Photographic Collection, Windsor Castle, who helpfully found references to the Awadh family's visit to England in 1856–58.

Charles Greig, who alerted me to images of the king in private hands, and who shared some Lucknow adventures with me.

Pramod Kumar KG, of Eka Cultural Resources and Research, who found a number of images of the king.

Shahanshah Mirza, his wife Fatima and his father Sahebzada Wasif Mirza, direct descendants of the king, for their unfailing hospitality, courtesy and encouragement, as well as their practical help in taking me to Garden Reach and answering queries on Shi'a rituals.

Mirza Kaukab Qadr, author of *Vājid 'Alī Shāh kī adabī aur saqāfatī khidmāt*, the most comprehensive catalogue to date of the king's works, and a direct descendant, who kindly gave me some images of Garden Reach.

Jaya Ravindran of the Reading Room at the National Archives, New Delhi, who has helped me find the research material for this book, as for previous books.

Mr Kenneth Robbins, a fellow Lucknow enthusiast, who shares his finds with me.

Dr S. A. Sadiq, a direct descendant, who has an impressive library and picture gallery on the royal families of Awadh and Murshidabad.

Emma Stuart of the Royal Library, Windsor Castle, who let me examine the beautiful *Ishqnama* manuscript.

Peter Wynne-James, the grand-nephew of Sir Trevredyn Rashleigh Wynne, who purchased the Sultan Khana at Garden Reach on the king's death, when he was appointed agent and chief engineer of the newly formed Bengal Nagpur Railway.

To all of the above-named, my most grateful thanks. Any errors in this book are the sole responsibility of the author.

LIST OF ILLUSTRATIONS

(Between pages 136 and 137)

1. The queen mother, Janab-i 'Aliyyah, enters the train at Southampton station. From the *Illustrated London News* 6 September 1856. Author's collection.
2. The queen mother and party at Drury Lane Theatre, London. From the *Illustrated London News* 14 March 1857. Author's collection.
3. The Awadh princes, Sikandar Hashmat and Hamid 'Ali, at the Art Treasures Exhibition, Manchester, July 1857. Photograph by Leonida Caldesi. Royal Collection Trust © Her Majesty Queen Elizabeth II 2013.
4. Prince Sikandar Hashmat, embellished photograph, i.e. the crown and robes have been painted on to an existing photograph. Private collection.
5. Wajid 'Ali Shah in Qaisarbagh. Painting on cloth, c.1851. From the collection of Kenneth and Joyce Robbins.
6. Wajid 'Ali Shah celebrates the Basant (Spring) Festival on the river Gomti. Sir William Sleeman, in red coat, sits next to the king. Hussainabad Picture Gallery, Lucknow.
7. The Great Vine and the Lanka, Qaisarbagh, Lucknow. Artist unknown, c.1862. © Alkazi Collection of Photography, Delhi.

LIST OF ILLUSTRATIONS

8. Wajid 'Ali Shah is recognised as heir apparent, c.1847. Gouache on paper. Private collection.
9. Prince Mustafa 'Ali Khan, elder brother of Wajid 'Ali Shah. Attributed to Felice Beato, March/April 1858. Albumen silver print 18.4 x 13.2 cm. © The J. Paul Getty Museum, Los Angeles.
10. Wajid 'Ali Shah greets Viscount Hardinge, the governor general, at Lucknow c.1847. Gouache on paper. © The British Library, London Add. Or. 742.
11. Wajid 'Ali Shah with wife (possibly Akhtar Mahal) and child. Photograph by Ahmad 'Ali Khan, early 1850s. From William Low, *Lieutenant-Colonel Gould Hunter-Weston* (1914).
12. Wajid 'Ali Shah, oil painting, possibly from a lost original by George Duncan Beechey. Hussainabad Picture Gallery, Lucknow.
13. Wajid 'Ali Shah and Safaraz Mahal, from the *Ishqnamah*, folio 263, Windsor Castle. Royal Collection Trust © Her Majesty Queen Elizabeth II 2013.
14. Wajid 'Ali Shah and Begam Hazrat Mahal from the *Ishqnamah*, folio 155. The caption reads: The likeness of Iftikhar-un-nisa' Khanum, Lady Hazratmahall, before the Sultan-e 'Alam, year 1261 of the Hijrah. c.1845. Windsor Castle. Royal Collection Trust © Her Majesty Queen Elizabeth II 2013.
15. Wajid 'Ali Shah in his *zananah* at Lucknow, late 1840s/early 1850s. Gouache on paper. State Museum, Lucknow.
16. The Sultan Khana today, Garden Reach, Kolkata. Author's collection.
17. Wajid 'Ali Shah, date and photographer unknown. Private collection.
18. Wajid 'Ali Shah in old age, date and photographer unknown. © Alkazi Collection of Photography, Delhi.

CHRONOLOGY

Wajid 'Ali Shah 1822–1887

1822	**born 30 July** at Lucknow, the second son of Prince (later King) Amjad 'Ali Shah and the prince's first wife, Malikah Kishwar (later known as Janab-i 'Aliyyah)
1830	sexually assaulted by the servant woman Rahiman
1837	**14 November**, preliminary marriage ceremony is delayed due to death of his uncle, King Nasir ud-Din Haider. His grandfather, Mohammed 'Ali Shah, becomes king, thus placing Wajid 'Ali Shah in line to the throne
1838	**January**, first nikah marriage to Khas Mahal is finalised
1839	first son, Nosherwan Qadr, born deaf and dumb
1842	Amjad 'Ali Shah becomes king. Wajid 'Ali Shah declared heir apparent, while his elder brother, Mustafa 'Ali Khan, is passed over
1843	heir apparent writes *Radha Kanhaiya ka Qissa*, a play based on an episode in Lord Krishna's life
1845	British Resident John Shakespear complains to the governor general about the heir apparent
1846	first performance of the play *Darya-i-Ta'ashshuq*, written by the heir apparent

CHRONOLOGY

1847	**13 February**, Wajid 'Ali Shah becomes king on the death of his father
	20 February, false report of human sacrifice at a Hindu temple
	8 April, chief minister attacked in his coach at Golaganj
	5 July, chief minister dismissed and 'Ali Naqi Khan becomes new minister
	8 November, Viscount Hardinge, the governor general, visits Lucknow and threatens annexation
1847/8	the *Ishqnamah*, a romantic autobiography, is written by the king
1848	land revenue reforms proposed by the king are rejected by the governor general. Building of Qaisarbagh Palace begins at a cost of 80 lakhs
	3 March, Dr Aloys Sprenger arrives to catalogue the royal libraries
	17 March, outgoing governor general refuses to meet the king or his heir
	27 May, king sends letter of welcome to Lord Dalhousie, the new Governor General
1849	**11 January**, William Sleeman appointed as British Resident at Court
	1 December, Sleeman begins his tour of rural Awadh
1850	Dalhousie travels through Cawnpore but declines to meet the king
	September, Janab-i 'Aliyyah orders her son, the king, to divorce six of his wives, including Begam Hazrat Mahal, mother of a young son
	Alambagh, a country house, is built and named after the king's first wife
1851	Sleeman warns the king against employing musicians in government posts
	5 June, the king marries a second nikah wife, Akhtar Mahal, then aged eleven

CHRONOLOGY

	30 July, Dalhousie sarcastically suggests that the king send his head in a crown to the Great Exhibition in London
	December, Dalhousie fails to visit Lucknow or receive anyone from the Court
1852	further criticism of the king by Sleeman. Qaisarbagh Palace completed and its gardens laid out
1853	the king's troops mutiny because they have not been paid
	14 April, two ambassadors sent by the king to Dalhousie are turned away
	July, the first Yogi Mela is staged in Qaisarbagh
	December, Sleeman sends a privately printed copy of his *Journey through the Kingdom of Oude* to Dalhousie
1854	**November,** Sleeman resigns because of ill health
	December, James Outram is appointed new Resident
1855	**January,** a 21-gun salute ordered to mark British victory in the Crimea
	February, Outram sends king a warning letter about bloodshed at Ayodhya
	Private Life of an Eastern King published in London causes a sensation
	July/August, clashes and bloodshed between Muslims and Hindus at Ayodhya. The king sends troops who kill between 300 and 400 Muslims
	21 November, Court of Directors order Dalhousie to annex Awadh
1856	**15 January,** Dalhousie orders Outram to prepare troops for annexation
	13 February, king refuses to sign annexation treaty
	28 February, Lord Canning sworn in as new governor general
	13 March, king and relatives leave Lucknow *en route* for Calcutta

CHRONOLOGY

	13 May, king arrives by boat in Calcutta; Canning refuses to discuss the annexation
	3 June, king moves to Garden Reach
	15 June, king's mother, brother and son leave Calcutta for London
	15 August, the royal party arrive at Southampton
	December, Canning tells the king that annexation is irreversible
1857	**16 January**, king's brother and son meet the Court of Directors in London
	10 May, the Great Uprising begins in Meerut and quickly spreads to Delhi
	16 June, king is arrested and taken to Fort William
	1 July, siege of the British Residency at Lucknow begins
	4 July, the royal party meet Queen Victoria at Buckingham Palace
	5 July, Begam Hazrat Mahal's son crowned king in Qaisarbagh Palace
	17 November, British Residency at Lucknow relieved
1858	**24 January**, king's mother dies in Paris hotel
	25 February, king's brother dies in London
	1–15 March, Lucknow recaptured by British troops. Begam Hazrat Mahal flees to Kathmandu
	2 August, East India Company abolished by Government of India Act
	1 November, Proclamation by Queen Victoria marks the end of the Uprising
1859	**9 July**, king released from prison, returns to Garden Reach
1860	**10 April**, severe fire at Garden Reach
	27 August, king sells the crown jewels returned to him by the British

CHRONOLOGY

1862	king mortgages Garden Reach house to meet his debts
1864	**5 October** great cyclone hits Calcutta, 60,000 people killed
1866	**June**, death of Safdar 'Ali leaves king facing huge debts
1867	king employs Amir 'Ali Khan as accountant and manager
	9 August, king warned by governor general to 'set his house in order'
1868/70	rebuilding programme at Garden Reach
1869	lavish spending by king on his menagerie
1871/3	second phase of rebuilding at Garden Reach
1874	death of heir apparent, Prince Hamid 'Ali
1877	king complains to governor general about Mowbray Thomson, his new agent
1878	king requests 50 lakhs to meet his debts, but is refused
	31 July, king divorces 27 wives in pension squabble
1879	**6 January**, two tigers escape from the king's menagerie
	10 April, management of king's affairs passes to Bengal government
	1 May, Commission set up to examine king's affairs
1880	**7 February**, Commission recommend changes in king's household
	December, king 'understood to be impotent'; further births will not be recognised
1882	king congratulates Queen Victoria after failed assassination attempt at Windsor railway station
1884	king sends letters of complaint to the governor general
1886	king's agent suggests measures to be taken on Wajid 'Ali Shah's death

CHRONOLOGY

1887	25 April, king falls ill
	20/21 June, Queen Victoria's Golden Jubilee celebrations
	15 September, looting at Garden Reach reported
	21 September, king dies at Garden Reach and is buried in Sibtainabad Imambarah, Calcutta
1888	**June,** properties at Garden Reach are auctioned off to shipping companies

GLOSSARY

Indian names and titles

Indian proper names can be complicated, with prefixes and suffixes. Take, for example, the name of Wajid 'Ali Shah's younger brother, General Mirza Muhammad Jawad 'Ali Sikandar Hashmat Bahadur. He was commander-in-chief of the Awadh Army, and thus a General. *Mirza* denotes a prince, because he was the son of a king. Muhammad Jawad 'Ali were his proper names and Sikandar Hashmat his title, by which he was generally known. *Bahadur* means 'brave' and was an honorific title, sometimes used with *khan*, meaning 'lord', so a distinguished man could be awarded the suffix *khan bahadur*, but this is not part of a proper name. Europeans were sometimes given the title *bahadur*, and so was the East India Company itself. The names of noblewomen are equally complex. Many had the honorific title 'nawab', seemingly a male name, which means 'deputy' (see below), so one needs to look for the feminine qualifier, which will be *begam*, *mahal* or *sahibah*.

Working men's names were often prefixed with their profession, so we get Maulawi Masih-ud-Din Khan Bahadur. *Khan bahadur*, as we have seen, is an honorific title. *Maulawi* ('lordly') is a learned man, often but not always, a cleric. Masih-ud-Din is the man's name, stripped of its titles. Finally there are the honorific state titles, so Amin-ud-daulah ('trusted one of the state') is the state title of Imdad Husain Khan, one-time chief minister of Awadh.

GLOSSARY

Indian children are also given affectionate pet names at birth, which are different from their proper names, and can, embarrassingly, often follow them into adulthood. We do not know what Wajid 'Ali Shah's pet name was; but as a poet he adopted the pen name of Akhtar, a celestial star or star of fortune.

amir	a ruler, chief or noble
bakhshi	paymaster
barahdari	an open-sided pavilion, traditionally with twelve arched openings
bhang	beverage prepared from leaves of the cannabis plant
bungalow	from *banglah*, a single-storeyed dwelling or temple, typical of Bengal vernacular architecture; later a building of two or more storeys, with a flat roof
cantonment	initially an area set aside for the use of the Company's army, including parade ground and barracks. Later it included residential accommodation for officers' families, with church, cemetery, library, ice-club, bandstand and gardens.
coolies	from *quli* for 'servant', labourers or porters
Court of Directors	the executive body of the East India Company in London, who liaised with the Board of Control, a government-appointed body overseeing the workings of the Company
daftar	office
dak (sometimes dawk)	the Indian postal system, that is, letters

GLOSSARY

	carried by runners, or by dedicated mail carriages
diwan	a collection of poems, a portfolio or a finance minister/accountant
durbar/darbar	a formal assembly of an Indian court of religion or royalty, also employed by British royalty in India to summon native rulers
firman	authorised royal edict, validated with royal seals and autographs attached
ghat	a landing stage onto a river, often with steps
godown	a shed, or warehouse
Governor General	based in Government House, Calcutta and from 1833 in charge of all Company administration in India. After the Company's abolition in 1858, the title of Governor General continued, now linked to that of viceroy, the British monarch's representative abroad.
hakeem	physician, native Muslim doctor practising the yunani (Greek) tradition of medicine
haveli	palatial mansion, walled villa or courtyard house, often an ornate, high-status residence
hookah/huqqah	pipe for smoking tobacco, the vapour of which is passed through scented water before being inhaled
howdah	covered litter, a box-like structure fitted usually to an elephant's or camel's back, containing seats, a canopy and curtains for passengers
hukumnamah	a written order or warrant

xxi

GLOSSARY

imambarah	building for Shi'a commemorations during Muharram and other ritual gatherings, often incorporating tombs
'itr	otto (of roses), attar, perfume from rose petals, developed at the Mughal court
'izzat	honour, status or respect
jagir	a gift of land for a person's lifetime
Janab-i 'Aliyyah	'Her Sublime Excellency', title for a Queen Mother, here for Wajid 'Ali Shah's mother
karindah	worker, agent or manager
kharitah	purse, envelope, charter or map, but here an important official letter
kincob	gold brocade
lakh	a hundred thousand, usually rupees
mu'afi	exemption, remission, a rent-free grant
maulawi	'lordly' or 'milord', a learned man, often but not always a religious cleric, also used as a title
mamtu'at	plural of wives married through the practice of mut'ah
marsiyah	dirge, solemn poetry usually recited during Muharram
masnavi	narrative poems, usually epic or romantic in theme
mela	a fête
mohubutnamah	a friendly letter
mohur	a gold coin, first struck in sixteenth-century India
Muharram	first month of the Islamic lunar calendar (hijri), a time of mourning, especially for Shi'as
mujtahid	a religious leader among Shi'a scholars, noted for interpreting the Qur'an and the Shi'ite tradition

GLOSSARY

munshi	a scribe or writer, also used as a title
musha'ira	a gathering of poets, often at night
mut'ah	a temporary marriage, underpinned by contract
nawab, nawwab	also Anglicised as nabob, originally meaning a deputy or governor. The first nawabs in Awadh and other states were deputies of the Mughal emperor. Also a term of respect for eminent Muslims.
nazr	a gift from an inferior to a superior
nikah	permanent marriage, underpinned by contract
paan	addictive chew made from shaved betel nut and other ingredients, wrapped in betel leaf, supposedly eaten to refresh the breath and aid digestion, but it eventually rots the teeth
pandal	large constructions of bamboo and canvas in the shape of a building
peshkar	a deputy
peshkari	the office of deputy
peshwa	chief minister of a Maratha state
purcha pyam	a written announcement
purdah	literal meaning is a curtain or veil, but it is also a metonym for confinement to the zananah
rahas	a religious musical play
Resident	an employee of the East India Company assigned to a native court to report back to the Governor General
Residency	home of the British Resident and his office where administrative work was carried out
risalah	a treatise or pamphlet, but here a cavalry troop, or regiment

GLOSSARY

ryots	native peasants
sayyid	title of respect for learned Muslim cleric, also a descendant of the Prophet
shamiyanah	an open-sided tent
takhallus	pen name adopted by writers
ta'luqdars	native revenue-farming landholders
tawa'if	courtesan employed for entertainments and dance performances, also derogatory term for a prostitute
taziatnamah	letter of condolence
ta'ziyah	symbolic tomb carried in a procession of remembrance by Shi'as during the first ten days of Muharram
waqf	a building, or plot of land, donated for religious or charitable purposes; an endowment
wakil	an agent or diplomat, or attorney
wali 'ahd	heir apparent
wasiqahdar	a pension-holder (not necessarily an elderly person)
wazir	minister of state
zananah	the female quarters in a house where only close male relatives can visit

INTRODUCTION

'Bougainvillea *Wajid Ali Shah*—a very showy, cultivated plant, with rose-coloured bracts, often grown indoors and in conservatories'

National Botanic Gardens, Lucknow

This is the story of a man whose memory continues to divide opinion today. Was he, as the British believed, a debauched ruler who spent his time with fiddlers, eunuchs and fairies, when he should have been running his kingdom? Or, as many Indians remember him, a talented poet whose songs are still sung today, and who was robbed of his throne by the English East India Company? Somewhere between these two extremes lies a gifted, but difficult, character—a man who married more women than there are days in the year—who directed theatrical extravaganzas that took over a month to perform, and who built a fairytale palace in Lucknow, which was inhabited for less than a decade. The last king in India, Wajid 'Ali Shah, was written out of the history books when his kingdom of Awadh[1] was annexed by the Company in February 1856. Some people even thought he had been killed the following year, during the Great Uprising (also called the Indian Mutiny). In fact he lived on at Garden Reach, a riverbank estate near Calcutta, where he spent the last thirty years of his life recreating the lost paradise that was Lucknow.

He remained a constant thorn in the side of the ruling British government with his extravagance, his menagerie and his wives.

Even so, there was something rather heroic about a man who refused to bow to changing times, and who single-handedly endeavoured to preserve the etiquette and customs of the great Mughals well into the period of the British Raj. When Wajid 'Ali Shah died in 1887, the year in which Queen Victoria celebrated her Golden Jubilee, a link which stretched back to medieval times was severed. The thousands of mourners who lined his funeral route at dusk on 21 September 1887, with their loud wailing and shouted prayers, were not only marking the passing of the last king but also the passing of an intangible connection to old India, before the Europeans came.

Awadh was one of three major states to emerge between 1717 and 1724 as the central Mughal government began to lose real authority. The death of the Emperor Aurangzeb in 1707 generally marks the end of the era of the great Mughals, and this was sensed by ambitious men who had worked for them as deputy officials. As the emperors became increasingly impotent, independent rulers established themselves in states around the periphery of empire. Bengal was the first, in 1717 under Murshid Quli Khan, the founder of a short-lived dynasty, whose successors were to be emasculated by the East India Company forty years later at the Battle of Plassey. The second was Awadh, which became virtually autonomous in 1722 under Burhan-ul-Mulk, who had been appointed deputy minister (*nawab wazir*) to deputise for the emperor, and who gradually assumed his master's role. His sixth-generation descendant was Wajid 'Ali Shah, the subject of this book. Awadh survived for a little over 130 years before its annexation, subject to increasing interference from the Company. The third state was Hyderabad, established under Asaf Jah in 1724; it survived the fate of Bengal and Awadh by remaining more or less independent until 1948.

What the three breakaway states had in common were dynamic and ruthless founders, all of whom came from outside the territories they were to make their own, with the vigour of

INTRODUCTION

new immigrants and the need to create a fresh power base. Both the nawabs of Bengal and Awadh were Shi'a, a minority, although powerful, sect within Islam, while Muslims themselves were always outnumbered in Hindu India. Revenue from land brought wealth to the new rulers, although it failed to trickle down to the majority of their subjects. Their capital cities, Murshidabad in Bengal, Lucknow in Awadh, and Hyderabad in its own district, began to boast extravagant architecture as palaces, mosques and *imambarahs* were erected, seemingly almost overnight. Builders, carpenters and craftsmen arrived, along with bankers and armament manufacturers.

Court culture began to develop too, inspired by the customs and patronage of the earlier Mughals, and there was rivalry between Lucknow and Hyderabad over which city was the true heir to the old Delhi Court. When Delhi fell to the East India Company in 1803, and the emperors became virtual paupers in their own capital, many of its poets moved to Lucknow, adding to its lustre, although there was some grumbling in verse about their changed circumstances.[2] All kinds of artists, including jewellers, musicians, painters, dancers, singers, skilled artisans and even cooks, settled in Lucknow, providing services to the rich men and women at Court and in the city. Some of these services were of course sexual, and the cult of the *tawa'if*, or high-class courtesan, blossomed here with women who were skilled in music, dance and repartee, among other things. A number of Wajid 'Ali Shah's many wives were to come from this group. There were also male and female brothels, and among the commonest diseases was 'syphilis complicated with Venereal taint', as an English doctor working in Lucknow reported.[3] It is not surprising that Wajid 'Ali Shah, growing up in this culturally rich but licentious environment, should become a noted poet and patron of the arts, with a fondness for pretty women. It would have been more surprising had he not. Lucknow has long been a byword for high culture, but it was not until a recent exhibition brought together artefacts from its so-called 'golden age', that is from about 1775 to 1856, that a proper appreciation of what this post-Mughal kingdom may actually have looked like could begin.[4] Exquisite jewellery, decorated glassware, delicate panoramic paintings, heavily-embroidered dresses and jewel-studded jade *objets d'art* are physical reminders of why the word 'Lucknow' still has such evocative powers today in the Indian imagination.

Ironically, none of the exhibits came from Lucknow itself, the city having been comprehensively looted during its recapture by British and Gurkha troops in 1858. Every book on the Great Uprising mentions the kingdom of Awadh, because its annexation is seen as the final element that set the revolt in motion. The annexation is discussed in detail in Chapter Three, together with the immediate events that led up to it. But a Company takeover had long been threatened, and Company interference in Awadh had begun as early as 1764 when Burhan-ul-Mulk's grandson unwisely took on British troops at Buxar and was thoroughly beaten. A compromise, similar to that which the Company had first tried out in Murshidabad was reached. Battalions of sepoy (Indian) troops—commanded by British officers—were to be stationed in Awadh ostensibly for its protection, in return for a financial tribute from the ruling nawab. In order to ensure that this was paid regularly, a British Resident was appointed to the Court of Awadh, and his position was described bluntly as having 'for its Object the cementing of the Friendship between the Company and the Vizier [*wazir*] and the obtaining of large Sums of Money said to be due from him'.[5] The unhappy relationship between the Company and the nawab wazirs, mediated or exacerbated by successive British Residents, formed the subject of my first book, *A Fatal Friendship: The Nawabs, the British and the City of Lucknow*. There was always something for the Resident to complain about to his superior officer, the governor general in Calcutta. One has to see the whole of Wajid 'Ali Shah's life as

INTRODUCTION

a life under surveillance by the British; and it is this uneasy relationship between the hedonistic king and the greedy, self-righteous Company, followed by the government of India, that forms the core of this book.

Although Wajid 'Ali Shah had left Lucknow for Calcutta long before fighting broke out at the end of June 1857, the Uprising was to affect him and his family profoundly and forever. Many of the soldiers who mutinied in the Company's Bengal Army came from Awadh, and when its mild-mannered ruler was unceremoniously stripped of his throne and his kingdom on the grounds of mismanagement, their first reaction was one of disbelief. Their second was anger. Lucknow was one of the most bitterly contested cities during the Uprising. Its British and Anglo-Indian inhabitants, together with Indian staff, were besieged in the Residency for four and a half months, from July to mid-November 1857, until they were rescued by a British task force at a second attempt. By this time Wajid 'Ali Shah was a political prisoner of the Company, locked up in Fort William in Calcutta, on what now seems like a spurious charge. His mother, brother and son had travelled to England on an unsuccessful mission to get the annexation reversed.

The Company's forces were not initially strong enough to recapture Lucknow from its defenders, who were led by a divorced wife of the king, Begam Hazrat Mahal. During the winter of 1857–8, with the British gone and their recent administrative changes abandoned, Lucknow reverted briefly to the old days, but without its king. Former ministers were reinstated in a provisional government, and a number of disbanded regiments from the Awadh Army were re-formed. Approaches were made to members of the royal family who had remained in Lucknow to select a new ruler. Even Wajid 'Ali Shah's disabled eldest son, Nosherwan Qadr, deaf and unable to speak, was briefly considered. Begam Hazrat Mahal was then persuaded to offer her twelve-year-old son, Birjis Qadr, as a nominal king, and he was crowned on 5 July 1857 in the Safed Barahdari at Qaisarbagh, the palace built by his father. Meanwhile, huge defensive ramparts of earth and timber baulks were erected around the city and many wealthy citizens were 'persuaded' to contribute to the war fund, while the properties of those who had left for Calcutta were looted. By the end of February 1858 the Company had mustered sufficient troops to mount an assault on Lucknow, and they were joined by the forces of the Nepalese ruler, Jang Bahadur. The city was recaptured after a bitter two-week struggle, and Begam Hazrat Mahal, with her son and her followers, escaped to Kathmandu.

The end of the Uprising was marked by a proclamation from Queen Victoria which was read throughout India on 1 November 1858 and offered a general pardon; but Wajid 'Ali Shah remained in prison for a further eight months. The governor general's not-very-convincing excuse was that Begam Hazrat Mahal had cited her ex-husband's name in her stand against the British. Wajid 'Ali Shah had never, for a moment, considered joining the Uprising. He maintained his position as a loyal friend to the Company. While he was still ruler, he had patriotically ordered 21-gun salutes to celebrate British victories during the Crimean War. Thus he was quick to condemn the Uprising that burst forth in 1857, even though it was largely inspired by his own downfall. 'We have learned with great concern that a rebellion has been created in Hindustan as well as in Oudh. We were ready to serve the British government to the best of our ability and power', he announced in a petition written from prison in November 1857.[6] He proposed to Lord Canning, the governor general, the formation of a new Awadh Army to fight the rebels 'under the Standard of the King', subject to the question of annexation being reconsidered. His suggestion was turned down. Yet the king seemed remarkably free from bitterness towards his British captors as he left Fort William, his prison for two years, to be driven home to Garden Reach.

INTRODUCTION

Wajid 'Ali Shah will always be seen in the context of British India: firstly that of the East India Company, then, after its abolition in 1858, the British government in India, which assumed responsibility for the country. There is a tendency to see the second half of the nineteenth century as the high point of Empire, not only in the Indian subcontinent, for the moment subservient to Britain, but in other parts of the world too. Yet how secure did the British actually feel? The theme of British unease runs throughout Wajid 'Ali Shah's life, and even after his death, revealing underlying anxieties. While he was king, the East India Company was criticised for allowing the perceived mismanagement of Awadh to continue, although it did nothing to support his attempts at land reform. During the Uprising of 1857 he was promptly arrested and held as a political prisoner for many months longer than was necessary. On his release he was monitored by a succession of British agents, who reported to the government in weekly diaries. His letters were censored and his movements were restricted. On his death, the Garden Reach estate was sold off and much of it demolished in a final attempt to eradicate his memory. Clearly a man who attracted this much attention from the British is an important figure in the history of India.

Many histories mention Wajid 'Ali Shah only in the context of his brief reign in Lucknow, from February 1847 to February 1856, a period of nine years—less than a decade. He was in his early thirties when he left Lucknow forever, and thus almost half his life was spent in voluntary exile in Calcutta. These last thirty years are much less well documented, although recently scholars have begun to examine this period, which for this author, at least, holds as much interest as the earlier and better-known accounts of his reign.[7] Immediately after the annexation, Company officials believed that the king would remain in Lucknow, relieved by the British from the burden of administering his kingdom and content with a large pay-off, in the form of a generous pension.

How the rich cultural life of the city might have developed further can only be speculated upon, but one suspects that Wajid 'Ali Shah would have provoked, or suffered, the same conflicts with British officials over his extravagance and consequent debts, and his shabby treatment of his wives and children.

As it was, a consistent British policy towards the king in exile was never developed, which led to fresh confrontations as each new crisis arose. This was partly due to changes of personnel at senior level in the civil administration, and also among the government-appointed agents to the king. New men would come along with new solutions to the problem, as they saw it. The king was the one constant, living into his late sixties, in spite of his hypochondria and the belief (and hope) among British officials that he was frequently on the verge of collapse and death. A very small number of Britons were sympathetic towards the king, including Captain Robert Bird, who spoke up for him; John Rose Brandon, who gave him practical help; and Major Charles Herbert, a government agent who worked with him to reduce his debts, and also produced a delicate little pen-and-ink sketch of his royal charge.

A number of biographies of Wajid 'Ali Shah (listed in the Bibliography) have been written by Indian authors, but no English writer has previously attempted to capture this prominent, yet elusive, character. As a young man he was a prolific writer, and some of his works are autobiographical, including the *Ishqnamah* and his prison diary *Huzn-i-Akhtar*, which are referred to in this study. Once re-established at Garden Reach, with a very substantial pension, his creative period seems to have drawn to a close.

This book is not a literary critique,[8] nor another examination of Lakhnavi culture, but a political study that attempts to move away from the many myths surrounding the king. There is a daunting amount of material relating to the annexation of Awadh by the East India Company, a topic which has been well

INTRODUCTION

picked over and does not need repeating here. Some of the more interesting papers concern the exchanges between British government officials when Wajid 'Ali Shah was creating his small, new kingdom on the outskirts of Calcutta, because these allow us to look into the mind of an Indian monarch and to understand how he himself defined his princely role. They also allow us to consider what held the 'kingdom' together long after it was removed from its original home in Awadh.

In their haste to remove all reminders of the king after his death in 1887, the archives at Garden Reach disappeared. We know that these were substantial and included the household accounts, copies of letters written and received over thirty years, lists of the king's numerous wives and children, receipts for the menagerie, wages for the servants and much else, including photograph albums. So information has had to be built up from other sources, including the National Archives in Delhi and the British Library in London. The policy of the East India Company, and later the government of India, was to send to London what was considered official or semi-official correspondence, while 'domestic' and often more interesting correspondence remained in India. The Delhi Archives have been fairly thoroughly explored and enjoyed too. Contemporary nineteenth-century Indian newspapers, in the National Archives at Kolkata, gave a different, gossipy slant on events at Garden Reach; and in England the invaluable *Illustrated London News* and *Punch* provided pictures and comments on the queen mother's ill-fated visit to Southampton and London. Contemporary photographs have been extensively studied, including a cache of the king's relatives which was recently identified in the J. Paul Getty Museum. Paintings have been examined, together with an uncatalogued, but valuable, collection of drawings in the Lucknow State Museum. Some information came from direct descendants of the king, now living in Kolkata and Lucknow, and several visits were made with them to what remains today of Garden Reach.

The structure of this book is mainly thematic, and the opening chapter places us immediately as witnesses to the unsuccessful mission of Wajid 'Ali Shah's relatives to England. We then trace the king's life through his passions for grand theatrical events, his wives, his menagerie (which he claimed gave him more enjoyment than his relatives), the trauma of annexation, his uncurbed extravagance, the frustration of his sons and the dismantling of his household after his death. Real life is messy: it doesn't always divide neatly into chapters, and past events can suddenly become relevant to the present, so there is inevitably some chronological overlapping in this story. Each chapter therefore has a brief summary and conclusion of its contents and each can be read separately. A time-frame of significant events is included.

To sum up, what kind of man was the king? Wajid 'Ali Shah was a survivor and, in his younger days, a highly talented and creative person. Had he been born a century later, he would undoubtedly have found his career in the film world, with the chance to realise, on an epic scale, the theatrical presentations he had directed in Lucknow. His attention to casting, stage design, costumes and musical numbers was that of a professional. Regrettably his attitudes towards the many women he met, including his wives, led to justified criticism and minor rebellions from the women themselves. For all his passionate love poetry, Wajid 'Ali Shah may have been one of those men who enjoy the pursuit and capture, but do not actually like women very much. He was pedantic about things that interested him; he was religious, and generous to a fault in funding religious festivals, but extremely careless where money was concerned. He never forgot that he was a king, and did not allow others to forget it. So we are left with a new picture: that of a man who was certainly not the debauched character painted by the British, but neither the great romantic hero of Indian memory. Perhaps, after more than a century, someone more interesting is beginning to emerge.

1

'THAT ENERGETIC OLD LADY'

The king's mother, brother and son travel with a large party to England, to plead for the return of the kingdom of Awadh, annexed by the East India Company. Curiously, the king decides not to accompany them. While they are in England, news of the Great Uprising in India (the Mutiny) is received, and the royal mission breaks up in disarray.

It is August 1856, the height of the holiday season for the wealthy in Britain. Queen Victoria is at Osborne House on the Isle of Wight. Robert Vernon-Smith, President of the Board of Control, the forerunner of the Secretary of State for India, is at Castle Menzies in Scotland, where the young Sikh prince, Duleep Singh, is also a tenant. Lord Palmerston, the seventy-two-year-old Prime Minister who began his political career as a Tory but moved steadily towards the liberal left, is also on holiday because Parliament is enjoying an unusually long recess. All seems quiet on the political front during the summer. Earlier in the year a peace treaty has been signed, bringing to an unsatisfactory end the Crimean War, fought between Britain, her allies and the Russian Empire. The Second Opium War and the short Anglo-Persian War are both in the near future, but for the moment Britain basks in the late summer sunshine as the steamship SS *Indus* docks at Southampton. An Indian queen, 'closely veiled' and surrounded by her ladies-in-waiting, is carried down the gangplank in a sedan chair. She is followed by her youngest son, commander-in-chief of an army which is being disbanded even as he steps ashore, and her grandson, heir apparent to a throne that no longer exists.

Accompanying this exotic party are the commander-in-chief's two Rajput wives, one of whom is pregnant and will give birth to a daughter two months later. The queen has brought her personal doctor with her, for she herself is over fifty and not in good health. But this is not a family holiday. It is a diplomatic mission, and among the hundred-strong group disembarking on the quayside are lawyers, courtiers and an English interpreter. Members of the Awadh royal family have brought their own entourages of servants with them, male and female. Among the group are several African slaves, who are, if anything, even more startling in appearance to the townspeople of Southampton than their owners.

The queen's name is Malikah Kishwar Bahadur Fakhr-uz-Zamani Nawab Taj Ara Begam, but she is always referred to as Janab-i 'Aliyyah, a respectful title for a queen mother that translates as 'Her Sublime Excellency', and this is what we shall call her. Her youngest son, the commander-in-chief, is General Mirza Muhammad Jawad 'Ali Sikandar Hashmat Bahadur, known as Sikandar Hashmat. The queen's grandson is the flighty, immature Mirza Muhammad Hamid 'Ali Bahadur, called Prince Hamid 'Ali. The royal family, their courtiers, servants, slaves and all are driven to the appropriately named Royal York Hotel, which stands in the town centre, and was perhaps chosen because of its name. It is the largest hotel in Southampton, a four-storey coaching inn built in the eighteenth century. A central passageway leads through to stables at the rear, and there is a handsome balcony at first-floor level—although Janab-i 'Aliyyah will not be appearing on it, as she is in *purdah*. Mr

White, the owner, has put the entire hotel at the disposal of the royal family, at a reputed cost of £100 for ten days.[1]

The first thing the royal party did on arrival was to close all the hotel's windows, and they remained closed for the duration of their stay. Even a late summer's day in England felt cold to people who had left humid Calcutta in the middle of June, sailed up the Red Sea in July, disembarked at Suez for the overland journey to Port Said, and passed through the Mediterranean, the Bay of Biscay and into the English Channel. Closing the windows also kept out some of the noise of the crowds who had followed the carriages from the waterfront, then stood outside the hotel cheering and waiting. The arrival of Janab-i 'Aliyyah and her party in the middle of the 'silly season' was a godsend to the national press. *The Times* reported almost daily at first on the sensation that she caused, manifested by the crowds that gathered each morning hoping for a glimpse of Indian splendour. It was, of course, added the newspaper disparagingly, 'mere vulgar curiosity on the part of the multitude who design only to see the dresses and appointments of the servants and followers and greedily drink in the absurd tales of the fabulous wealth and jewels of the royal party which have been industriously circulated'. The magazine *Punch* was baffled and expressed its surprise at all the fuss in doggerel verse:

> What means that shouting of the crowd?
> The people cheer the Queen of Oude.
> The British people always cheer
> All sovereigns who come over here.
>
> Why cheer the people Oude's Ex-Queen?
> She hates, like poison, to be seen,
> In privacy she fain would dwell
> Within the Royal York Hotel.[2]

Its rhetorical question was partly answered in another frightful 'poem' with tortured rhyme and scansion:

> The Queen of Oude
> She cries so loud
> For justice like a QC
> And claims her right
> And wants to fight
> The Marquess of Dalhousie
>
> The Queen of Oude
> Has brought a crowd
> That shares her strange halluci-
> Nation that she
> Shall shortly be
> Avenged on Lord Dalhousie
>
> The Queen of Oude
> Is disendowed
> Of regions rich and juicy
> Their milk and honey
> I mean their money
> Squeezed out by Lord Dalhousie.[3]

This second effort at least had the merit of partly explaining to those who did not keep up with Indian affairs what the queen was doing in England and why she had seemingly followed the former governor general, James Broun-Ramsay, Marquess of Dalhousie, when he retired after eight tumultuous years of service in India.

Those who did know that one of Dalhousie's final acts before leaving Calcutta was to annex the last remaining kingdom in India, the kingdom of Awadh, also knew that Janab-i 'Aliyyah was no longer its queen. The plump, middle-aged woman was the queen mother, chief wife and now widow of the late King Amjad 'Ali Shah. She was also the mother of four children, including Sikandar Hashmat, the commander-in-chief without an army. It is her eldest son, still in India, who is the subject of this book—the last king in India, Wajid 'Ali Shah. But his mother holds centre stage for a moment, not least because Janab-i 'Aliyyah is a forceful, strong-minded character, perhaps even more so than her son, the king. Her lineage and connections were impressive. She was a granddaughter of nawab Sa'adat 'Ali Khan, the sixth and most engaging of Awadh's rulers. Born in 1803, she was married to the tenth ruler, Amjad 'Ali Shah, and widowed at the age of forty-five.

Now an Indian widow, particularly from an aristocratic family, can be a powerful figure. A charming autocrat, she is feared and revered in equal measure by her family. Proud of her own ancestry, often more so than that of her late husband, she insists on the proper forms of address, correct etiquette and unquestioning obedience from her children, particularly her sons. It is an extremely brave, or foolhardy, son who goes against his mother's wishes, particularly in matrimonial affairs. Often still handsome into old age, and impeccably dressed, the widow gathers visible and invisible courtiers around her, paying homage. She knows the histories of all the important families and is entertaining company, when she chooses to be—full of anecdotes and gossip. Curiously, many such widows are addicted to nicotine, and Janab-i 'Aliyyah was one of them, never without her hookah and her maid-servant to attend to it. She did not drink alcohol, and it was remarked that she ate her meals with a spoon, instead of using her fingers like those around her. She remained in purdah all her life, as ladies of her background did, surrounded and served by women. Even the entrances to the *zananah* apartments (female quarters) in the palaces were guarded by female soldiers—African women who had been imported into India by Arab slavers, put into uniform and armed with muskets.

Moving, according to the seasons, between three palaces in Lucknow, Janab-i 'Aliyyah was said to dislike ceremonial events, which in any case she could only observe from behind a purdah screen. She tried to avoid travel outside the royal enclosures and gardens, but if she did have to leave home, for religious events or family occasions, she was carried in a closed palanquin by servants or in a silver *howdah*, on elephant-back. She held her own female *durbars*, or court audiences, where women from all over the kingdom, rich or poor, could come to her with petitions, complaints and gifts. She was literate, and after her husband's death in February 1847, the widow spent many hours reading the Qur'an. She also interfered outrageously in her elder son's matrimonial affairs and had already tricked him into divorcing eight of his wives of whom she did not approve, including Begam Hazrat Mahal, the mother of a young son.[4] In spite of palace politics, it was a comfortable life for a woman of her class and expectations, and infinitely luxurious compared to that of the majority of her countrywomen. So what drove her, in the heat of the summer of 1856, from her Lucknow palace to Mr White's Southampton hotel?

The annexation of Awadh by the East India Company was the defining point in the lives of Wajid 'Ali Shah, his relatives, courtiers, servants, soldiers and thousands of other people. Nothing would ever be the same again, particularly in Awadh and in its capital, Lucknow. The outrageous event, the taking away of a kingdom from a king whose ancestors had been crowned by the British, led directly to Janab-i 'Aliyyah's decision to seek redress from another queen, Victoria. 'I will go to England', she is reported to have declared. 'The Queen of England is also a mother. I will ask her to give me back my kingdom.'[5]

Janab-i 'Aliyyah had appealed against the annexation of Awadh as soon as the dreadful news was announced by Colonel James Outram, the British Resident to the Court, on 1 February 1856. She immediately requested an interview with the Resident, which could not be face to face, even for so important an event. An interpreter was present, because the queen mother like her sons, did not speak English. Even through the two filters of the curtain and the translator, Outram was said to be moved by the appeal, but he had no power to reverse the decision of the governor general, Lord Dalhousie, who in turn was under the orders of the East India Company's governing body, the Court of Directors, acting with the sanction of the cabinet of the British government. The kingdom was annexed (as we shall see in Chapter Three) without bloodshed, on 7 February. Five weeks later Janab-i 'Aliyyah left Lucknow with her two sons, the king and his brother the commander-in-chief, on the first stage of the journey to England. She was never to return.

The reason why the queen mother ultimately travelled to England without her son, the king, has never been satisfactorily explained. Although Lord Canning, who had replaced Dalhousie as governor general, was not keen on Wajid 'Ali Shah travelling to England to plead his case, he did not actively prevent him from doing so. At first Canning did not believe that the king would even get as far as the capital of British India: 'I have no expectation that he will go to England and not much that he will make his appearance in Calcutta', he wrote to Vernon-Smith in March, some days after the royal party had left Lucknow.[6] James Outram even doubted that he would travel beyond Cawnpore,[7] the large British cantonment on the bank of the Ganges, where the party had halted after its first over-night coach journey. 'He is unwell', Outram told Canning, 'and it is reported that the fatigue of making this, the first journey of his life, barely 50 miles and the discomfort of his accommodation compared with the luxuries of Lucknow are the cause of the illness and that he is so disheartened by them he will be glad to go back again, but for the shame of it.'[8] Outram was wrong on both counts. The king had travelled twice to Cawnpore and back, once to meet an earlier governor general there, and the Resident had gravely underestimated Janab-i 'Aliyyah's determination, using her son, to win back 'her' kingdom.

When Canning learned in April that Wajid 'Ali Shah and his party had moved downriver to Benares and were waiting there for a steamer to take them to Calcutta, the new governor general still remained fairly sanguine. It would take the king 'at least a fortnight to make the journey by water' at this time of year, and he would have to travel round the Sunderbans, he told Vernon-Smith. In this particular river passage 'with a strong north-wester blowing, it is likely that His Majesty may have such a foretaste of a voyage by water as will more than anything else deter him from a visit to England'. The best solution would be for the king to return to a 'quiet retreat at Lucknow', although Canning feared this was exactly what would *not* happen, as long as he was surrounded by 'adventurers and harpies' no doubt attentive to the 25 lakhs of rupees (about a quarter of a million pounds sterling) that was being carried down to Calcutta, mostly in gold bullion and jewellery.[9]

Wajid 'Ali Shah arrived in the capital on the evening of 13 May, and probably went straight to Spence's Hotel, an imposing Grecian-looking building conveniently adjacent to Government House and its occupants, Lord and Lady Canning. The next day Thomas Menzies, who had been hired by the king as his agent, sent a letter to George Edmonstone, Secretary to the Foreign Department, announcing his master's arrival in Calcutta. The letter was passed up to Canning, and passed down again with a pencilled note: 'Mr Menzies is not recognised. The Govt. of India know nothing of Mr Menzies. No acknowledgment.' Two days later, having received no reply, Thomas Menzies sent another letter to Edmonstone asking for permission for Wajid 'Ali Shah to visit Fort William, the military headquarters of the East India Company. 'Perhaps you will be good enough to let me know to whom I should apply for such authority?' he asked politely. Another note was pencilled on the back of Menzies' second letter: 'An agent's first act should be to show some credentials. Mr Menzies had addressed the Govt. more than once without doing so; but the Govt. knows nothing of him, or of his functions; and until it does is not called upon to recognise them or notice him. No answer should be sent.'[10] Menzies, an Anglo-Indian, was being subjected to the British government at its most pompous and obscurantist. Without being told why his letters could not be answered, he could not remedy the situation.

Puzzled at the government's silence and surprised at the lack of acknowledgement on his arrival, the king spoke to nawab Munawwar-ud-daulah, a wealthy landowner, former commander-in-chief of the Awadh Army and one-time chief minister in Awadh. In turn, Munawwar-ud-daulah sent one of his own officials, the respected *munshi* Baqir 'Ali, to the Foreign Department office to make an appointment with its Secretary to find out what was wrong. Edmonstone's written report to Canning after the event was defensive and self-excusing, demonstrating the sensitivities around anything to do with the king. 'After some hesitation', he wrote, '[I] determined to admit him; as I should have admitted any other respectable native gentleman waiting upon me at my office.' Edmonstone clearly suspected something was up, because he asked his undersecretary, Mr Shaw, to sit in on the interview. At first Edmonstone denied knowing who Munawwar-ud-daulah was, despite the positions he had held in the former kingdom. Then he said he did not have the authority to set up an interview with him, or with Canning himself, 'without asking permission in the first instance'. Baqir 'Ali was staggered by this. 'What? [I] have placed the whole matter before you, and you can't give me any answer?' Limply Edmonstone replied, 'I have given you my answer.'[11]

How long this cat-and-mouse game might have gone on, one can only speculate. The deadlock was broken by the governor general, who 'let the king know through some of his people' what the proper procedure was, and agreed to receive a petition from Munawwar-ud-daulah on the king's behalf. In it, Wajid 'Ali Shah explained how, after losing his kingdom, he 'consented to undergo exposure to the burning heat of the sun in the very height of the hot weather, with the desire of getting within the shade of your Lordship's [Canning's] benevolence'. Even though he was 'oppressed with mental afflictions and sorrows and bodily ills which no pen can describe—to say nothing of the severe fatigues and the various great inconveniences incident to travel', the king had bravely set out 'disregardful of the dangers of the land and water' to meet the new governor general in Calcutta. One wonders how great his mother's efforts had been to spur him on, when he could have retired gracefully to an easy life in Lucknow with a pension.

In response to the petition, Canning did not fail to remind the king that the latter had been advised by his predecessor, Dalhousie, not to come to Calcutta. When Wajid 'Ali Shah expressed his disappointment at the lack of courtesy, he was tartly informed by Canning: 'I have to remind Your Majesty that your arrival in this city was not reported to me in any authentic [way] or by any accredited agent of Your Majesty, nor until the receipt of Your Majesty's letter or customary form; and that without such intimation, a salute or other recognition of your Majesty's presence, would have been opposed to the usual observances. Now that Your Majesty has been pleased to inform me of your arrival here, I have ordered that a Salute of 21-guns shall be fired tomorrow at 4.pm from the ramparts of Fort William in honor of Your Majesty.'[12] This exchange took place a week after the arrival of the Awadh party, and the following days were taken up in settling into hired houses at Garden Reach, rented from Chand Mehtab Bahadur, the Maharaja of Burdwan.

By the beginning of June, Wajid 'Ali Shah had got his 21-gun salute, 'for the thing nearest the poor King's heart is the expenditure of gunpowder in his honour', Canning told Vernon-Smith. Thomas Menzies was still hanging about the royal villa, but was shortly to be imprisoned for debt. Canning reported gleefully that the erstwhile agent's creditors in Calcutta 'have shown even less respect for his full powers than I did'.[13] But a new advisor and agent had already been appointed, and one whose reputation had preceded him. Captain Robert Wilberforce Bird was an officer in the Bengal Army and considered competent enough to act as assistant Resident in Awadh when the Resident was on tour. Bird was a dapper young man, slim, with a fashionable walrus moustache, and he was also a fluent Persian speaker who had translated some of the earliest letters from the Resident to the new king. (Persian was the Court language in Awadh, as it had been at the later Mughal courts.)

The governor general was briefed on Bird's seemingly charmed career, and the man himself. He had recently resigned from the army, on a pension, to pursue his new career as the king's agent. He was an old friend of Wajid 'Ali Shah, and the two used to meet at the Lucknow racecourse, united in a common love of horses and horse racing. Bird had even been living in a house provided for him by the king, near the cantonment racecourse, which had infuriated his superior officer, William Sleeman, who expected the young man to live in the Lucknow Residency with the other British officials. But Robert Bird could get away with a lot because he was connected, through a relative's marriage, to Sir Frederick Currie, a powerful figure in the East India Company hierarchy who became the last Company Chairman in 1857. After numerous complaints by Sleeman, Robert Bird had been transferred from Lucknow to Ajmer by Lord Dalhousie, which was a demotion, but it got him out of Sleeman's way.

Canning noticed that Captain Bird was said to have been given 'too much to horse-dealing and in that character to have been sharp in his practice and exorbitant in his charges to the Oude Durbar and I believe this influenced Lord Dalhousie in displacing him, but these are matters on which I cannot speak positively'.[14] He added that 'extravagant stories' were going around Calcutta about what Bird was going to get from the king as salary. It was said he had already been paid 1 lakh of rupees (£10,000), and there would be 'much more if he succeeds in recovering the throne for his client'. Having appointed Robert Bird as his agent, Wajid 'Ali Shah planned to send him to England to begin lobbying sympathetic Members of Parliament, the East India Company's Court of Directors, the British press and anyone else who might be able to help.

This was not such a wild venture as it might seem at first. As the East India Company extended its grip by annexing large parts of the subcontinent through wars, treaties and depositions of ruling princes, there had been a steady stream of missions to England from unhappy Indian chiefs, seeking reparation and reinstatement of their lost status. Because objective British justice was held up as an ideal for British rule in India, it was not surprising that Indians who felt they had been unfairly treated would seek redress in the Mother of Parliaments, the Law Courts, or from Queen Victoria herself.

There had been thirty such missions by groups of Indians to England before 1857. A modern historian has noted that 'Many were convinced by British assertions that justice would ultimately be obtained and wrongs righted if only superior authorities in Britain learned what their British subordinates in India had been perpetrating. Enough of these appellants did indeed obtain redress and/or advance (or at least promise of these) that further Indians were encouraged to make this journey.'[15] The Awadh royal family had itself sent four previous delegations between 1822 and 1838, one of which had included an aunt of Wajid 'Ali Shah. The present party led by Janab-i 'Aliyyah was the fifth to travel from Lucknow to London, and the queen mother, veiled as she was, certainly knew more about life in Britain than the majority of Britons knew about life in Awadh.

By early June Robert Bird had been sent on ahead of the group to begin lobbying Liberal Members of Parliament and to prepare the way for the dispossessed monarch. At this point Wajid 'Ali Shah still intended to travel to London, but something happened during the next ten days to make him change his mind. Canning got a hint of it from 'an informant' stationed at Garden Reach, who may have been planted to report on the household in its early days. Bird had drafted out a document by which Wajid 'Ali Shah was to transfer £17,000 to London for Bird's initial expenses. Shortly before his steamer, the SS *Nubia*, sailed, he sent the document to the king for the royal signature and seal. But to Bird's surprise, when he went to collect it he was barred from seeing his old friend and now employer by Janab-i 'Aliyyah, who told him the king was not going to sign the money transfer. She offered to send a smaller sum of money in charge of one of the eunuchs and a munshi who would dole it out as necessary. Bird had been relying on this enormous sum to cover his expenses and flew into a 'towering passion declaring the King deserved all his misfortunes, even the loss of his Crown and for his own part he was glad to be rid of so wretched a creature'.[16] He then stormed off to catch his ship.

Just under two weeks later, on 15 June, the governor general was astonished to learn that Janab-i 'Aliyyah, her son Sikandar Hashmat and grandson Prince Hamid 'Ali had secretly boarded a steamer at night, and were already sailing down river to catch the SS *Bengal* to Suez. The royal party and their estimated seventy staff had the steamer to themselves, for the boat's owner had not taken on any other passengers. Canning could not explain the reason why the departure of the group had been carried out so secretly, unless it was feared that the British might try to stop them. Wajid 'Ali Shah had pleaded illness, suffering from an attack of dysentery when he reached Calcutta, but there is a suggestion that he was fearful of being humiliated by the British and of losing face among his peers and former subjects if his case was rejected in London. His illness was probably more diplomatic than dysentery, but there is no evidence that the British would actually have prevented him from leaving India. A more authentic reason for his decision not to travel to England is hinted at in a contemporary radical newspaper, *The Englishman and Military Chronicle*, which was no friend of the Company. The king's chief minister (and father-in-law) 'Ali Naqi Khan had not been allowed to travel to Calcutta with the royal party in March. He had been arrested in Lucknow by James Outram, ostensibly to help in sorting out the arrears of payment for the palace staff. The minister was released from arrest on 7 June and was preparing to leave for Calcutta when he was re-arrested, this time on charges of bribery and corruption while in office. But the real reason, according to *The Englishman*, was 'the desire of our Government to keep away from the ex-King's person a man who in spite of his many faults, cannot be accused of want of attachment to the late ruler of Oudh'. It was widely believed in Lucknow that 'Ali Naqi Khan was being deliberately held there on trumped up charges in order to prevent him from advising the king and accompanying him to England. 'Good God, how wantonly has this unfortunate Oriental King been dealt with at the hands of the British Government!'[17] wrote an anonymous correspondent.

Clearly there had already been arguments between mother and son that led to Bird's extravagant expenses being curtailed, and it is not difficult to imagine another showdown between the two on the final evening before the steamer sailed. Wajid 'Ali Shah felt that he could not leave without his minister, while his mother refused to delay any longer. Canning had been puzzled by the secrecy of the embarkation, but a more wily observer like James Outram would have surmised that Wajid 'Ali Shah intended, almost to the last, to travel to England and therefore the matter had to be kept hidden from the British in case they attempted to prevent him from boarding the steamer. Once the depleted royal party was safely on its way, and could not be recalled, the king wrote to Canning asking that his relatives should be 'well received and attended to in England', to which the governor general replied that he could 'rest at ease on that score'.[18] Having given this assurance, he wrote to Vernon-Smith hoping that the latter 'would verify the promise to the illustrious strangers arriving in England in August' and that 'the Court of

Directors should do what they can to prevent an appearance of slight'. (Vernon-Smith has added in pencil on this letter, 'They did just the contrary.') Canning also noted that when the party reached England Robert Bird would probably join it, in spite of the row, and this is what in fact happened. Bird was too valuable a contact to ignore, with his family links to the East India Company's Court of Directors, but he also needed financial backing from the fabulously rich ruler of Awadh, even if it was not to be the £17,000 he had initially hoped for.

In his rant against the king at Garden Reach, Canning's informant reported that Bird had shouted that he did not know 'what he should say to Roebuck and Otway in the King's favour'. The Right Honourable John Roebuck and Sir Arthur Otway were both Liberal MPs, and both with a keen interest in India. Roebuck had been born in Madras at the beginning of the nineteenth century, and as a young man in England deliberately sought out radical and utilitarian allies. Whatever the party in government at the time, his general attitude was to oppose it. Otway had served in India for five years, and after studying law became a powerful supporter of the India Reform Society. This society had been founded in 1853 by the writer and activist John Dickinson. Despite not having direct experience of India, Dickinson was influential enough to get Dalhousie to set up a public works commission looking at deficiencies in administration, and particularly the lack of viable transport in the subcontinent. The year 1853 was also when the East India Company's charter was due for renewal by the British government, and this brought together a number of liberal bodies opposed to the monolithic, reactionary nature of the Company. Manchester was a particular focus for opposition because of its vested interests in the cotton trade, which it believed the Company was doing little to support. But the charter was renewed, and the old guard continued ostrich-like on its seemingly immutable way. Vernon-Smith told Canning during the Parliamentary debates on India that 'we routed the missionaries and we gave battle to the Manchester men'.[19] So there were sympathetic voices in Britain ready to speak out against Company misrule and to support individual Indians seeking justice in England. It was Bird's job to solicit their help, and the fact that Wajid 'Ali Shah was an extremely rich man did not go amiss. Two more Liberal MPs, Sir Erskine Parry and Sir Fitzroy Kelly, had been trying to help the nawab of Surat pursue a claim in Parliament even as the Awadh party was en route for England. Although they were unsuccessful, and the Surat plea was dropped, Vernon-Smith told Canning that 'the case of an Ex-King who brings over 25 lacs of Rupees ... must make Sir E. Parry and Sir F. Kelly's mouths water to hear of it'.[20]

At first it seemed that the king did have a good chance of success. *The Englishman* was encouraging, writing on 7 June 1856: 'The King of Oude is still endeavouring to obtain an interview with the Governor General. In this we think he is ill advised, for he can obtain no redress here. The sooner he appeals to Parliament the better, his case is exactly of the kind which will strongly influence them, for it can hardly be believed when they are made fully aware of the facts, that a body of English gentlemen will suffer themselves dragged through the mud by Lord Dalhousie, in the face of all Europe ... there is a general belief here that the King will have his own again, a belief growing daily in force, and circulating widely in the City and the districts.' But five days later, the mood was changing. 'If the King really means to exert himself in his own behalf, which his delay inclines us to doubt, he should be prepared to refute imputations, which however false and calamitous will, if not denied and refuted certainly make a great impression in England.' On 13 June the paper's editor asked pointedly: 'What is the dethroned King doing at Calcutta?' There was 'intense interest in Lucknow' as to whether he would have his Kingdom again. 'I really do think that the chances he had of obtaining justice are fast disappearing! His want of action will possibly prove his ruin!' Two days later Janab-i 'Aliyyah set out without the main plaintiff in their case against the British government. The Lucknow correspondent wrote a week after her departure that, although the king was not forgotten there, 'People think it foolish of him to have stayed behind while his family went to England.'

If Janab-i 'Aliyyah's party was depleted—without the king and without Captain Bird—it did at least have the irrepressible John Rose Brandon and his wife Mary Ann on board. Brandon was a working-class man, born in 1809 at Southwark on the south side of London Bridge, and thus entitled to call himself a cockney. He had first travelled to India as a young lad of fourteen and claimed to have joined the East India Company's army, rising to the rank of captain.[21] Four years later he was sent home, but returned to India in 1832 and found his way to Lucknow where he was employed by the frivolous eighth nawab, Nasir ud-Din Haidar. Brandon's father was a market gardener, and on the strength of this John Rose Brandon was employed to lay out the gardens in the Lucknow cantonment at Mariaon. He was then appointed by the nawab on a monthly salary of 500 rupees and put in charge of 'rare plants' in the palace gardens. Here he met George Harris Derusett, another vivid working-class character, who was known as the 'Barber of Lucknow' and was hairdresser to the nawab.[22] The relationship between the two men, both Londoners, both born without a privileged background but canny and enterprising men, flourished on a foreign soil. Nasir ud-Din Haidar paid Brandon and Derusett generously, and both exploited him shamelessly, returning to England in 1837 with a sizeable fortune. After the death of Brandon's first wife, he married Derusett's daughter Mary Ann, in 1843, and returned to India two years later to set up business in Cawnpore. Although he had been banished from Lucknow for fraud by his former royal employer, Brandon returned and was able to resume his earlier position as head gardener at the palace, this time under the new nawab,

Wajid 'Ali Shah, and with the sanction of Robert Bird, then assistant Resident. An unlikely friendship sprang up between the gardener and Captain Bird which was 'creditable and *profitable* to both parties', as a contemporary newspaper hinted.[23]

On being expelled from Lucknow again, this time by the unrelenting Resident William Sleeman, who described him as 'the mischievous Mr B.', Brandon settled in Cawnpore and established himself as Brandon & Co. railway contractors and agents for the North Western Dak Company, a passenger and mail service using horse-drawn carriages between Lucknow and Cawnpore. In his spare time he founded an English language newspaper, the pro-nawabi *Central Star*, published twice a week with a bi-monthly news digest, and he was also proprietor of an hotel. Today he would be praised as an entrepreneur and successful self-made businessman, but the prejudice of British officials and inherent snobbery of the time meant that he was seen as a disreputable, almost comical, figure. Canning commented to Vernon-Smith that Brandon had left his railway contract 'in the lurch to take up the cause of the ex-Royal family, not unselfishly we may presume', and that he was 'the guide and protector of the present mission' to London by the royal family.[24] Brandon has not been given credit for his role in driving forward, literally, the Awadh deputation. It was in carriages belonging to the North Western Dak Company that Wajid 'Ali Shah, his relatives, servants and a few courtiers left Lucknow for Cawnpore on the night of 13 March 1856, with Brandon sitting beside the coachman. It was in Brandon's bungalow at Cawnpore that the king spent his first night on British soil. It was Brandon, according to James Outram, who had encouraged the king 'to adopt a course of negative opposition and passive resistance' to the British, and who had assured 'His Majesty that, if deputed to England as his Agent, he will, without doubt, obtain his restoration'.[25] This is how Brandon and his wife came to be onboard the SS *Bengal* as it steamed towards the port of Suez four months later.

'THAT ENERGETIC OLD LADY'

As president of the Board of Control, a post equivalent to that of a cabinet minister, Vernon-Smith was the man most closely concerned with Janab-i 'Aliyyah's mission to England. He was warned about her arrival by Lord Canning, early in August 1856: 'I do not know whether you will object as much to a visit from the Queen Dowager of Oude as to one from the King; but I am afraid that by this time that energetic old lady must be with you. I knew nothing of her intentions until she was onboard of the Steamer ... but had I been aware of them I should not have crossed them. Had I done so openly it would immediately have been made the ground of a complaint that restraint and constraint were used against the royal family, in spite of all professions to the contrary; whilst it would have been expected that I feared the result of an appeal to London: to have attempted to do it privately would have stimulated her all the more to go.'[26]

Janab-i 'Aliyyah's arrival, with her eclectic party, was duly reported to Canning by Vernon-Smith, who insisted on referring to her as 'the Queen'. 'She has just arrived', he told the governor general, 'and I am out of her way now' (he was still in Scotland), 'but Outram recommends me not to receive her *en Reine*. The difficulty will be with our own Majesty who sometimes patronises these deposed despots. The Chairs [of the Board of Control] are rather annoyed at your writing so strongly in her favor, when you yourself declined to receive the ex-King.'[27] Canning protested that he had not refused to meet Wajid 'Ali Shah, because the king had not asked for a reception and that 'were he to do so, he should have one tomorrow'. The king's mistake had been to send an ex-minister to Government House, without proper accreditation. But this frank and highly confidential exchange raises some interesting issues.

Was there ever a possibility that the annexation of Awadh could have been reversed? Although Dalhousie's aggressive policy of annexing Indian states had been heavily criticised both in Britain and Europe, Wajid 'Ali Shah would not get his kingdom back.

The new British administration was already in place in Awadh, reforming the collection of land revenue, the corrupt judicial system and the appalling prisons discovered as officers systematically surveyed the city of Lucknow. Over the next year the king's army was broken up, his servants paid off and palaces requisitioned or part-demolished in the interests of hygiene, a new found British preoccupation. What the king could have gained was a more generous pension, the right to remain in his Qaisarbagh Palace, the right to exercise jurisdiction in specific places and to continue his life much as it had been before, but without the burden of trying to administer the kingdom of Awadh.

Janab-i 'Aliyyah had not known, in her passionate declaration to seek the kingdom's restoration from Queen Victoria, that the British queen had no power to restore Awadh to her son. This was not how things worked in Britain, and Janab-i 'Aliyyah's realisation of this fact after arriving in England was a bitter blow. Lady Login, an old friend of the queen mother from her Lucknow days, told Vernon-Smith that Janab-i 'Aliyyah was 'most wretched and discovered she was duped and did not know where to turn'.[28] She told Lady Login that she thought she had the governor general's leave to travel to England, which was not actually the case, as we have seen. Janab-i 'Aliyyah also said that she had vowed to meet Queen Victoria before returning to India, and Vernon-Smith thought there was no reason why an audience could not be arranged as long as the queen mother promised to leave quietly afterwards. He admitted that he was 'perplexed' about the 'Queen of Oude', as he called her. Lord Dalhousie and his cronies seemed determined to treat her and her party 'most cavalierly', whereas Vernon-Smith said his own inclination was to be 'most courteous to fallen royalty and respectful to the energy which has induced her to venture into foreign lands and over strange seas to plead her own and her children's case'.[29] He dismissed hopes that Awadh would be restored to any members of the family, but said he would address any complaints of ill-treatment and undue severity towards them while in England.

As Canning had anticipated, Robert Bird joined the royal party on its arrival at Southampton and was put in charge of the business of presenting the Awadh claims to Parliament and the Court of Directors. Brandon was sent off to London to look for suitable accommodation and after a couple of weeks selected Harley House, a large mansion standing in its own grounds at the Regents Park end of the Marylebone Road. The house had previously been occupied by another distinguished foreigner, the Duke of Brunswick, who gave his name to the adjacent Brunswick Place, and it was to be let unfurnished at an annual rent of £550. There had been no shortage of comment on and description of the royal party during their ten-day stay in Southampton, while Brandon searched for a house. *The Times*, having run daily articles, then seemed to lose interest; by the end of August it was reporting wearily, 'The excitement which followed the arrival of this illustrious family has almost entirely subsided. The strangely dressed natives stroll and lounge about the street without apparently the slightest notice being taken of them. The policeman's occupation whose duty it is to guard the exterior of the residence of the oriental visitors, is gone.'[30]

But Janab-i 'Aliyyah had not been without visitors during the Southampton days. A number of distinguished people had made their way to the Royal York Hotel, some of whom had no Indian connections at all, but were driven by a combination of courtesy and curiosity to meet the queen mother, or at least to view a veiled figure behind a curtain. Visitors included Admiral Charles York, the Earl of Hardwicke and his wife, Lady St John of Bletso, Field Marshall Sir George Pollock, who had led troops back into Afghanistan in 1842 after the fatal retreat from Kabul, Sir George Wombwell, whose family had Lucknow connections, and Rear Admiral John Ayscough. The mayor of Southampton, Richard Andrews, who had been called upon to manage her disembarkation from the SS *Indus*, was allowed to shake a female hand extended through the purdah curtain. *The Globe*, after noting these visitations by the British aristocracy, commented, 'There is a certain propriety in receiving with courtesy unfortunate strangers from a far distant land; but it is one thing to show hospitality to ladies and gentlemen in distress, and another to convert them into a spectacle.'[31] The visits, it went on, were not to gather information about the queen mother's mission. Had they been, then Captain Bird was standing by, as an early version of a publicity agent, although in the language of the day he was described as 'the guide, philosopher and friend' of the party.

Captain Bird, for all his faults and tantrums, did his best to present the royal family's point of view. He stood on the balcony of the Royal York Hotel and in a long, extempore speech tried to explain the reasons behind the delegation from Awadh to the crowd standing below: 'a crowd that knew as much about the real facts of the case as they did of the political condition of Thibet and who therefore accepted the *ex-parte* statement of the Major [Bird] with cheers', sneered *The Globe's* reporter. 'It was a daring concept to bring the late Court of Oude bodily before the British public, and appeal directly to their passions, to their best attribute—the love of fair play—against the mature judgement of the much vexed and long-suffering Government of India.' In his speech, Bird went on to list the services rendered by the Awadh family to Britain through the East India Company, no doubt listing the enormous and largely unredeemed loans it had made. He skirted over the protection offered to the royal family by that same Company, and the undoubted corruption and oppression in the kingdom. 'Suppose', he asked rhetorically, 'that the Emperor of the French were to deprive Queen Victoria of her throne to save Britons from misrule...'[32] A cry went up from the crowd and Bird had won them over.

The Times had underestimated the continuing curiosity of Southampton's citizens, because it subsequently reported that the street opposite the Royal York Hotel was blocked by spectators as the royal party left by special train for London on Saturday 30 August. A fleet of horse-drawn cabs took the hundred-strong party to the station, with servants sitting on top and waving farewell to the crowds. Brandon, returned from London, directed the proceedings, but Mr Watkins, the stationmaster, refused to clear the platform as Janab-i 'Aliyyah entered the first-class compartment. After some fruitless attempts to hold back the crowds, the tallest servants lined up holding calico sheets to form a human corridor along which the queen mother passed. Two enterprising English lads who had climbed up unseen on to the roof of the carriage to peer over were disappointed at the closely veiled figure who was helped into her compartment. An artist from *The Illustrated London News* sketched the scene for its readers and it was lithographed in the issue for 6 September. No one speculated on how a middle-aged Indian woman might feel embarking on the first train journey of her life in a foreign country.

On reaching Waterloo Station, the south London terminus, the large party made its way northwards to Harley House. Saturday evening was not a good time to arrive at an unfurnished mansion in Victorian England. Brandon had not had time to organise anything, and all shops and businesses were shut on Sunday. The queen mother must have spent a miserable day, listening to the 'considerable number of people' who had gathered outside and were gawking up at the windows. Early on Monday workmen and upholsterers were called in to organise the furniture, while servants and interpreters set out shopping in hansom cabs. Brandon held a press conference, telling journalists he had been 'connected with the family for several years in the kingdom of Oude', glossing over the fact he had been expelled from it twice, once by a previous nawab and once by the Resident.[33]

The principal people in the Awadh mission, apart from the royal family themselves, were a mixture of other relatives, senior court officials and servants. Nawab Julus-ud-daulah was the king's aide-de-camp, who had left his master in order to travel to England. Nawab Mahdi Quli Khan was in charge of Janab-i 'Aliyyah's household staff, nawab Jur'at 'Ali Khan was the chief eunuch, Hakeem 'Ali Wasma the queen mother's medical adviser, and Mir Farzand 'Ali Khan the Persian writer. Prince Hamid 'Ali, the heir apparent, had his own staff, including two eunuchs (Haji Tawakkul 'Ali Khan and Nilum 'Ali Khan), two soldiers as bodyguards, and his own medical adviser and tutor. The prince's uncle, General Sikandar Hashmat, had a similar retinue. All of these important servants would of course have brought their own servants with them, so that the figure of just over a hundred staff was quickly reached.

Strangely, Brandon forgot to mention one of the most important members of the delegation, Maulawi Masih-ud-Din Khan Bahadur, who was to take a leading part in the battle with British officialdom. Masih-ud-Din had been employed in the Persian Department of the East India Company in Calcutta for twelve years, receiving from the Company the honorific title of Khan Bahadur. In 1844 he was dismissed from his post for leaking the contents of a letter from the governor general of the time to nawab Amjad 'Ali Shah, father of the present king, before its official dispatch. He returned to work in Lucknow, where his family had served former nawabs for several generations, but was dismissed 'from all employment about the Court of Lucknow' in 1847 by the Company—a measure of how much it could interfere in the nawabs' domestic matters. When Wajid 'Ali Shah attempted to reinstate Masih-ud-Din as his agent or representative immediately after annexation, the Company simply refused to recognise him or to answer his letters.[34] Masih-ud-Din was a clever, sophisticated man, fluent in English, Persian and Urdu, and he is one of only three senior officials to appear in a group photograph taken in London, with the king's brother and son, in 1857. He was also to have the sad task of arranging the funerals of two out of the three members of the royal family the following year.

Skilled though he was, Masih-ud-Din was only a representative of the king, an agent or *wakil*. By not pressing his case in person, Wajid 'Ali Shah almost certainly lost the chance of bargaining for a better deal. The Awadh mission lacked focus from the start. There were too many people involved: Robert Bird, with his brief to approach the Liberal MPs and his family connection to the Court of Directors; John Rose Brandon, who claimed to the press that he was the 'interpreter and general agent' to the royal party; Masih-ud-Din, the king's agent whom the British deliberately did not recognise; and of course Janab-i 'Aliyyah, the queen mother, whom the British *could* not recognise, because she was in purdah and could only act through intermediaries. In addition there was her son General Sikandar Hashmat, a tall stout man in his mid-thirties who spoke no English; and the heir apparent, Prince Hamid 'Ali, who also spoke no English and was described as 'bashful in the presence of strangers'.

The Awadh delegation was of course unaware of what was happening behind the scenes at the Board of Control and the Court of Directors in Leadenhall Street. Vernon-Smith was not unsympathetic, as we have seen, and on the queen mother sending him a letter announcing her arrival, he wanted to send Sir George Clark, a former governor of Bombay, to see her, as a mark of respect, but was dissuaded by 'the Indian authorities' at the Court of Directors. When Janab-i 'Aliyyah made a direct request for an interview with Vernon-Smith, he turned her down. A firm of British lawyers, Gregory, Gregory, Skirrow & Rowcliffe, who advertised themselves as 'Parliamentary Agents', was hired. Although they had some success in obtaining papers on which an appeal to Parliament could be based, the months dragged by with little apparent progress. There was also the problem of funds. Like many Indian visitors before them, the royal party found living in England much more expensive than they had ever anticipated. No longer heading a rich kingdom, they had not made the necessary financial adjustments to their changed circumstances; entire hotels were booked, London mansions rented, special trains laid on, fleets of hansom cabs used, top lawyers hired—it all added up. And Wajid 'Ali Shah, who was funding the delegation, found himself suddenly deprived of regular income from land revenue at the very time when he needed more money to establish himself in Calcutta.

A petition from the king had been sent to the Court of Directors on 10 December 1856. In response the Court directed that a pension of 12 lakhs per annum (£120,000) should be offered to him in return for the loss of his kingdom. Vernon-Smith told Canning that he thought this was a 'magnificent proposal', but at the same time hoped the governor general would *not* 'consider the liberal grant … to the Oude family' a concession to the queen mother's pleas. On the contrary, it was 'the feeling of this country in which I must say I share' that the Awadh family should be decently compensated. Queen Victoria herself was 'most anxious he should be more liberally treated and I think it good policy, if we take Kingdoms, to pay Kings'.[35] So Wajid 'Ali Shah's financial future was assured, but in London the Awadh delegation continued to pursue the fruitless task of trying to reverse the decision of annexation.

On 16 January 1857, five months after their arrival, General Sikandar Hashmat and his nephew, Prince Hamid 'Ali, were entertained to lunch by the Court of Directors at the Leadenhall headquarters of the East India Company. They were met by Sir Henry Rawlinson, the chairman and former agent at Baghdad, with Robert Bird in attendance. *The Times* reported that the royal couple, magnificently robed in crimson velvet and laden with jewels,[36] were formally received at East India House, introduced to a number of the Court's directors and shown around the Company's museum. They lunched in the Finance Committee's room, not perhaps the most tactful place to entertain men whose ancestors had often financed the Company in happier times, and whose loans would not now be repaid. William Bathe of the nearby London Tavern in Bishopsgate provided the catering, and the meal was served 'in a style of great elegance', ending at 3.30 p.m. when the royal party returned home.[37] This was all very well as another 'oriental spectacle', but went no further towards the plea for restoration of the kingdom.

To keep the royal family in the public's view, a number of letters from and about the Awadh mission were published in newspapers, including *The Times*, with long and abstruse arguments against annexation and the perfidy of the East India Company. The Oude Blue Book, the official justification for annexation, had been presented to both Houses of Parliament in 1856.[38] It has been called 'an indictment against the King of Oude's Government, [and] is composed of all the imputations, past or present, vague or minute, real or rumoured, or even absolutely false, which the Company could collect by ransacking its archives or by stimulating the zeal of its officials to seek for elsewhere'. This was Robert Bird's description, published in 1857 in a book that he co-authored entitled *Dacoitee in Excelsis or the Spoliation of Oude by the East India Company*. Although the book is attributed to Samuel Lucas, barrister at law, it is clear that Bird's input was considerable. Lucas was one of the 'Manchester men' and had spent five years setting up secular schools there. He was editor of a radical newspaper, *The Morning Star*, and a man known for championing worthy but unfashionable causes. He was thus a good choice to put forward the king's side of the story. Although Lucas had no Indian experience, it was hoped that his position as a barrister would lend more weight and impartiality to the book than had it been published under Bird's name. (Bird had already published his own 24-page booklet, *The Spoliation of Oude*.) The word 'dacoitee' was of course a dig at Bird's old enemy, William Sleeman, who was credited with putting down the dacoits or thugs (both Hindustani words) who preyed on travellers in rural areas of India.

The Oude Blue Book was indeed an indictment of Wajid 'Ali Shah's administration and a justification for annexation, beginning with a statement by Dalhousie and detailing Outram's own cursory investigations into the kingdom and his dealings with the royal family. It contained Minutes of Council meetings in Calcutta and letters to the governor general from the Court of Directors in London. No complaint against the king was left unturned. Wajid 'Ali Shah's response to the Blue Book was drawn up in the autumn of 1856, with the help of his lawyers. The measures that the king had taken to remedy former wrongs were listed at length and the Company's accusations were rebutted, together with denials of specific allegations. It was printed in Calcutta as the *Reply to the Charges against the King of Oude* and sent to Queen Victoria on 7 January 1857, with an accompanying illuminated manuscript letter. The king's agent, Masih-ud-Din, wrote a similar book called *Oude: Its Princes and Its Government Vindicated*, published in 1857 by the Covent Garden firm of J. Davy & Sons.

A 'state visit' to the Theatre Royal in Drury Lane took place at the beginning of March 1857, as a useful way of publicising the continuing presence of the Awadh family in England. It was the end of the pantomime season, and the performance was based on the old ballad 'Babes in the Wood', in which Robin Hood traditionally appears. Janab-i 'Aliyyah was accompanied by her son and grandson and 'a large suite, including two or three European ladies'. *The Illustrated London News* carried a lithograph of the august audience in the royal box and adjoining boxes, reporting that it was the first appearance of Her Majesty at any public place, which created 'considerable interest and curiosity', as it was designed to do. 'The effect of so many and varied Oriental costumes was rich and peculiar, and the blue and silver tissue hung entirely over the Royal Box for the purpose of shrouding the Queen from vulgar gaze gave an air of mystery to the dark faces, rich dresses and flashing jewels which were dimly seen through it.' The royal party sat through the whole show, watching with 'interest and astonishment'.[39]

Later the same month Vernon-Smith paid a visit to Janab-i 'Aliyyah, at Queen Victoria's prompting. He was clearly aware of the pantomime outing and commented tartly, 'Nothing could be more savoring of a second rate theatre than my reception at Harley House and Mrs Brandon, the Lady of the Bedchamber was one of the most impudent people I ever saw.' Mary Ann, who was known to have a fondness for the bottle, was evidently in good form. Vernon-Smith was still cautious about the British royal family being seen to acknowledge the Awadh mission, and ministers he consulted were against it, but he admitted that if Queen Victoria still wished it, 'after her confinement', he would arrange an audience.[40] Victoria was 'rather anxious as she thinks the Court of Directors prevent her showing [the queen mother] a courtesy she would be inclined to otherwise'. Vernon-Smith had already noted Victoria's tendency to patronise 'deposed despots', and he certainly did not want to encourage her to add to her 'Indian family' of Maharaja Duleep Singh, the Raja of Coorg and his daughter, princess Gauramma. Victoria had already met the two Awadh princes at a *levée* in June, at which Duleep Singh was present.

When news arrived of what, at first sight, seemed like a local revolt in India, Vernon-Smith thought this might be an excuse to cancel the meeting between the two royal ladies. He asked Canning for his opinion. 'If you have still any reason to believe the Oude people instigated this revolt, as Her Majesty [Victoria] is so anxious to show favor to the Princes here, that such a story, if true, would be a wholesome check to any demonstration of respect.'[41] At the same time, he thought that the change in British government after the general election in the spring of 1857 would not benefit the Awadh mission. He doubted if any new MP would be prepared to take on the case, even though the Whigs had won a decent majority over the Conservatives. Sir Arthur Otway, on whom hopes had been pinned, had lost his seat.

Finally the audience between Queen Victoria and Janab-i 'Aliyyah was announced for 2.45 p.m. on the afternoon of Saturday 4 July 1857 at Buckingham Palace, with Vernon-Smith presenting Awadh's queen mother and the princes to Victoria. It was now clear that the Indian Uprising was much more serious than at first suspected. The British queen had noted the massacre of Britons at Meerut in her journal at the end of June, together with the declaration of independence by Bahadur Shah Zafar, the king of Delhi. It was therefore a quixotic gesture by her to meet the Awadh family, particularly when its head, Wajid 'Ali Shah, had been confined in Fort William, Calcutta by Canning for the last three weeks as a 'precautionary measure'.[42] Luckily it was agreed in advance that there would be no mention of politics, only regal salutations and polite conversation. Purdah was suspended during the audience, and Prince Albert, his two eldest sons and a gentleman-in-waiting stood behind Janab-i 'Aliyyah's chair. Sir George Clark acted as interpreter. Victoria entered with her seven younger children, including the two-month-old princess Beatrice. Janab-i 'Aliyyah threw back her veil and kissed Victoria's hand. 'She was much weighed down by her heavy dress, her crown and Jewels, being very small', wrote Victoria. 'She has fine eyes, painted, as is customary. The grandson also wore a sort of crown and both the Princes had long loose robes, like dressing gowns, on.'[43] A letter and a 'handsome ornament of pearls' with a perfume flask (an *itrdan*) was handed over to Victoria as a gift, and then it was all over.

A longer account of the audience was later published in Urdu by the historian Kamal ud-Din Haider, who had received a verbatim account, probably from one of the female attendants. Victoria had impressed the Awadh family with her simple crinoline, described accurately as a 'circular dress'. Conversation had been limited to a discussion on boating, the uncomfortable sea journey from Calcutta and whether Janab-i 'Aliyyah had visited many English mansions. Victoria apparently offered to arrange visits to some of them for her.[44] It was very different from Janab-i 'Aliyyah's original intention to plead with another mother to restore her son's kingdom.

Shortly after this meeting, and perhaps inspired by Victoria's conversation, there was an expedition by the Awadh group to Manchester to see the Art Treasures exhibition, the largest collection of paintings ever assembled in Britain. A special hall was constructed to house the 16,000 exhibits, with an extensive gallery running around it, supported by decorative ironwork. Here the two princes, Sikandar Hashmat and Hamid 'Ali, posed for a photograph with fourteen members of their retinue, including Julus-ud-daulah and Masih-ud-Din. The young heir to the throne, Hamid 'Ali, looks nervous and is clutching the sleeve of a top-hatted Englishman, possibly Sir Thomas Fairbairn, chairman of the exhibition's executive committee; Sikandar Hashmat has linked arms with another Englishman. It is both a formal, yet touching, image of what was probably the last happy occasion for the princes.[45]

On 6 August, Lord Campbell, Chief Justice of the Queen's Bench, presented a petition to the House of Lords from the Awadh royal family. However, the great revolt in India had changed everything. What had been a straightforward mission, to have the annexation of Awadh reversed and the king reinstated, had turned into a desperate plea to prove the king innocent of any part in the Uprising and to get him released from incarceration in Fort William. The unjustness of the annexation paled into insignificance beside the fact of an imprisoned monarch. Janab-i 'Aliyyah, Sikandar Hashmat and Hamid 'Ali expressed their 'deepest pain and regret' at the news of the defection of the native troops in the Bengal Presidency. They were surprised that Wajid 'Ali Shah's name had been mentioned in connection with this, and were confident from what he had told them that he was entirely innocent. The House of Awadh, they added, was faithfully attached to its connection with Great Britain; and for any wrongs they felt they had suffered, they looked to Queen Victoria and Parliament for redress. They begged to know what offence the king was charged with, so that they could have the opportunity of proving his innocence and corresponding with him. It was a short, dignified petition and Campbell, in presenting it, said that the petitioners' sentiments were perfectly respectful and unobjectionable, although he thought the government of India had acted correctly over annexation. No one would be happier than he if the charges against the king, which were not specified, were proven to be unfounded.

But there was little appetite in Parliament, sitting during the summer holidays, to pursue the case. Campbell himself was unenthusiastic about the petitioners' cause and said he had only submitted it 'out of duty'. How much his fees were, as an eminent lawyer, is not known. Certainly the petition was presented in so much of a hurry, as he admitted, that it was not properly worded. It was rejected on a technicality. 'Their Lordships declined to receive it on account of an objection having been taken to it by Lord Redesdale, because it did not style itself the "humble petition."' The word 'humble' had been inadvertently omitted, and Campbell had not spotted this.[46] Almost a year to the day after the mission's arrival in Britain, its hopes were finally crushed. Its three-pronged attack on the Court of Directors, the Queen of the United Kingdom and the House of Lords had all been deflected by the most subtle weapon the British can deploy—studied politeness.

There were more pressing problems too. The lease on Harley House was due to expire at the beginning of September, so new, cheaper, accommodation was found on Warwick Road West, in Paddington, which was not such a smart area as Marylebone.[47] Wajid 'Ali Shah had managed to transmit nearly £5,000 for the mission's continuing expenses, but more was still needed. Humiliatingly, the king was forced to borrow from his jailers, the East India Company.[48] He asked for, and got, a loan of just over £7,000, 'pending the sale of a number of gold pieces and old gold mohurs', which he planned to sell in the Calcutta bazaars; the money was remitted to London in January 1858. Masih-ud-Din's book *Oude: Its Princes and its Government Vindicated* was banned shortly after publication as a subversive work, and unsold copies were seized and destroyed, although not before one had been dispatched to the imprisoned king who, surprisingly, was allowed to receive it from Colonel Cavenagh's hands.[49] Janab-i 'Aliyyah's health became a cause for concern and Sikandar Hashmat wrote to his brother about this at the end of the dreadful year of 1857. 'May the all merciful God restore her to me in health and safety', replied the king. He said that news of his mother's illness had caused him to forget his own suffering, incarcerated in Fort William.[50]

In the same letter, he told his brother that he was dismissing Brandon, and that the balance of money advanced for his salary was to be clawed back, together with any papers that might be in his possession. We do not know what Brandon's offence was that caused his final dismissal, but he had made a 'representation' to Wajid 'Ali Shah, perhaps complaining about the tensions within the Awadh mission. The obvious lack of progress and the king's continued imprisonment and consequent helplessness were bound to lead to friction. Masih-ud-Din wrote to the Court of Directors asking them to ignore any letters that might come from Janab-i 'Aliyyah because she had fallen under the influence of a group opposing him. Masih-ud-Din was in charge of the funds sent by the king, and it may have been financial quarrels that subsequently arose. But the situation was not helped by Wajid 'Ali Shah appointing a new 'chief agent' to deal with his affairs in England, on a salary equivalent to £100 a month. This was Colonel Richard Ouseley, a familiar name at the Lucknow Court because it was his uncle, Sir Gore Ouseley, a good friend of earlier nawab Sa'adat 'Ali Khan, who had built the splendid country house of Dilkusha, south of Lucknow. Richard Ouseley seems to have been suffering from an ongoing mental problem.

He had recently been suspended from the Bengal Army. In the autumn of 1857 the king wrote that he was 'very uneasy concerning Major Ousely [sic] whose mind has, he understands, been seriously affected owing to which he has demanded large sums from the queen mother and others and in many respects conducted himself in a very extraordinary manner'.[51] The last thing the Awadh mission wanted, in the midst of their troubles, was a mad Englishman. Not surprisingly, the mission refused to pay him any salary and, six months later, Ouseley was withdrawn from his post.

The Awadh mission split into two factions. Janab-i 'Aliyyah wanted to visit France and then Mecca, on her journey home to Calcutta. Lord Clarendon, Secretary of State, and responsible for issuing passports, told Queen Victoria at an informal meeting that he had 'evaded' the issue of the queen mother's request for a passport, because she had not asked for it as 'a British subject'.[52] The Parliamentary Act of 1847 had allowed certain foreign nationals from British-ruled countries to be awarded British subject status, which was valid throughout the Empire and was known as 'Imperial Naturalisation'. There was absolutely no reason why the Awadh royal family should have sought British nationality. None of them intended to settle in Britain, yet Clarendon made a fuss about this. He could simply have issued a certificate granted at the time to non-Britishers who requested protection by the United Kingdom while travelling, which was a single piece of paper signed by the Secretary of State, requesting foreign officials to allow the bearer to travel without hindrance. But he chose not to do so. No doubt he was reluctant that the queen mother should become an object of sympathy, particularly as European public opinion was critical of Britain's conduct in India.[53] As a result, Janab-i 'Aliyyah's journey to France was delayed and she only arrived in Paris in the third week of January 1858, after getting clearance from the French Embassy in London.

Less than half the Awadh mission travelled to Paris with the queen mother. Between forty and forty-five people accompanied her, landing at Dieppe and taking the train to Paris. Janab-i 'Aliyyah was taken off the train in an 'hermetically sealed palanquin carried by hand, by eight men in a team from the railway', reported the French newspaper *Le Journal des Débats*. The party arrived in style on 22 January, and on their journey from the Gare St Lazare two 'magnificent carriages' led the procession, enclosing seven or eight veiled ladies. In the first carriage was 'a baby between eight to ten months old, richly dressed, and wearing a gold headpiece, topped by a crown of gold'.[54] The following day the same newspaper reported the death of Janab-i 'Aliyyah at 1.00 p.m. on Sunday 24 January at the hotel in the rue Lafitte. She had died, it was reported, after succumbing to a long-term 'decline' which had resulted in anxiety and tension ('*de vives inquiétudes*').[55] Janab-i 'Aliyyah was a stout woman of fifty-five who took little or no physical exercise (despite her description by Canning as 'energetic') and was addicted to the hookah. There had been earlier accounts of her having to be helped by her ladies as she walked.

The funeral and its preparations were reported in detail by the French journal *L'Illustration* on 6 February, with accompanying sketches.[56] The queen mother's body was taken into the courtyard of the hotel where a fire had been lit, and numerous candles illuminated the scene. After the corpse was washed it was covered for the last time by a veil, and a guard of honour stood over it. On the day of the funeral the simple white wood coffin was covered with a cloth of red and gold silk, and carried to the hearse on the shoulders of eight dignatories. All these events were watched by weeping attendants and Janab-i 'Aliyyah's son and grandson. The funeral took place at sundown on 27 January in the Muslim quarter of Père Lachaise cemetery. The delay in burial was probably caused by formalities over a suitable burial site. Only a year earlier Georges-Eugène Haussmann, then the Préfet de la Seine, had ordered that a special area within the cemetery be set aside for 'the burial of deceased persons of Paris professing the Mahomedan religion', and this is where the ceremony took place, under a simple canopy, after prayers had been said. Sikandar Hashmat was particularly affected and was supported during the funeral ceremony by Inayat Husain and other members of his suite. Thirteen carriages of mourners had accompanied the coffin to the cemetery, among whom were the Turkish and Persian ambassadors. Clarendon cannot have failed to register, with dismay, this solid show of support from Muslim representatives in Europe. The hearse itself was drawn in a carriage by six black horses. There had been another death in Paris too, that of the infant daughter of Sikandar Hashmat, the one-year-old princess Rif'at-ara Begam Sahibah, who was buried in the same tomb.

The bereaved relatives returned to the Warwick Road houses in London. It is not clear why they went back, unless it was to persuade the rest of the group to return to Calcutta with them. But worse was to come. On 25 February Sikandar Hashmat died suddenly. His death certificate shows the cause as 'water on the chest and fistula'. No post-mortem was carried out, and 'water on the chest' is a vague Victorian term covering pleurisy and pneumonia. It could have been contracted in Paris and worsened by cold weather at the queen mother's open-air funeral. Masih-ud-Din made heroic efforts to get the prince's body embalmed and transported to the Paris cemetery, where his mother had so recently been laid to rest.

And finally, one last tragedy. In what is called today the Paddington Old Cemetery at Kilburn, in north London, a small, flat tombstone was discovered and identified a few years ago. It looks as if it has been moved from its original location. Its inscription reads: 'Sacred to the Memory of Princess Omdutel Aurau Begam daughter of the late General Mirza Sekunder Hishmut Bahadoor, brother to his Majesty King of Oude, who died the 14th April 1858, aged 18 months'. This was the daughter of one of the General's two Rajput wives, who had been pregnant on arrival at Southampton. The little tomb is now known as that of the Paddington Princess.

The Awadh mission, deprived of its two senior members, fell into disarray. Prince Hamid 'Ali was nominally in charge, but Masih-ud-Din still held the funds sent by the king. There were claims and counterclaims, and both the prince and the agent went to court. Servants who had accompanied the group from India sued for unpaid wages, and after a final, futile plea to Parliament that his father should receive a fair trial[57] the prince returned to France, where he had to be coaxed back to India by his father. Robert Bird remained loyal to the king, despite his earlier outburst. He gave two lectures at the Southampton Athenaeum, in the spring of 1858, in which he exonerated the king of any responsibility for the revolt and trenchantly expressed unfashionable views about the Uprising, as well as repaying a few old scores against Sleeman and the whole business of annexation. He retired to become a country gentleman in the south-west of England.[58] John Rose Brandon, released from royal service, sailed for New Zealand with Mary Ann and his family, where he led as colourful a life as he had done in India.

The Awadh royal tomb was identified in Père Lachaise cemetery by the author, with the help of French friends, several years ago. It is a large, square, raised platform of crude brickwork that bears no inscription, and apparently never has done. It was erected in April 1858 by Masih-ud-Din, who paid a local stonemason to do the work. In an odd postscript of 1884 the Préfet de la Seine, Eugène Poubelle, wrote to the British ambassador in Paris saying that the tomb was in a very poor state, regrettable in itself, and particularly as it took up a lot of ground. Since the kingdom of Awadh was now under English protection, perhaps the ambassador would care to take measures towards its upkeep?[59] The message was passed through various officials to Wajid 'Ali Shah, together with estimates for demolishing the tomb's superstructure, rebuilding it and facing it with stone. The work would cost between £264 and £448 depending on whether or not marble was used. When this modest amount was put to the king, he claimed to be unaware that any tomb had been constructed over the remains of his mother, and declined to contribute anything towards the repairs. A British peer stated that there was no justification for expenditure from the public revenues of India, and there the matter rested.

Janab-i 'Aliyyah's death in a foreign country, after a fruitless mission, is a sad one. The bad timing that dogged her son's life was clearly at work here too. Although the annexation of Awadh could not be reversed, Wajid 'Ali Shah could have negotiated better terms from the British government had he come to England himself in 1856. A speedy and more favourable settlement in his favour could, just possibly, have deflected some of the anger of the mutineers in Awadh. There was certainly sympathy in Britain for the Queen Mother, even from Queen Victoria, who insisted on meeting her against the wishes of her advisors. But news of the Uprising put an end to any hopes of success for the visitors from Awadh.

2

PAGEANTS AND PANTOMIMES

Wajid 'Ali Shah as poet and theatre director in his newly-built Qaisarbagh Palace. On his father's death in 1847 he becomes king and immediately runs into trouble with the British Resident at Court. The governor general visits Lucknow and gives the new king two years to reform himself and the kingdom, or face its annexation.

One of the most intriguing images from nawabi Lucknow is both unnamed and unsigned. It is a large painting by Indian standards, more than three feet wide and nearly two feet high (95 cm by 54 cm), and painted on cloth. It cannot be called a miniature, although the many figures depicted in it have the detail and individuality of this genre. Even the cloth's large size is not big enough for the unknown artist's vision, and two strips have been carefully added to either side.[1] It is a night-time scene, but the central courtyard of Qaisarbagh Palace, with its gardens and pavilions, is glowing with lighted lanterns. It is a bird's-eye view, looking down from an elevated angle, so we can see over the walls and into the fantastic scenes being played out within. The courtyard depicted still survives, and is actually a rectangle, but it has been compressed in this painting so that it appears square.

A few uniformed soldiers are on duty outside the eastern gateway, but the action is inside, where Janab-i 'Aliyyah's son, the king, Wajid 'Ali Shah, is being carried shoulder-high on a portable throne. Gorgeously dressed and jewelled, his long ringlets spread over his shoulders, he appears a god-like figure, an impression heightened by the golden halo or nimbus around his head, the artistic convention to denote royalty. The gold ceremonial umbrella held over his head is another royal indicator. He is surrounded by male attendants, although a few women are there too, looking up at him adoringly. One of the grandiose titles conferred on him at his coronation was *qaisar-i-zaman*, the Caesar of the Age, and this is where the name Qaisarbagh (Caesar's Garden) originated, together with the conceit that the king was a latter-day Roman emperor. There are hundreds of people in the courtyard, perhaps as many as a thousand, crammed into the pavilions, standing on the Merman Bridge over the small canal (the delightfully named Fountain of Beauty, *chasmah-yi husn*) and seated under *shamiyanahs* (open-sided tents). And yet, despite the crowds, everything is orderly. There are distinct groupings: the sweet-sellers in one corner, fruit-sellers in another, a procession with flags near the far gateway, and a small exclusive group seated on a white sheet enjoying a hookah. A few of the king's many wives are strolling on the terrace of the largest pavilion, the Safed Barahdari, and a small group are climbing the stairs of the Lanka, the bridge that joins four folly-like towers together. Every archway is hung with globular glass lanterns, and these are strung across the terraces too. Flaming torches on slender poles are placed along the flat roofs of the two shorter terraces.

There is an air of anticipation. Wajid 'Ali Shah has only just entered the courtyard and is making his way through the crowds and slowly over the Merman Bridge to a large pavilion topped with brass domes that stands in its own courtyard. Visible through the arches of this pavilion is an inviting yellow divan, on which the plump royal figure will shortly be resting as the first part of the evening's entertainment unfolds. Later he will move to a golden throne under a tall canopy.

PAGEANTS AND PANTOMIMES

We know tantalisingly little about the entertainments held in Qaisarbagh Palace and other palatial buildings in Lucknow, apart from the fact that they cost a huge amount of money to stage and went on for a very long time. The majority were private events to which only certain people were invited, like courtiers, ministers, relatives and the king's already numerous wives. British officials were not welcome, even if they had wanted to attend, and as a result there are almost no written descriptions and certainly none in English. Modern Indian writers, trying to piece together what happened during that brief period in the early 1850s, have become bogged down in academic arguments, or so distracted by technical terms as to be almost unreadable to the layperson. But the fact remains, evidenced by the Qaisarbagh painting, that extraordinary performances did take place here, written, orchestrated, choreographed and directed by Wajid 'Ali Shah himself.

By the time he came to the throne in 1847, he had already written two long romantic *masnavi* (narrative poems), entitled 'The River of Love' (*Darya-yi-Ta'ashshuq*) and 'The Ocean of Affection' (*Bahr-e 'Ishq*), both based on various fictional couples and their amatory adventures. Following literary convention he wrote under a pen name, choosing the appropriate name of Akhtar, which means star. He then had the idea of dramatising 'The River of Love' and presenting it as a musical play, or *rahas*. There is a long and still vibrant tradition of folk theatre in India, particularly retelling the story of Lord Krishna, and troupes of travelling players from certain castes would stage these plays in designated areas of towns and villages. Originally a rahas referred to a Krishna play, but by the mid-nineteenth century the word was in general use for a drama with music, and a *rahas manzil* (performance building) was equivalent to a theatre or opera house. But Wajid 'Ali Shah's conception was too grandiose to be confined in a single building. He was to use the newly-built Qaisarbagh Palace and its courtyards as a gigantic open-air stage set, where consecutive scenes were played out in different parts of its gardens, and some even in different parts of the city itself.

A rare eyewitness account comes from a nobleman, nawab Iqtidar-ud-daulah, who described the performance that took place in February and March 1851.[2] It was staged in fourteen sessions, with intervals of a day or more between each session, and took a month and ten days to complete. Not every scene was staged in Qaisarbagh, according to the nawab, who said that other, older palaces were used too. The Daulat Khana Palace, completed in the 1780s, was transformed into a *Paristan* (Fairyland) for one evening's act. In addition to this, a number of artificial buildings were constructed, using canvas stretched over bamboo frames. This was an Indian speciality, creating temporary structures that were painted like stage-sets to create certain illusions for spectators. A remnant of this almost lost art can still be seen annually in Kolkata during the festival of Durga Puja, where enormous *pandal* are constructed to resemble well-known, or fantasy, buildings. One description of a royal wedding in Lucknow, in 1795, recalls that along the processional road 'were raised artificial sceneries of bamboo work very high, representing bastions, arches, minarets and towers, covered with lights in lamps, which made a grand and sublime display...'[3] So Wajid 'Ali Shah was drawing on a well-established tradition in designing the settings for 'The River of Love'. A 'high and huge fort', with mock cannons set on its bastions, was created, together with 'the natural phenomena of a desert, a forest and an apple tree laden with fruit'.[4]

The performance, wrote the nawab, began with music played on 'European instruments', which would have been provided by one of the king's regimental bands, who had been trained to play marching songs, including 'The Girl I Left Behind Me' and 'God Save the Queen'.[5] Then a chorus of 250 women, elaborately dressed in coloured silks embroidered with gold thread, danced to the music of the *sarangi* (a short-necked stringed instrument) and the drum. This was only the prologue. The play itself followed the rocky path of the lovers Ghazalah and Mahru and other leading characters at an imaginary court, including the king, queen, princes, princesses, courtiers, astrologers, pandits, dervishes, demons, fairies, harem attendants, mace-bearers and others. Indeed it resembled the Lucknow Court so closely that the spectators may have wondered if they themselves were part of the play or if the play mirrored their own lives. Certainly it emphasised the semi-magical qualities of Wajid 'Ali Shah, a man who had the power to create another kingdom within his own kingdom. There were numerous diversions woven into the play, including jousting and archery competitions, and huge tableaux of marriage processions, with real elephants, and ceremonies carried out after the birth of children. Everyone appeared in new clothes: the soldiers taking part in the mock battles had new uniforms, the 'fairies' had embroidered wings fringed with gold and silver stars, and the demons wore fearsome papier mâché masks. Elaborate props were used in each scene, and with hundreds of costumed 'extras' we can see how this one-off performance cost £12,000, and why it took a year to prepare.

No proper evaluation can be made of this extravaganza. After all, there is nothing so ephemeral as a piece of theatre after the stage-set has been dismantled and the players have gone home. But the implications were far-reaching. Wajid 'Ali Shah had the authority, imagination and financial resources to create something that present-day theatre directors can only dream of: a whole new palace as his stage, and other palatial buildings around the city for specific scenes. Although this performance was not open to the public, stories of its grandeur would have leaked out from those building the stage-sets and from the palace servants. Whatever its artistic merits, 'The River of Love' provided work for many, with the promise of more to come. A dramatised poem based on the king's own life, 'The Story of Love', was presented as a musical play in October 1851, and the third poem, 'The Ocean of Affection', sometime between 1852 and 1855, all with the same grand staging.

Wajid 'Ali Shah's theatrical talents first emerged when, as a young man of twenty-two, he arranged a private function for his younger brother, Sikandar Hashmat, in 1843. For the event, the heir apparent directed a play about Lord Krishna and his sweetheart, Radha. A group of Brahman actors from Mathura were hired, and four of Wajid 'Ali Shah's favourite wives played leading roles in the drama, with Yasmin Pari and Hur Pari as the milkmaids.[6] This was an important moment in the history of Indian theatre. For the first time, a Muslim monarch was directing a play about Lord Krishna and his amorous affairs, an event which could only please his many Hindu subjects. The king became fascinated by the story of Krishna, the great lover, no doubt identifying himself with the romantic hero and a magnet for women, to the extent that he was sometimes referred to as Kanhaiya, one of Krishna's many names. On 18 July 1853 the Qaisarbagh courtyard was thrown open to the public for a *mela*, or fête. There are more accounts of this, simply because it was a public event, although eyewitnesses differ on what it was called: the Yogi Mela, Royal Mela, Qaisarbagh Mela, or the Sawan Mela, because it was held in the Hindu month of Sawan, as the monsoon started to break. The date was chosen to mark the anniversary of Wajid 'Ali Shah's official recognition as heir apparent, and the mela was held again in 1854 and 1855.

The king describes the inspiration behind the mela in his autobiography, the *Ishqnamah*.[7] He writes that one day he was seated in the garden of Hazratbagh, under the shade of a banana tree, reading his own love poetry. He became so inspired by the words that he tore off his robes like Majnun, the mythical lover of Arab and Persian literature. Semi-naked apart from a loincloth, Wajid 'Ali Shah is joined by two female companions, and the trio smear each other with ash, in imitation of a *yogi*, a Hindu holy man. More women rush out into the garden to participate and a group of musicians join in the frenzy of naked bodies. Even two of his Muslim courtiers are depicted smeared in ash and holding peacock fans in honour of the king, who has become the chief yogi. As evening approaches, Wajid 'Ali Shah reclines with his female yogis (*joginis*) by the banks of a stream, watching fireworks, and he is visited by a number of inquisitive men, who cosset him like a bridegroom.

It is all a strange conceit and has given rise to a number of unsubstantiated stories.[8] What we do know is that Wajid 'Ali Shah enjoyed this ritual so much that it was repeated at the Yogi Mela, with increasing elaboration. The ash-smeared king pretended to hide in an imaginary 'mountain', a stage prop of canvas and bamboo, and was eventually 'found' by two of his ladies, which led to great rejoicing with more fireworks, music and cannon firing. Meanwhile the public was entertained in the palace gardens by jugglers and acrobats, singers and musicians. It was a party atmosphere with food- and trinket-sellers moving through the crowds. Stalls were set up along the paths, and families picnicked on the lawns. It was not all good clean fun though, because the event attracted hundreds of prostitutes, pimps, 'licentious men' and 'effeminate persons dandily dressed who were singing and dancing'.[9] Everyone was asked to appear in saffron clothes to continue the theme of a Hindu gathering of holy men and women.

A similar event was held to mark the Hindu festival of Basant (Spring), this time on the river Gomti, where everyone was again dressed in yellow. The celebration is shown in a detailed painting now in the Hussainabad Picture Gallery, Lucknow. Wajid 'Ali Shah sits on the upper deck of a gilded barge, with his male relatives and ministers. Next to him sits a solitary East India Company officer in red, who has now been identified as the Resident William Sleeman, accompanied by his wife Amélie and another European lady.[10] The royal barge, its prow decorated with a Renaissance-style angel blowing a flute, is surrounded by other vessels laden with members of the household, the queens, the courtiers, musicians and dancers. A bear and a camel are perched perilously on a flat-bottomed boat. The river banks are lined with elephants and cavalry, each soldier in smart yellow uniform and yellow shako. It was another acknowledgement by the king towards the majority Hindu population of Awadh, and it bolstered his reputation as a syncretic ruler celebrating popular Hindu festivals. It explains the affection in which Wajid 'Ali Shah was held by the majority of his subjects. For a few brief years it seemed as if the golden period of nawabi rule, which had flourished under the king's great-great-uncle, Asaf-ud-daulah, had returned.

Like many of his predecessors, and like other rulers, Wajid 'Ali Shah decided to build a new palace to mark the beginning of his reign. In most cases the monarch's name is as important as the palace. One thinks of Ludwig II of Bavaria and his fairy-tale buildings, particularly the Herrenchiemsee Castle, inspired by Versailles. But Wajid 'Ali Shah has never received due credit for his extraordinary creation of Qaisarbagh Palace, which lies south of Hazratganj, the main road of nawabi Lucknow. There are several reasons for this. The city's architecture, as a whole, was not properly evaluated for many years.[11] Instead of informed criticism and praise, it was described in general terms as degenerate, debased, full of 'execrable taste' and 'ridiculous absurdities' and demonstrating only a 'grotesque grace'.[12] Writing specifically about Qaisarbagh, in 1955, the architectural critic John Terry deplored 'the full horror of the impact of stucco and European Baroque' and the 'wild incompetence of the work'.[13] An earlier writer commented, 'Judged from an architectural view-point the result [Qaisarbagh] is a gigantic failure; it could hardly be otherwise considering the indolent and flabby nature of its parent Wajid Ali Shah.'[14] The correlation between so-called debased architecture and a decadent ruler was so frequently made, and so often repeated, that it is only now that photographers and writers are starting to look objectively at Lucknow's last palace complex.[15] As well as being vilified in print, Qaisarbagh also had the misfortune to be chosen as the headquarters of those fighting against the East India Company's rule in 1857–8. For this reason, it was deliberately targeted by the British when they resumed control of the city and partially demolished it, in a spiteful act of architectural vandalism.

The period between the completion of the palace and the annexation of Awadh was brief, no more than four years, and during that time Wajid 'Ali Shah had little inclination to show tourists around his new home. Our knowledge of Qaisarbagh, therefore, depends on images taken by European photographers immediately after the city's recapture, a short description by the writer Abdul Halim Sharar, whose maternal grandfather worked there, and a survey carried out a few years ago by an Indian architect.[16] The early photographs cannot convey the colour of the buildings, with their neat green shutters, fanciful orange curtains, brass domes and shining white balustrades. The architect chosen by the king to realise his vision was almost certainly Ahmad 'Ali Khan, the first amateur photographer in Lucknow and perhaps in the whole of India. He was known affectionately as Chhote Miyan, or 'little master', and is believed to have also designed the Husainabad imambarah, a religious building, for Wajid 'Ali Shah's grandfather. Certainly Ahmad 'Ali Khan was the superintendent of the imambarah, but almost nothing else is known about him, except for a hint that he may have been a relative of the king. We know very little about the actual construction of Qaisarbagh either, except that it took four years to build, from 1848 to 1852, and is supposed to have cost about £80,000 (8 lakhs), an impressively large sum. However, this would have provided an army of workers with a living, including brick-makers, scaffolders, stucco-workers, painters, gilders, foundrymen, carpenters, upholsterers, lantern-makers and gardeners, all of whom required food and accommodation, to be provided by a second tier of people.

The whole complex consisted of a large rectangular courtyard flanked on each side by terraces of two-storeyed houses, with additional adjoining courtyards, government offices, gateways and bazaars. It incorporated three existing buildings, two of them the tombs of the king's great-grandfather and his wife, and a splendid mansion erected by a former chief minister. There were a number of unique features within Qaisarbagh, now known only from photographs, including the Mermaid Gate (*Jalpari Darwaza*), the trick spiral staircase that led nowhere, the Palladian-inspired pigeon house, and the Great Vine supported on its wooden framework. There were small free-standing mosques, inlaid marble pavilions, summer houses with tiled roofs, little kiosks and numerous statues of shapely women.[17] At the centre of the great courtyard is the Safed Barahdari, the White Pavilion, which was originally intended as a 'house of mourning' during the Muharram rituals.[18]

Much of the European criticism levelled at Qaisarbagh was that its architecture was 'theatrical' and reminiscent of the Vauxhall pleasure gardens on the southern bank of the river Thames. There were terraces that appeared as solid structures, but in reality were only painted facades, creating an illusion of greater depth than was actually the case (a trick familiar to stage-set designers). The Lanka provided a perfect setting for actors to appear suddenly at rooftop height, and the free-standing pavilions could be decorated and lit from inside, like separate stages. Today, with the benefit of the Qaisarbagh painting and descriptions of the musical extravaganzas held there, we can see that 'theatrical' was exactly what Wajid 'Ali Shah intended. He would have been delighted by the description.

It is easy to get seduced by the king's fantasy world of romantic poetry, love songs and dancing girls into thinking that this represented Awadhi life in the mid-nineteenth century. After all, these are the things that come most readily to mind whenever Wajid 'Ali Shah is portrayed in novels, plays and films.[19] But he also had a kingdom to govern, and it was the revenue from this kingdom that enabled him to live the luxurious life that he did, to fund his theatrical productions, to build Qaisarbagh Palace and to support his many wives and numerous relatives. So how much princely training did Wajid 'Ali Shah actually receive when he succeeded to the throne on 13 February 1847, following the death of his father?

He was born on 30 July 1822 when his great-uncle, Ghazi-ud-Din Haidar, was the ruler of Awadh. Wajid 'Ali Shah was not then in the direct line of succession, and so he received no special treatment during his early years. He was not born to be king, and it was not apparent that he was in line for the throne until he was fifteen years old, when his grandfather was placed on the throne by the East India Company after an attempted palace coup. Wajid 'Ali Shah was conventionally educated at home, learning Persian, the language of the Court, and enough Arabic to read the Qur'an. His father's old tutor, nawab Imdad Husain Khan, was employed to teach the boy, who showed an early talent and love of music, dancing and literature. A touching story—based only on hearsay—relates that during lessons he kept tapping his feet to an invisible orchestra, and this so annoyed his tutor that the latter slapped him across the head, leading to a permanent loss of hearing in one ear.[20] Certainly he was known to be hard of hearing as an adult, and British Residents were aware of this when talking to him, repeating their statements if necessary. It was a handicap that he had to adjust to when supervising musicians and singers. Another misfortune was his size. From an early age Wajid 'Ali Shah was plump, an inherited trait which missed out certain members of the family but settled inexorably on others. His great-great-uncle, Asaf-ud-daulah, had become quite gross, even as a young man. Another uncle, Iqbal-ud-daulah, who had led one of the earlier Awadh missions to England to pursue a claim to its throne, was found to weigh 23 stone when he stepped onto a weighing machine in Manchester.

Wajid 'Ali Shah was formally appointed heir apparent (*wali 'ahd*) to the throne of Awadh in May 1842. A number of ceremonies at the old Farhat Bakhsh palace marked the occasion. A fragile painting, passed down to descendants, records the scene of the chubby young man holding a slip of paper, his passport to the throne, and standing next to his father, King Amjad 'Ali Shah. He was twenty-one at the time and already the father of three sons, the eldest of whom, Nosherwan Qadr, was born disabled. This formal recognition of a successor may seem an archaic ritual, but in fact it was necessary to ensure that the throne of Awadh passed smoothly to the appointed heir on the death of the king. The unpleasant scene, only five years earlier, during a failed coup, was still vivid in people's minds. The British Resident at the time, Colonel John Low, had had to call out Company troops to force the pretender, Munna Jan, off the throne in the Lal Barahdari, the coronation hall.

In the present ceremony acknowledging Wajid 'Ali Shah as heir, his elder half brother, Mustafa 'Ali Khan, was being passed over. He had been born to a concubine of Amjad 'Ali Shah, probably before the king's first marriage. Genealogical records simply note that, although a nominal heir, he had been 'repudiated' by his father and his claim to the throne dismissed. The poor man was imprisoned by the British in the Lucknow Residency during the siege of 1857, and was described after his release as living 'on small means and continual hopes'. There was always the possibility that people unhappy with a king's rule might form themselves into a group around a pretender to the throne, and this is why it was so important to make a public ceremony of recognising Wajid 'Ali Shah as the legitimate heir to his father, and his throne.

The heir apparent was given a number of impressive-sounding, but meaningless titles, cruelly mocking his real lack of power. These included Abu-l-mansur and Sahib-i-alam (master of the universe). He was also appointed as deputy (*peshkar*) to his father, in the expectation that he would shadow his father in the latter's administrative duties. We do not know how diligently he applied himself during the five years' apprenticeship. He was certainly busy writing romantic poetry, as we have seen, fathering more children with new wives and directing his first play featuring Krishna and Radha. He also ordered the construction of three mansions for himself and his wives: one for the winter season, the Shahinshah Manzil (King of Kings' House); one for the summer, the Makan-i-Khass (Special House); and one for the rainy season, the Falak Sair (Heaven-wandering House). None of these houses can be identified today, and it is possible they were demolished to make room for Qaisarbagh. Wajid 'Ali Shah's first identifiable residence, when he left his father's palace, was in Hazratbagh, south of the main road, which was already lined with large mansions.

Whatever he was doing, even before he became king, was annoying the British Resident of the time, John Shakespear, who complained to Lord Hardinge, the governor general: 'The prospect that the present reign offers is truly a melancholy one and in case of anything happening to the King, I should much dread that the future will become still more clouded. The Heir Apparent's character holds out no promise of good. By all accounts his temper is capricious and fickle, his days and nights are passed in the female apartments and he appears to have resigned himself to debauchery, dissipation and low pursuits, and for some time past has been on distant terms with his father.'[21]

Thus Wajid 'Ali Shah was already marked out in British eyes as an unsuitable heir to the throne and this description was to follow him for the rest of his life. He seems to have done little to alter this impression at the time. As deputy of the king there are no accounts of his touring the countryside and probing the administration, as the later British Resident, William Sleeman, was to do with devastating results. Holed up in his new palaces, dreaming of love, music and drama, his lack of enterprise only increased the distance between the bubble-like atmosphere of the Court and the reality of peasant life outside the city.

Given the political importance of Awadh, the kingdom was surprisingly small: some 24,000 square miles, less than the size of Scotland. But Awadh had been consistently nibbled away at since the East India Company became interested in it in the mid-eighteenth century, and it had been halved in size under a treaty of 1801 between the Company and the nawab Sa'adat Ali Khan. Yet neither party seemed quite able to accept this psychologically, with the result that Awadh was seen by the British government as an immense, intractable problem, while the nawabs continued to behave as if they still had the bounty of the whole of northern India coming into their treasury coffers. The population was estimated at about 10 million people in the early 1850s, and of these possibly as many as 700,000 lived in or near the unwalled city of Lucknow before annexation.[22] The Company's own census of 1856 provided the lower figure of 370,000, but because the returns were destroyed in 1857 we cannot be sure how this was arrived at. Whatever the correct total, it was still a considerable number, and surprisingly it was more than double the population of Delhi, the old walled Mughal capital. Apart from Lucknow, the other courtly city of note in Awadh was Faizabad, to the east, which had been the previous nawabi capital before 1775.

Geographically Awadh lay in the Gangetic plain, a flat, fertile area bordered to the north by another kingdom, that of Nepal, with a fuzzy indeterminate frontier which was to provide a useful escape route in troubled times. As the nawabs' interest in the countryside declined and British interference in internal politics increased, separate power-bases emerged in rural areas. Landholders, known as *ta'luqdars* or petty rajas, lived in fortified houses and sometimes actual forts built of unbaked brick surrounded by thick hedges of prickly cactus and impenetrable bamboo. Most kept their own groups of armed men, or men who could be called upon to fight when necessary. If the enemy was not another ta'luqdar seeking to increase his holdings, or simply gain revenge for a grievance, then it was often the land revenue collector who had to venture out with his own armed soldiers to bring in the money to support the king and his government. Smaller amounts of revenue came from customs duties, bazaar taxes and travel tolls (payments for using a road, bridge, or being rowed across a river), but it was the land revenue that provided the bulk of the treasury holdings, and this was assessed from the amount of land held by individuals.

Of course there was corruption, injustice, bribery and murder inherent in such a system, and where the collection of revenue was farmed out to contractors, corrupt men grew enormously wealthy. Yet somehow it continued, an unwieldy contract between the government and the people, poorly managed at times, with inevitable outbreaks of violence, but one that had survived for generations, and with which the rulers at the centre found little reason to interfere. Although the kingdom was divided into five main areas, for the purposes of revenue collection and the maintenance of civil and criminal law, Awadh had a centralised government. Power was vested in the king, and the king and his ministers were in Lucknow, which naturally acted as a magnet for those seeking work, patronage, justice and shelter.

The government departments of Lucknow provide a fascinating picture of how a post-Mughal kingdom was run.[23] In some ways it was similar to a large modern organisation, with its post room for incoming mail and its Finance Department; in others there were unpleasant hints of a police state. Wajid 'Ali Shah inherited twenty-three distinct departments, and set up another three. They reflected the dichotomy between rule by an absolute monarch through his ministers, and controlled access by the public for civil matters, like registering a land deed or applying for a permit to purchase wine (which was not on open sale). There were three offices that dealt with 'intelligence gathering' or spying, to use a less technical term. The largest was the Political and Espionage Department (*daftar-i bait-ul-insha'*), which tried to anticipate what the British Resident was thinking and analysed confidential matters of state. It was accepted practice to plant servants in the British Residency who would report back to the Court, just as the Resident had his own men planted in the palace.

An independent office, whose staff were not attached to any of the ministries, sent its spies out into the city streets to gather and assess information on what the population was saying and doing. Any matters worth consideration were passed to the head of department who forwarded them on to the king. And the king had his own personal spies too, who collected news of daily happenings in the palace, including the women's quarters, and submitted secret reports direct to their master. In addition, there were daily summaries from the government departments and courts of justice in the city, which were written up for the *roznamah*, the journal or diary of events.

There were five major departments: the Treasury, the Secretariat, the Chief Minister's office, the Finance office and the Paymaster General's office, which dealt with all military matters, including the appointment and dismissal of army officers. Less important departments covered land claims, superintendence of the 52 police stations in Lucknow, the Frontier Police Force, urban armed patrols, litigation regarding loans, land registry, permits for various controlled commodities, excise and customs, and revenue. The royal mint (*bait uz-zarb*) retained its offices in the old part of the city, west of the Chauk, where it had been originally established in Mughal times, although the king tried to bring it up to date by renaming the area Akhtarnagar, or Akhtar's city, after his poetic pen name.

The all-important Land Revenue Department was split between three offices: the Treasury, which appointed officers to collect the money; the Finance Department, which kept current accounts of annual collections and rents; and one of the News departments, which appointed clerks attached to the collectors who toured the countryside with them, submitting written reports to the centre. This looks unwieldy at first, but there was a rationale behind it, and a system of checks and balances to ensure that not too much money was siphoned off before it got to the Treasury. Similarly, the seemingly odd arrangement whereby the Paymaster General's office appointed army officers was a deliberate move to prevent the army from establishing its own power-base and thus presenting a possible threat to the monarchy. These were systems that had been inherited virtually unchanged from the provincial governments of the Mughals. They were based on experience, sometimes painfully gained, and were well-suited to an autocracy like Awadh.

The emphasis on police and armed patrols was an expedient response to the lawlessness that Sleeman was to discover during his tour of Awadh. The Frontier Police Force had been specifically set up on his advice as Resident, and its duty was to curb the activities of thugs and dacoits, mopping up any groups remaining after his successful campaign against them, which had earned him the nickname of 'Thuggee' Sleeman. In the city and in country towns, the streets were patrolled night and day by armed men, on horseback and on foot, who had the authority to arrest trouble-makers. The latter were confined in police station lock-ups until brought to trial, or released after bribing the guards.

After the king, the two most powerful men in Awadh were the *wazir* (chief minister) and the *diwan* (chief financial officer). Traditionally—that is, since the start of nawabi rule in Awadh in the 1720s—the post of diwan was filled by a Hindu from the elite *kayasth* caste. Not only this, the post became hereditary too, handed down from father to son, sometimes skipping sideways to accommodate a son-in-law, but remaining within the family. Raja Balkrishan was the diwan during Wajid 'Ali Shah's nine-year rule, and loyally he refused to serve under the British after annexation. The office of Paymaster General (*bakhshi*) was also in Hindu hands and also hereditary, its last incumbent being

Dhanpat Ray, whose father and grandfather before him had served the nawabs. The appointment to a ministry post was of incalculable value. It offered almost unlimited opportunities to build up a personal fortune through bribes and payments by underlings seeking work. It gave the minister the chance to promote his own relatives into posts (Raja Balkrishan was reported to have nearly a hundred clerks in his office who were related to him in some way), and with luck it provided a job for life and one's sons. The money laid out in achieving such a post, in the form of lavish gifts to the sovereign, was worth the rewards the office would bring.

It was a highly sophisticated system of government, and reassuring to the young Wajid 'Ali Shah who inherited it on his father's death in February 1847. The deliberate compartmentalism of the departments and the rich rewards for those in office meant that there was no threat to his rule from this quarter and, as we have seen, very little chance of an army coup either. What the king did have to worry about were factions within his own family, and the much greater threat from the East India Company, with its increasing interference in the administration of Awadh.

Amjad 'Ali Shah's death was not unexpected. He had been suffering from cancer for some time and died in the Farhat Bakhsh palace at 5 p.m. on Saturday 13 February. Four hours later Wajid 'Ali Shah was escorted up the steep steps of the Lal Barahdari to the throne room, with its gorgeous ceiling of painted cherubs. A contemporary report says that the crush of well-wishers was so great that the iron banisters flanking the stairs gave way.[24] At his night-time coronation further titles were announced for the king, who now became Father of Victory, Supporter of Religion, the Grandeur of Alexander, the Just King, Caesar of the Age, as well as Sultan of the Universe. These epithets were announced to the faithful during the Friday sermon the following week. The coronation was a time for gifts. Government ministers and officers of state received ceremonial robes from the monarch, and honorific titles. Rupees were given to the royal artillery and the sepoys of the 23rd Native Infantry regiment, who were on duty at the Lal Barahdari. Their British officers, Lieutenants Nicolson and Hilliard, each got a handsome shawl and embroidered handkerchief. Two days later, ministers were confirmed in the offices they had held under the former ruler, which indicated that no immediate changes were planned.

One of the new king's first acts was to set up a trust to look after his father's mausoleum, the Sibtainabad Imambarah on the main road in Lucknow. It was an extensive structure with two large gateways, the first fronting the main road, Hazratganj. Inside the second gateway was a large walled courtyard, with cells built into the walls, so that pilgrims coming to pay their respects to the late king could lodge here for a few nights. Across the courtyard, and furthest away from the road, stood the imambarah on a raised platform, where Amjad 'Ali Shah was laid to rest. The tomb had been constructed during his lifetime, as was customary. Wajid 'Ali Shah told the newly arrived Resident, Colonel Richmond, that he was depositing 7 lakhs (about £70,000) in the Residency treasury 'by way of a perpetual Loan' to the East India Company. The interest of 5% on the loan was intended to cover the wages of 170 men to be employed at the tomb.[25] There was a superintendent, a deputy, a lawyer, a muezzin to call out the prayer times, eleven men to read the Qur'an, watchmen, sweepers, gardeners, masons, carpenters, water carriers, musicians and a hundred soldiers. An allocation of £500 was made for the month of Muhurram and the same amount for ceremonies to mark the death anniversary of the late king. A second pious act was to send a sum of money (£2,375) to Baghdad, to be distributed to pilgrims visiting the holy places at Karbala. Again, this was paid into the Company treasury, and the Resident was charged with sending it to Major Henry Rawlinson, the political agent in Turkish Arabia, as the area was known under the Ottoman Empire.

But after that, the new king's political life, with all its problems, began. The dreamy poet was faced almost immediately with the reality of his situation, a ruler already marked out by the British as a failure. The East India Company was pursuing an increasingly aggressive policy towards supposedly autonomous states and kingdoms. Sindh had fallen into its grasp in 1843, and after the death of Maharaja Ranjit Singh, the 'Lion of the Punjab', dissension among his successors and an increase in the Sikh army led to confrontation with the Company. The political agent in Lahore reported that there was disorder in the countryside and corrupt behaviour at Court, exactly the same charges that would shortly be levelled at Wajid 'Ali Shah. The first Anglo-Sikh War was quickly concluded by the Treaty of Lahore, in March 1846, and the guns and cannons captured by the British during the two major battles were brought in triumph to Calcutta, where they were exhibited on the parade ground in front of Government House. Wajid 'Ali Shah learned that he was to be presented with one of the Sikh guns, the grandly named Koh Shikan ('mountain-denting') cannon. It duly arrived on Christmas Eve and we hear no more about it. Although ostensibly meant as a compliment to the new king, the hint must have been clear to him. The Company, which had begun as a trading concern at the beginning of the seventeenth century, was becoming ever more voracious in its appetite for Indian territories.

There was trouble nearer home too. Barely a month after his coronation, a letter arrived from one of the city's newswriters reporting on a seemingly dreadful event. A jeweller called Chhote Lal had cut the throat of a seven-year-old Brahman boy and sacrificed him to 'the Idol Purasnath' [Parsunath] in a newly-built temple.[26] Without stopping to think how absurd this was, Wajid 'Ali Shah immediately sent two of his Muslim staff with a group of workmen to demolish the temple. Perceiving what was about to happen, fifty or so jewellers left their shops and marched in a body to the palace to complain about the false report and the demolition. They were turned away by palace guards and told to return home. The following day, Wajid 'Ali Shah sent his retainers and workmen out again and three more temples were destroyed, and property found in them was brought to the palace. Taking advantage of the disturbances, one of the king's favourite companion-servants, Mir Mahdi, sent a hired thug called Farzand 'Ali to Haidarganj, where a number of Shiva temples and personal property belonging to Hindus were destroyed. The superintendent of police, 'Ali Riza Khan, sent in an urgent petition confirming that no atrocities had taken place, and that the jeweller caste of Hindus would not kill an insect, much less shed human blood.[27]

But the damage had been done. A much larger procession of jewellers, some eight to nine hundred-strong, marched to the palace, and Colonel Richmond, the Resident, thought that a 'general disturbance' was likely, particularly if the jewellers recruited other Hindus to their cause. The situation was only defused when the chief minister managed to calm the demonstrators down and send them back to their homes and shops. Richmond rushed to the palace for a crisis meeting with the king—the first of many—and asked what Wajid 'Ali Shah thought he was doing. The king admitted straight away that he had ordered the temples to be demolished because it was 'his desire to save the lives of innocent little children, who', he was informed, 'would be sacrificed under the wheels of the Idol's car'. This was a reference to the great Jagannath's wheeled chariot taken out in procession once a year. Wajid 'Ali Shah was hopelessly confused and Richmond told him so. He blamed the king for inflicting hardship on his subjects without checking if the first report was correct. Wajid 'Ali Shah retorted that he was surprised Richmond would defend 'shedders of blood', but on being assured again that the jewellers would not kill even an insect, he backed down and ordered an investigation. The king asked his chief minister why he had not been warned that the initial report was flawed, to which the minister retorted that it was not his job to do so, and that he was not responsible for orders issued through other persons. The king's late father had appointed his old tutor, nawab Imdad Husain Khan, then in his sixties, as chief minister in 1842, with the title of Amin-ud-daulah. He had been Wajid 'Ali Shah's tutor too, the man who had slapped him round the head. It was clear from the above exchange that the relations between the tutor, now an elderly man, and his former pupil, now king, were not good.

Richmond himself was under fire from the governor general, Viscount Hardinge, who told him that he should have reacted as soon as the first temple was destroyed on 20 March 1847. In defending his own position, Richmond said it was 'very evident that many of His Majesty's present attendants who have been raised from the lower ranks are endeavouring to exert their influence over him to their own advantage'.[28] He learned that the favourite of the moment, Mir Mahdi, had previously been a drummer, playing for dancing girls. Having risen rapidly through the Court hierarchy, Mahdi had wanted some land near his home in Haidarganj that was occupied by the Shiva temples, and had been acting without the king's consent in ordering their demolition. In the end the situation calmed down, though Richmond reported that 'an evil feeling still seems to prevail amongst many of His Majesty's subjects'. Wajid 'Ali Shah had the grace to express his regret for the destruction of the temples, saying that 'his youth and inexperience in state affairs had led him to commit himself in this matter', and he trusted that the government of his country would be better administered in future.[29] He put Mir Mahdi under temporary house arrest. There is no doubt that the king could be gullible—there were to be plenty more examples of this—but could he really not know, at the age of twenty-five, that the Jain caste, as some of the jewellers were, would literally not kill an insect or any other living being?

Within a month of this crisis being defused, something even worse happened. Early on the morning of 8 April 1847, the chief minister, Imdad Husain Khan, was on his way to the palace for an appointment with the king when his carriage was held up by four men armed with daggers.[30] The attack took place in Golaganj, in the old part of the city, and someone ran down to the Residency to tell Richmond what was happening. Mindful of being reprimanded for not acting quickly enough in the temple incident, Richmond was on the spot immediately, with his assistant Robert Bird. The two men found that the minister had been dragged out of his carriage and pinioned on his back on a low parapet in front of the Malikah-yi-Zamani imambarah. Assessing the situation, Richmond sent for guns and soldiers from the cantonment, four miles away, and while he waited for them to arrive, he began negotiations with the kidnappers. The four men said they had no livelihood and demanded 50,000 rupees (about £5,000) and safe passage to Cawnpore, in British territory. The ransom money was speedily brought by the minister's relatives, arriving on elephant-back, and Dr Login, who was attached to the Residency, was then allowed to treat the frightened minister. Richmond promised the men that their lives would be spared if they let the minister go, and shortly afterwards the four 'desperate characters' were escorted into the Residency with the ransom money.

An emergency meeting was arranged for midday at the palace between Richmond and Wajid 'Ali Shah, who appeared as shaken as his minister and 'much alarmed'. A compromise was reached that the men should face a fair trial, but would be spared the death penalty. The king's wakil (agent) was summoned to the Residency to escort the men out. However, they had not gone more than a couple of yards beyond the Baillie Guard gateway when they were set upon by the wakil's own men and severely beaten with sticks, whips and sword hilts before being taken to the lock-up. The ransom money was placed in the government treasury. The affair left the British Resident looking foolish. He had given his word, albeit it to kidnappers and under duress, but then had not been able to keep it. When he tried to intervene with the king the following day as the men came to trial, Wajid 'Ali Shah told him that all investigations of crime in the kingdom were carried out according to Shari'a law, and that he, the king, could not influence this. The four men now appeared to be something other than common criminals, or at least men with a real grievance. They protested that 'good men were not now employed by the Oude Government', and gave as an example the recent appointment of Farzand 'Ali as the new deputy superintendent of city patrols. It was Farzand 'Ali who had demolished the Shiva temples and, instead of being punished, he had been rewarded with a good job. The men, all Muslims, added that they were flattered the king should put *them* in irons, the implication being that there were much greater rogues in government. The chief minister intervened on behalf of his kidnappers, and three were sentenced to life imprisonment while the other was sent home, but was to be 'closely watched'.

Poor Richmond was told off again by the governor general, Viscount Hardinge. He had been right to promise that the men's lives would be spared, but then he should have ensured this by immediately getting them to a place of safety outside Awadh. Clearly Hardinge was ignorant of the layout of the Residency, and the difficulty of ensuring that a coach to Cawnpore, the nearest British cantonment, would not itself be hijacked en route. In turn, Richmond rounded on the king again, in what was becoming a familiar pattern of blame and accusation. He reminded Wajid 'Ali Shah of the treaty drawn up in 1837, which was to prove hugely controversial later on, and which gave the British government the power to interfere 'when necessary for the proper government of the kingdom'. Richmond added piously, 'I did not omit to point out to His Majesty that without the active support of my government, His Majesty could not stand for one day, instancing his own request that the two guns and the regiment of native infantry might remain in the city for the purpose of preventing tumult and plunder until such time as he could make some arrangement for the maintenance of tranquillity.'[31] It was a horribly rude awakening for a man who only a few years earlier had been directing fairies and milkmaids in private theatricals.

Wajid 'Ali Shah responded by withdrawing into his palace, where according to the Resident he was 'surrounded by a body of low intriguing men, players on Native Instruments and Women he has given himself up to all sorts of excesses allowing the first mentioned parties to carry every species of intrigue and entirely neglect all care, or thought of the government of his kingdom'.[32] He added that nawab Imdad Husain Khan was unable to administer anything because the king's favourites had taken over his role and were issuing their own orders without the minister's knowledge, leading to 'great confusion and discontent'. The 'singing and dancing men' were preventing the minister from meeting Wajid 'Ali Shah 'by keeping the King duly employed in dancing and singing and such like amusements while His Majesty's Minister was waiting for orders on matters of government'.[33] It did sound as if reality and fantasy were coinciding in a gigantic pantomime, with a cast of villains and a large and unruly musical chorus.

Unlike the post of finance minister (diwan), that of the chief minister (wazir) was much less secure. One of the reasons was that the East India Company had become so powerful in the kingdom that it was able to veto appointments and propose its own candidates. Nawab Imdad Husain Khan could count himself lucky that he had survived for five years, with only one short break. He was a steady, rather than brilliant, administrator and his master, the late King Amjad 'Ali Shah (1842–7), had been a quiet, pious man to work for, sensibly keeping his head down from the British. Now things were very different. The old man was being made a fool of by the new king's friends, and with the new regime in place, younger men were looking for opportunities at Court. One of them was 'Ali Naqi Khan, a slim, handsome man with a long face. He was an ambitious young courtier of impeccable background who was later to strengthen his ties to the king by becoming his father-in-law. He first set his sights on becoming wakil and, according to Richmond, was offering large bribes for the purpose. But a greater prize beckoned. On 3 July, the Resident was startled to learn that nawab Imdad Husain Khan had been dismissed and 'Ali Naqi Khan appointed as chief minister.

Richmond hurried round to the palace again, along what was becoming a well-trodden route, and berated Wajid 'Ali Shah. It was, he said, against the spirit of a fifty-year-old treaty that a chief minister should be appointed without the approval of the Resident.[34] Wajid 'Ali Shah had been king for less than six months, condemned as hopeless before he even got to the throne, threatened with the loss of his kingdom because of promises made by his predecessors and frightened by the prospect of civil unrest. But he was also a man of principle—something for which the British never gave him credit, preferring to call it obstinacy when he made a stand—and this was something on which he was not going to back down. When 'Ali Naqi Khan was criticised for his lack of administrative experience, the king robustly argued that there was no reason why men of 'ordinary ability' should not be able to do such a job.[35] The former minister had been at fault in not maximising the collection of land revenue, and was said to have accepted bribes from district administrators. The army had fallen into disorder too, though this was not strictly within the chief minister's remit. Richmond seemed taken aback, and he was faced with a fait accompli two days later when he learned that the seals of office had been taken away from Imdad Husain Khan, which effectively meant that the minister could no longer act in the king's name. Grudgingly, the Resident had to accept the situation, although he did win two concessions: firstly, that 'Ali Naqi Khan was to act 'in conformity' with the Resident's advice, and secondly, that both Mir Mahdi and Farzand 'Ali were to be dismissed over the temple demolitions. The Resident learned from his palace spies that this had been done, and 'Ali Naqi Khan was duly installed in his new office on 5 August 1847.[36] He was to prove a loyal friend to his master, accompanying him into exile within the decade and sharing his subsequent imprisonment in Calcutta.

The governor general, Viscount Hardinge, was due to retire in January 1848 and return to England. He was the last governor general to accompany the commander-in-chief on the battlefield, which he had done during the First Sikh War. It was customary for departing governors to make a farewell tour, and Hardinge intended to visit Cawnpore and Lucknow in November 1847. As soon as this was known, Richmond began holding the visit over the king's head, both as a threat and as an inducement to reform. But Wajid 'Ali Shah was not the only one anticipating the visit with some dread. The Resident, too, would be under scrutiny, and so far he had not done very well. Like most Residents Richmond had a military background, not a diplomatic one, but this was his chance to show that he had a difficult monarch under control. He attacked on several fronts. Wajid 'Ali Shah had appointed some of his musical friends to high positions in government and the army, and a month before Hardinge's arrival the Resident was anxious to have them removed. He warned Hardinge about 'the unlimited control which the dancing and singing men so often alluded to by me in the various reports had obtained over the king...'[37]

Wajid 'Ali Shah defended the appointments. When Richmond asked him sarcastically if he considered that Haji 'Ali Sharif, a 'common singer', was a proper person to be put in charge of leading a cavalry regiment (*risalah*), the king said 'Yes'. He also pointed out that the officer's proper name was Musharraf ud-daulah Haji Sharif (a man who had made the pilgrimage to Mecca), that he had previously led Wajid 'Ali Shah's bodyguard, that he was a native of Abyssinia, and that he was not a singer.[38] Richmond had to back down over this, but then sent the king a list of names of 'dancing men' who were not to work in any government office. It included Ghulam Riza, commander of the Ghanghor Platoon, who had asked his horsemen to pay for the privilege of serving under him and Anjum ud-Daulah, the king's messenger to the Residency, who had once held back a letter from the king for three days. One appointment that did get through was that of the eunuch Diyanat ud-Daulah, who was put in charge as collector of customs and excise. The eunuch, also an African, was to prove another loyal supporter of the king for the rest of his life, though Richmond noted with disapproval that the first thing he did was to farm out the customs collections. It was agreed that the 'singing and dancing' men should be removed from the official posts to which they had been appointed, but would be retained in their 'private capacity' with the king, who was planning further theatrical entertainments.

By September, as Hardinge's visit approached, Richmond felt that things were improving. The king had stopped sulking in his palace and was going out more, seeking 'for amusement in out of door occupations and recreations'.[39] 'Ali Naqi Khan was settling down into his new role, and appeared 'a man of honest purpose [who] professes his entire willingness to be guided by my advice in matters relating to the better government of the country, but he is deficient in experience, [and] not sufficiently firm in office to set these petty intrigues at nought'.[40] He was as anxious as the Resident to get the land revenue sorted out, and to limit the excessive demands of local collectors. He also improved and reinforced the Oude Frontier Police, as Hardinge had suggested.

For his part, Wajid 'Ali Shah issued a proclamation that there was to be no more bribery in the army and that new recruits no longer had to buy their way in. More controversially, in order to save money, he reduced the pensions of his relatives, which were paid monthly from the Awadh treasury. A vast number of dependants were entitled to receive sums of money for their support. Often this would be a small amount, a few rupees a month, but it was a matter of pride to be seen as a *wasiqahdar*, a royal pensioner. Widows of former kings, of course, had to be supported, but there were other people, too, whose tenuous claims went back over a century because they were related to the nawab Shuja-ud-daulah who had died in 1775. Normally the Resident would welcome any attempt to reduce royal expenditure, but now he reported that the king's relatives had gone 'on strike' and were refusing to accept their reduced stipends. Although Richmond did not say so, this might be why the king had started going out more, in order to avoid being ambushed by indignant aunts and cousins. He was, however, persuaded to settle a pension on nawab Imdad Husain Khan, the former chief minister, and to release the old man from the house arrest under which he had been placed.

One of Richmond's preoccupations, when not dealing with more urgent matters, was the line of succession following Wajid 'Ali Shah's coronation. At a public breakfast given by the new king in April, Richmond noted that his eldest son, eight-year-old Nosherwan Qadr, was absent. This was the unfortunate lad who had been born deaf and dumb, and was consequently regarded as 'weak in intellect'. It was the second son, seven-year-old Falak Qadr, 'a fine intelligent-looking boy', who performed the ceremony of offering *itr* (perfume) to the guests at the end of the meal, a graceful gesture normally carried out by the heir apparent.[41] Because the eldest son was clearly not fit to succeed to the throne, Wajid 'Ali Shah needed to nominate his second son in a written proclamation. Richmond hesitated to approach the king, 'out of respect to his feelings on so delicate a matter', but it had to be sorted out. It was a constant concern among British officials that Wajid 'Ali Shah's health seemed so precarious, an impression assiduously fostered by the king himself, who frequently complained of various illnesses. In an exchange of letters to which the king was not privy, the Resident and Sir Henry Elliot, Secretary to the Foreign Department, agreed that if the king died before his second son Falak Qadr came of age, then 'a Council of influential and competent people about the Court' should be brought together, under the Resident's leadership.[42] The Council would not be able to pass any orders without the Resident's agreement, and the Resident himself would hold the king's seals of office.

Supposing that Wajid 'Ali Shah *was* to die prematurely, Richmond pondered, it would thus provide an opportunity for 'the gradual introduction of reforms and the princes should receive a liberal Education under responsible supervision'. This was to remain a pleasant fantasy on the part of the Resident and the governor general. The idea that an English education was superior to that provided by Indian tutors was a recurring theme in nineteenth-century India, not just in Awadh, but throughout the so-called Princely States.[43] To the Resident's relief, Wajid 'Ali Shah issued a written statement making it clear that because his eldest son 'from the will of fate is unable to speak or hear and is not fit to undertake the administration of the affairs of the Kingdom', Prince Falak Qadr would become the heir apparent. 'From the bounty of the Almighty many children have been given to me', the king boasted, 'yet they are young.'[44] Sadly, Falak Qadr was to die from smallpox two years later, and the disabled elder boy was killed by a cannon shot during the Uprising of 1857.

Elaborate arrangements were made to welcome the governor general. Henry Elliot was sent to Lucknow in advance of the visit, to brief the king and to catch up with the Resident's news and views. At some point, the question of what the king should wear during his interview with Viscount Hardinge had arisen, and Hardinge's own views had been sought. Richmond passed them on to the king.

'As regards shoes, the Governor General desires me to state that if His Majesty and his sons put on English patient [*sic*] leather shoes, His Lordship will not object to their wearing them in his presence. This much the Governor General is prepared to concede to the merely nominal equality between himself, as the representative of the Paramount power and the King of Oude. The Governor General however desires that it may be clearly understood that under no circumstances can he admit of shoes of Hindustanee make and pattern being worn in his presence, whatever the rank or title of the wearer may be.' If anyone *had* worn Hindustanee shoes before, when meeting the governor general, then that was no precedent for the king's guidance now.[45] 'Ali Naqi Khan, as the chief minister, was also allowed to wear English shoes during the durbar, if the king permitted him to do so. Naturally this guidance on shoes has subsequently been the subject of much amusement and critical analysis among historians and anthropologists, and rightly so too, but it is also a useful indication of the minute measures of control that the Company was exerting at the start of Wajid 'Ali Shah's reign.

A royal encampment, lavishly decorated, was set up on the Awadh side of the Ganges, opposite the British cantonment town of Cawnpore and near the bridge of boats, which was then the only semi-permanent structure across the river. Wajid 'Ali Shah arrived at the camp on 6 November during heavy, unexpected rain, and it was not until 10 November that he was summoned to the governor general's equally grand camp on the British side of the river.[46] He was accompanied by his brother, Sikandar Hashmat, commander-in-chief of the Awadh forces, and the ill-fated little prince, Falak Qadr. Also among the party were 'Ali Naqi Khan, Captain Robert Bird as translator, and Colonel Richard Wilcox, astronomer at the Lucknow Observatory. After feasting with the governor general, his staff and dignatories from the cantonment, the royal party was presented, as was customary, with trays of gifts. The following day, Hardinge paid a return visit to the Awadh camp, accompanied by his two sons. The same elaborate ceremonies took place, with trays of gifts for the governor general and his family. If the two camps, with their large tented enclosures and flying pennants, situated on either bank of the river, reminded spectators of a medieval jousting tournament, then this was not so far from the truth. It was, in fact, the beginning of the last encounter between the East India Company and the rulers of Awadh, which was subsequently to be played out between the two, armed with opposing ideologies instead of staves. Both parties punctiliously still observed the rules of the game, although there could be only one victor.

The governor general travelled on to Lucknow, and a watercolour now in the India Office Library shows the moment when Viscount Hardinge was greeted by Wajid 'Ali Shah, in the great hall of the Chattar Manzil palace.[47] The king, in a long robe and wearing a plumed crown, is warmly embracing the governor general, who is more soberly clad in a morning suit of black. The arched hall is full of courtiers in turbans, and Sikandar Hashmat is just visible in the throng, wearing a crown. Young British officers from various regiments, uniformed and impeccably groomed, are looking on, while Indian officers proudly display unfurled standards. It has been suggested that the occasion might represent the presentation of new standards by the East India Company to its regiments, stationed in Awadh. Certainly it is a very formal occasion, and the unknown artist has cleverly avoided having to show the royal footwear by inserting a low balcony, which effectively hides Wajid 'Ali Shah's feet from view.

The meeting between Hardinge and the king took place on the afternoon of 22 November, and lasted for two hours. It was attended by Henry Elliot, 'Ali Naqi Khan and Richmond, who reported the scene. A twelve-page written letter from the governor general was read out, in Urdu, to the king, and was reiterated in a Persian translation delivered later. Wajid 'Ali Shah, said Richmond, 'whose expression or countenance is usually dull and animate [*sic*] exhibited the liveliest interest during the recital of the paper. Afflicted with deafness and particularly invited to say what passage he could not hear or understand [he] gave signs that he comprehended each sentence at its conclusion and asked no portion to be repeated.' He appeared 'much affected', said Richmond, and did not speak during the reading.[48] It was a mind-numbing document—at first seeming to be a rational review of treaties between the rulers of Awadh and the Company dating back to 1801, but in reality a series of scarcely veiled threats. The governor general had been well briefed by the Resident. He knew all about the destruction of the 'Hindoo pagodas', as he called them, at Haidarganj. He knew about the 'dancing and singing men' turned out at Richmond's request and the appointment of 'Ali Naqi Khan against the Resident's advice, and he also knew about the strength of the king's army, which was being kept up 'contrary to the treaty of 1801'. Sportingly, Hardinge said that he did not wish to make the king answerable for the wrongs of his ancestors and recognised his inexperience as ruler, but the perceived maladministration of Awadh had to cease, and in particular the land revenue system was to be overhauled so that peasants knew how much they were to be taxed. Before leaving the palace, Hardinge indicated to the king which of the royal presents on offer he had decided to accept; then, according to Richmond, Wajid 'Ali Shah 'retired apparently much gratified with the interview'.

The king was given a week to respond to Hardinge's complaints, and a grace period of two years in which to implement the reforms. Richmond reported that the king wrote a letter of thanks to the governor general and suggested a feast 'to commemorate our Glorious Victory on the Sutlej before our advance on the Punjab' but unfortunately Hardinge's stay in Lucknow was so short that this was not possible.[49] However, since the king had mentioned the Punjab (which was subsequently added to the Company's Indian portfolio), the Resident noted that this was 'a good opportunity to remind His Majesty how careful we were to maintain Native Princes in the exercise of their power provided it could be done with due regards to the happiness and protection of the people'.

Ironically, it was the Company's own aggressive policies that extended the postponement of the threat of annexation well beyond the two-year period specified by Hardinge. In succession, the Company fought the Second Anglo-Sikh War, which took place in the winter of 1848–9, and then embarked on the Second Anglo-Burmese War four years later (1852–3). In both conflicts the Company was the victor, and subsequently both the Punjab and the area designated as Lower Burma needed troops and administrators to consolidate the gains. This drew attention away from the comparatively minor problem of Awadh, where its ruler was compliant to the Company and presented no military challenge. Yet it was an annoyance—a nagging, unresolved irritation for the new governor general, Lord Dalhousie, who took up office in January 1848, and for his employers, the Court of Directors. Although external events had led to an interregnum of eight years, the annexation of Awadh was still a goal to be achieved. British politicians may have forgotten why it was important to annex Awadh, and the impetus for reform had long gone, but Lord Dalhousie had remembered.

While Wajid 'Ali Shah was allowed by the British to coast along, producing extravagant musical events, writing poetry, building Qaisarbagh and marrying innumerable wives, the threat of annexation always hung over his reign. Perhaps it was this that intensified the creative fervour in Lucknow, a fin de siècle *moment in the middle of the nineteenth century. Meanwhile, to continue the theatrical analogy, while the king was busy centre stage, his nemesis, Sir William Sleeman, was waiting in the wings.*

3

THE SORROWS OF AKHTAR

A new Resident, William Sleeman, is appointed and submits a damning report on Awadh and the king to the governor general. The blow falls, the kingdom is annexed, without bloodshed, by James Outram, and the king and his relatives travel to Calcutta. A year later he is imprisoned in Fort William following a suspicious incident. His release, after the Great Uprising is over, marks the start of his thirty-year exile in Bengal.

The East India Company had had Awadh in its sights since the middle of the turbulent eighteenth century, when policy was decided on the battlefield and through unlikely, but expedient, alliances. Wajid 'Ali Shah's great-great-grandfather, the nawab Shuja-ud-Daulah, had challenged the East India Company at Buxar, in Bengal, in 1764. Fighting alongside his temporary allies, the nawab of Bengal, Mir Qasim, and the Mughal Emperor Shah Alam II, Shuja-ud-Daulah was defeated by the Company's army, commanded by General Sir Hector Munro. This led to the start of British interference in Awadh and the stationing of Company troops there, at the nawab's expense, ostensibly to defend the province. It was to lead, within a few years, to the installation of a British Resident at the Awadh Court, who reported directly to the governor general in Calcutta. It also led to various treaties (always in the Company's favour), and to huge loans extracted from the nawabs by the Company.

It was a nawabi loan of £2.5 million that had financed the British expedition against Nepal in 1814. Another loan of £1.5 million paid for the First Burmese War (1824–6), and a further loan of £100,000, brought British troops back to India following their defeat in the First Afghan War. Seven loans were made by Awadh to the Company between 1814 and annexation. Some loans were paid back in the form of pensions to individuals or land grants, while others were quietly transmuted into 'gifts'. But even so, a decade after annexation, the British government was found to owe Awadh nearly £2 million, including interest. To British embarrassment the paperwork for these loans was not readily available when called for years later. It was 'scattered over various documents'[1] or lost somewhere between the Financial Department in Calcutta, the Shimla record office and the office of the chief commissioner of Awadh, who of course had the perfect excuse that all the Residency records had been destroyed during 1857. While the money for these loans had come from the nawabi treasury, they had been authorised by the nawabs, and when loans *were* repaid, they were repaid to the nawabs themselves, the dividing line between state income and personal nawabi income seemingly non-existent. This goes some way towards explaining Wajid 'Ali Shah's nonchalant attitude towards money. He was certainly a spendthrift, and an easy dupe in financial matters, but at the back of his mind he knew how generous his ancestors had been towards 'borrowings' by the Company and felt, justifiably, that the Company's successor, the British government, owed him reparation.

Exchanges between the Company and the nawabs were not completely one-sided, however. In 1819 Wajid 'Ali Shah's great-uncle, the ruling nawab Ghazi-ud-Din Haidar, became king of Awadh. The bauble of a crown had been dangled in front of him by the Company and he took it eagerly. The Company's gesture was not entirely altruistic, but was an attempt to wean the nawabs away from their allegiance to the Mughal emperor. By the second decade of the nineteenth century, the once great empire had been reduced to little more than the confines of the Red Fort in Delhi. The Company had abandoned the pretence that it ruled in the name of the emperor, and now struck coins in its own name. Nevertheless, there was a powerful, emotive residue of awe and respect towards the descendants of the great Mughals. The Company suspected that the Mughal heir, Prince Jahangir, who had taken a potshot at Sir Archibald Seton, the British agent to the Court of Delhi, might form an anti-British alliance with other disgruntled Muslim rulers. In a classic example of divide and rule, the Company encouraged nawab Ghazi-ud-Din Haidar to declare his independence from the nominal Mughal emperor and to name himself 'King of Awadh'. (Other regional rulers were offered the title of king too, including the *nizam* of Hyderabad, but only Awadh accepted.)

The nawab could not have been more delighted. Hugely elaborate preparations were made for his coronation. An area north of the river Gomti was marked out as a great tented enclosure for guests attending the event, and it is still known today as Haidarabad (Haidar's settlement), after the new king. The Lal Barahdari, a pleasant red-painted pavilion within the palace complex, became the throne room, with a newly painted ceiling of plump flying cherubs. Because there were no precedents for crowning a Muslim monarch according to Christian rituals, the ceremony became a curious blend of Indian and English elements.[2] A coronation robe of heavy blue velvet with an ermine cape was ordered from London[3] and a Persian-inspired crown was designed by the Court artist in residence, Robert Home. Home also designed chairs with blue velvet seats and backrests of gilded fish for the guests attending the ceremony. The throne was an extravaganza of beaten gold panels richly embellished with jewels placed under a pearl-embroidered canopy. Over

£1 million was allotted by the nawab for expenditure on the coronation, but in spite of all the pomp and ceremony there was little significant political change. The new king began to strike coins in his own name, using his own regnal year, and he acquired a coat of arms too; but as an English officer observed, 'Ostensibly, his Nabobship has been promoted from the rank of servant to that of lord, virtually he has only changed masters…'[4] Nevertheless the nawabs were now royalty, and were to be addressed as 'Your Majesty' even by the governor general. With the departure of the King of Delhi to exile and death in Burma after the Uprising of 1857, Ghazi-ud-Din Haider's great-nephew was indeed the last king in India.

The crown, with its fashionable egret plumes, had been placed on the head of the first king by a young cleric, Sayyid Muhammad Nasirabadi. He was described, misleadingly, as a 'high priest', although Islam does not officially recognise religious hierarchies. Nasirabadi was a *mujtahid*, the learned son of a pious Muslim family. The symbolic act of crowning a new king (which in England is carried out by the Archbishop of Canterbury) was to remind the congregation and the British Resident that the nawabs, too, were men of faith. They were Shi'as, who regarded 'Ali (the son-in-law of the Prophet Muhammad) as the first legitimate Imam. The schism between Shi'as and Sunnis resulted from a dispute about leadership after the Prophet's death. Within the Shi'a sect came further divides, but the majority of Shi'as, including the Awadh family, trace the leadership descent from 'Ali to the twelfth Imam, and are known as Twelvers, or Isna 'ashariyah. Ghazi-ud-Din Haidar actually claimed descent from the seventh Imam, Musa al-Kasim, which gave him an impeccable pedigree. Although Company officials were aware of the different sects of Islam, not least because they had had to intervene in clashes between Sunnis and Shi'as during Muharram of 1828, they chose to ignore the importance of religion in the lives of the nawabs. They missed the connection between Lucknow and

Iraq,[5] which was regarded by the nawabi family as their original homeland and which was still a place of refuge and retirement. Indeed, an unsuccessful contender for the Awadh throne spent the last years of his life living in a house that later became the British Residency in Baghdad.[6]

The links between the Shi'a community in Iraq and the ruling nawabs in Lucknow were strengthened by men like Sayyid Dildar 'Ali Naqvi, father of the cleric who had crowned the first king in 1819. It was Dildar 'Ali, a Lucknow scholar, who had persuaded the fourth nawab, Asaf-ud-daulah, to fund the building of a canal in the Iraqi city of Karbala. The small waterway is still known today as the Asafi Canal after its donor, and this pious gesture ate up huge amounts of nawabi money, despatched from the Lucknow treasury. It was followed by equally generous amounts for other projects at the holy cities of Najaf and Karbala. The regular transfer of money to Iraq, through the British political agents in the Ottoman Empire, is a continuing theme throughout the whole of the nawabi period and, as we have seen, one of Wajid 'Ali Shah's first acts as king was to distribute money for Shi'a pilgrims at Baghdad. It was not a one-way traffic either for Iraqi workmen were brought to Lucknow as builders to recreate the religious edifices of their homeland. A building in the old part of Lucknow is a close copy of the Shrine of the Two Imams at Kazmain, now on the outskirts of Baghdad. Wajid 'Ali Shah inherited this rich and substantial background, which gave him status among Shi'as in India, Iran and the Ottoman Empire. This was not only by virtue of his descent, but also from the generosity of his predecessors towards the holy places of Islam, something that his British detractors signally failed to acknowledge. He had a position to maintain, both as a temporal king and as a descendant of the seventh Imam.

Wajid 'Ali Shah's personal feelings as a Muslim—and a Muslim ruler—are harder to gauge and somewhat contradictory. Under his predecessors, and particularly his late father, the *muj-*

tahid had done very well, both financially and politically. They had played an important part in Court life, often prompting or initiating the building of mosques, imambarahs, schools and theological colleges, as well as advising on correct procedure during the mourning month of Muharram. Wajid 'Ali Shah felt confident enough to stop payment of the government-funded poor tax established by his father, which the mujtahid had administered, mainly to their own benefit. He was later to stop funding the Shi'a seminary, also set up during his father's reign, which had received regular grants from the treasury. He reintroduced the restricted sale of opium, wine and *bhang*, which had been forbidden by Amjad 'Ali Shah. At the same time, as we shall see, Wajid 'Ali Shah was not above invoking specific Shi'a laws when it suited him. He remained a teetotaler all his life, and we have no reason to disbelieve his descendants who say he was a pious, God-fearing man who prayed five times a day. Whether he drew on the comfort of his religion during difficult times is harder to say. There was certainly more than an element of self-pity in much of his writing, but he lived within the boundaries of his faith, observing, and being seen to observe, the obligations of a Shi'a. Later in life Wajid 'Ali Shah would himself be regarded as a mujtahid, and one of his books deals with the problems of religious jurisdiction.[7] Interestingly, its place of publication, which was at the king's Garden Reach estate near Calcutta, is given as *daru 'l-hakumat*, the conventional term for an area where Muslim edicts are in force.

During the first critical period of his reign, when he needed all the help he could get, Wajid 'Ali Shah had had to rely on the unsatisfactory British Resident Colonel Archibald Richmond, himself under pressure from the governor general. Richmond was good at finger-wagging and dishing out criticism, but far less adept at making positive suggestions, or encouraging initiatives by the new king. In the two years before William Sleeman became Resident, in January 1849, Wajid 'Ali Shah embarked on a number of projects that could have been nurtured and developed by a more sympathetic British advisor. One such initiative, started with the best of intentions, was to erect a number of 'complaints boxes' in public places in Lucknow. These were called *mashghalah-ye-noshervani*, a grandiose Persian term that translates as something equivalent to 'the royal prerogative'. Like letter boxes, with a small slit in the top, the idea was that the general public could post letters and petitions which would be read by the king himself (his prerogative) and passed on to the appropriate government department for action. There were also two silver letter boxes that were carried at the front of royal processions on a stick, where the public could post their complaints. Although there is no tangible or written evidence for these boxes, mention of them appears in oral accounts from eyewitnesses, captured by several historians of Awadh.[8] It was an imaginative gesture by a young king. If it seems naïve now, then it is no more so than today's British government inviting email petitions from the electorate. Unfortunately, the complaints boxes had to be quietly removed after they were found to be full of obscene suggestions.

A more significant gesture was Wajid 'Ali Shah's attempted reform of the Awadh Army, again something upon which Colonel Richmond, as an officer, could have advised. Although micro-managing many aspects of the king's life, the East India Company did not interfere with his military arrangements, because it did not perceive the Awadh Army as a potential threat. In this the Company's judgement was correct. There had been no hint of army insurgency either against the nawabs or against the Company since the battle of Buxar, nearly a century earlier. Ostensibly recruited to protect the kingdom of Awadh, in fact the last time the army had been called on to do so was during the second Rohilla War in October 1794, when it arrived twenty-four hours too late to participate in the only battle of that short-lived event. Thus the army's role had not been defensive for many years, but it was retained to assist in land revenue collection from reluctant landholders, to keep the peace throughout Awadh and to provide a colourful backdrop during royal processions and ceremonies. The uniform of the Awadh Army was based on the European model and consisted of a short blue jacket with gold frogging worn over long white trousers and a shako with a plume on the head of the officers. The palace guard soldiers wore a similar uniform, with the shako and plume but with blue trousers.

Shortly after his enthronement the king was reported to be visiting the Lucknow parade grounds regularly on horseback to inspect his troops. A small painting in the Hussainabad Picture Gallery in Lucknow shows him doing just this. He raised a number of new regiments to support those already well established, and gave fanciful names to the new platoons, like Palton Akhtari, Palton Wajidi and Palton Gulabi (the Rose Platoon).[9] Relatives and Court favourites like Prince Miftah-ud-daulah and the eunuch Diyanat ud-Daulah were appointed as commanders of the regiments. A number of European and Anglo-Indian officers were in charge of platoons, or serving in them, including Captains Magness, Barlow, Hearsey and Orr.[10] The king's father-in-law, 'Ali Naqi Khan, was appointed officer in charge of the Habshiyan Risalah, the Black Regiment, made up of Africans who had been brought into India by Arab slave traders. The history of Africans in Awadh has only recently been uncovered,[11] but it is clear that they had long been employed in the nawabi army, as they were in the nizam of Hyderabad's army. From the mid-nineteenth century there were anecdotal reports that the king's personal bodyguard was made up of African women, who were described as 'Amazons' by British eyewitnesses. These reports were previously dismissed as fanciful, but now that the king's liking for African wives has been established (see Chapter Four), we can imagine how he would have enjoyed being surrounded by these female black warriors. The Rose Platoon was commanded by Haji Husain Ali, and this was almost certainly the king's own female bodyguard, riding out in their smart red jackets and 'tight-fitting rose-coloured silk trousers'.[12] Wajid 'Ali Shah's love of the theatrical meant that he had probably designed their uniforms too.

Money was lavished on the soldiers, apart from providing them with uniforms. 'Arms and Accoutrements' were purchased by the king from the Company's Cawnpore magazine, specifically for the African Regiments at a cost of £900.[13] Other soldiers got prizes and titles for exhibiting particular skills. The king told Richmond that he had found the army in a bad state when he took over, and at first he contemplated reducing the army corps by degrees, to make the remainder more efficient and serviceable, but when he learned of the difficulty of collecting land revenue with fewer men, he changed his mind and increased his force.[14] The Resident argued that it was the police force that should be strengthened, not the army. Richmond pointed out that because the East India Company's three Presidency armies (Bengal, Bombay and Madras) had been considerably enlarged since 1837, the king's own Awadh Army could be correspondingly reduced. But this did not happen, and on annexation it was found that the army consisted of 52 regiments with 60,349 serving officers and men.[15] (Although the Awadh Army was disbanded on annexation, it is clear that some platoons re-formed during the Uprising that began in Lucknow in June 1857. These included the Akhtari, the Ghanghor and the Nadri Paltons who joined other forces to oppose the British.) By the time of Hardinge's visit in November 1847, the king's military enthusiasms had been effectively quashed, and apart from appointing regimental commanders he took no further interest in the army and ceased to visit the parade ground. Bribery crept back in again with new soldiers having to buy their way in, but the army remained loyal to the king.

The third and final innovation was to be a reform of the land revenue collection. Without being specific, Viscount Hardinge had talked about the Company's duty to protect the *ryots*, the peasants who actually farmed the land. Because of the way the revenue was collected, with some money sticking to the hands of everyone it passed through before it got to the nawab's treasury, the peasants were thought to be dreadfully exploited. This was certainly true in some cases, though it was not universal throughout Awadh. Landholders were canny enough to realise that they needed productive, reasonably healthy workers to till the land, and that ultimately their own financial standing depended on the men and women who pulled the plough and planted the spring and autumn crops.

In the spring of 1848 Wajid 'Ali Shah decided to introduce the 'English system' of revenue collection, where officers appointed directly by the Resident were responsible firstly for assessing the potential worth of the land, and secondly for collecting the revenue. (This is how the term District Collector originated.) Robert Bird was sent to Agra to meet the lieutenant governor of the North Western Provinces, James Thomason, and to work out how the scheme could be implemented. Sensibly it was proposed to start with the areas of Awadh that adjoined British territory, then to work inwards towards the centre of the kingdom. Following Thomason's suggestions, Bird returned to Lucknow with written proposals, got them approved by the minister 'Ali Naqi Khan, and was about to present them to the king for implementation when the Resident decided that the new governor general, Dalhousie, should look at them first. Whether the scheme got as far as Dalhousie is unclear. It was forwarded to Henry Elliot, Secretary to the Foreign Department, who peremptorily rejected it, saying, 'if His Majesty the King of Oude would give up the whole of his dominions, the East India Government would think of it', but that it was not worth while to take so much trouble about a portion.[16] Bird was later to comment that Elliot's remarks amounted to a snub not only to himself, but to the king, his minister, the Resident Richmond and the lieutenant governor Thomason. There was no more talk of revenue reform and the old method of collection remained unchanged until annexation, when the new government immediately implemented the 'English system'.

While he had dismissed the king's proposals out of hand, there was one thing that Wajid 'Ali Shah did have that interested Elliot greatly, and that was his huge collection of books. If the king had chosen to inspect his Lucknow arsenal in the second year of his reign, he might have found Dr Aloys Sprenger, the clever Austrian orientalist, poking around inside the large building and trying to avoid the rats. Sprenger had received orders on 6 December 1847 from the government of India appointing him as 'Extra Assistant to the Resident at Lucnow, as a temporary measure, for the purpose of cataloguing the extensive collection of works in Arabic and Persian literature in the king of Oudh's libraries'.[17] (Sprenger had arrived in India in 1843 and was appointed principal of Delhi College, thanks to his knowledge of oriental languages.) He was exactly the right man to take on the formidable task of cataloguing the three nawabi libraries, which had been built up since the 1770s by men of culture and unlimited wealth. Some of the treasures from the libraries of the Mughal emperors had found their way to Lucknow, including the famous Padshahnamah, which was presented as a gift by nawab Asaf-ud-daulah to the visiting governor general of the time, Sir John Shore.[18] This was an indication of similar riches which Elliot hoped would be found in Wajid 'Ali Shah's libraries. Elliot, as we have seen, had been in Lucknow since the middle of 1847, preparing the Resident and the king for Viscount Hardinge's visit in November of that year. As a keen historian, Elliot would have been shown the royal libraries, and was told about other, private, collections in the city.[19] After Sprenger's death in 1893, a second catalogue was published, a *Report... into the Muhammadan libraries of Lucknow*, many of which of course were lost during 1857–8.

There is practically nothing historians will not do to get their hands on new material, and the libraries of Lucknow were beyond temptation. It is of course possible that Elliot, during meetings with the king, suggested that his libraries should be catalogued and Wajid 'Ali Shah, as a man of letters himself, agreed. If so, no written agreement has been found, and Sprenger makes it clear he was 'ordered' by the government of India to compile the catalogue. There is no mention of the king inviting him, as one would expect. He arrived in Lucknow on 3 March 1848 and spent nearly two years working there. As European scholars became aware of the treasures held so carelessly, it seemed, by libraries in the East, there was a surge of interest. Sprenger told Elliot that the French government had sent 'gentlemen to Algiers, Egypt and Constantinople to examine the Libraries and Mr Fahn of St Petersburg published in 1845 a List of Oriental works which the Russian Government had purchased for the Imperial Academy'.[20] He added that 'The devastation of manuscripts in the East and more particularly in India is so rapid that anyone who takes the slightest interest in Literature or in the honor of the government must want a record.' We read this with mixed feelings today. The cataloguing and purchasing of oriental books and manuscripts from these countries by European governments can certainly be seen as a manifestation of arrogant colonialism. But at the same time Sprenger was quite right about the way many of these manuscripts had been left to deteriorate. The 'library' in the Lucknow arsenal was upstairs in the northern wing, and the books were not on shelves but in about forty dilapidated boxes known as 'camel trunks—which are at the same time tenanted by prolific families of rats … At the end of the hall there are bags full of books completely destroyed by white ants.'

It was unfortunate, and indeed strange, that Wajid 'Ali Shah was not more interested in the collections made by his ancestors. It was the librarians' job to make sure that the number of books remained constant, and so they were counted at intervals, but not catalogued. Sprenger found that many valuable books had been extracted and replaced by worthless ones. He learned of a librarian who had stolen books worth 1,100 rupees and sold them to pay for his daughter's wedding.[21] Elliot urged Sprenger to work as quickly as possible, because the Court of Directors is 'anxious to see the result of your labors'.[22] By March 1851 the first volume of what was to be a five-volume catalogue was ready for publication, listing about 10,000 volumes. (The expense of publication, which Sprenger had grossly underestimated, meant that the Court of Directors would not pay for the remaining four volumes.) Today Sprenger's catalogue is all that remains of the nawabi libraries. A contemporary report from 1857 describes 'thousands' of volumes from the royal library that were either burned or thrown into the river during looting by rebel Indian soldiers, long before the British started their own looting in 1858.[23]

Quite apart from Elliot's personal desire to see what the royal libraries contained, there is the calculated assumption, indeed the certainty, that before too long their contents would be added to the treasures of the East India Company. Sprenger told Elliot in September 1848 that he saw his role as preserving 'a sketch of the literature, libraries, learning and educational systems of the Rulers of India to whom the British government has succeeded'.[24] This episode, minor in the scale of tragedy that would overwhelm Wajid 'Ali Shah, but nonetheless significant, demonstrates that the king's fate was written from the moment he took the throne, if not before. Not only had he been damned by the Company when still heir apparent, he had been threatened and lectured at by the Resident and governor general before he had completed a year's reign. His attempts at reforming the collection of land revenue, the very basis on which Awadh functioned, were scornfully dismissed. It was almost as if the Company willed him to fail. No wonder he took comfort in those areas that he could still control: the grand theatrical extravaganzas, the fairy palaces, the endless supply of young women and the melancholy delight of poetry.

On 11 January 1849 Major General Sir William Sleeman took over the post of Resident at the Court of Lucknow. Although he had wished to retire from the Company's service, being sixty-one at the time of his appointment and not in good health, Sleeman was considered too valuable a political officer to let go. Lucknow was to be his last posting: a well-paid, prestigious end to his remarkable career. Unlike his predecessor, Sleeman had a number of advantages: he was fluent in Urdu and Persian and so able to converse directly with the king and, just as importantly, able to pick up information from palace staff, courtiers and the man in the street. He had a formidable literary reputation. His first published work was an examination of tax collecting in India, published in 1829, and this had been followed by a number of books, including the popular *Rambles and Recollections of an Indian Official* (1844). His work in suppressing thuggee in Upper and Central India in the 1830s led not only to his accounts detailing how this was achieved, and the peculiar, coded language of the murderers, but had also given him the nickname of Thuggee Sleeman. His article in 1843 for the new natural history journal *The Zoologist* explored the stories of so-called wolf-children, raised in the dens of wolves.

Sleeman had joined the Bengal Army as an ensign in 1809 and arrived in Calcutta that year as a young man of twenty. He had been stationed in Awadh in 1818 and 1819, and claimed to have seen much of the correspondence between the then Resident, Colonel Baillie, and the Army commandant. He moved from military to civil service and had been Resident at Gwalior for six years before the Lucknow appointment. During the short interregnum after Richmond left Lucknow and before Sleeman took over, Captain Robert Bird was acting Resident. He was already Assistant Resident and was sufficiently trusted by Wajid 'Ali Shah to act as emissary on various missions. He was referred to at one point as the nawab's wakil, or agent. After Sleeman's arrival Bird reverted to assistant again and the two men worked together until the fatal falling out which saw Bird banished to Ajmer. After this there was clearly no love lost between the two, so Bird's statements on Sleeman have to be read with this in mind. Nevertheless, something rings true about his comments on the latter's mission to Awadh. 'Colonel Sleeman was appointed Resident in 1849, and his appointment sealed the doom of Oude and of its dynasty. Colonel Sleeman was the emissary of a foregone conclusion. He affected to inspect and make a report, but the character of his report was determined for him before he entered Oude. He professed to examine, but he was under orders to sentence; he pretended to try, but he was instructed simply to condemn.'[25]

In appointing Sleeman to Awadh, Dalhousie told him that the king had been given a specific deadline by which to improve his administration, and if his government was not 'very materially amended before two years had expired', the British government would take over and rule on his behalf. He added, 'There seems little reason to expect or to hope that in October 1849 any amendment whatever will have been effected. The reconstruction of the internal administration of a great, rich and oppressed country, is a noble as well as an arduous task for the officer to whom the duty is intrusted, and the Government have recourse to one of the best of its servants for that purpose.' There was more flattery to this effect, and Dalhousie referred 'to the great changes which, in all probability, will take place'.[26]

William Sleeman was too intelligent a man to act as a mere stooge in carrying out Dalhousie's intentions. What he envisaged was that he would shortly be in charge of the complex but rewarding job of bringing Awadh into the Company's fold, of introducing an 'English system' of land reform throughout the entire kingdom, of curbing corruption, supporting the peasants and mollifying Wajid 'Ali Shah, who would become a mere nominal ruler. After all, Gwalior, Sleeman's former posting, had been successfully subsumed into British India, while maintaining the ruling Shinde (Scindia) dynasty. But the threatened deadline of October 1849 passed without any action being taken. Dalhousie had hesitated. After the successful annexation by the Company of the Punjab six months earlier, it might seem a little greedy to add Awadh in the same year. A new, provisional deadline of December 1851 was promised.[27] But as the months passed, Dalhousie felt there was no necessity for immediate action. 'Before very long', he confided to his diary in January 1852, 'it seems certain that the King himself must solicit our interposition, in which case we shall act more authoritatively, and with less caviling than if we should take the initiative.'[28] He thought that Sir Frederick Currie, then a member of the governing council at Calcutta, would oppose the move. Later the Second Anglo-Burmese War would become a further excuse for postponing any solution to the problem. Sleeman thus found himself in the uncomfortable position of Resident to the Court of Awadh, when he might have expected to be running the kingdom by the end of 1849.

On his arrival in Lucknow Sleeman learned that the king was indisposed, and by the end of January he reported to Henry Elliot that Wajid 'Ali Shah 'continues very ill, but no danger seems to be apprehended. The disease is accompanied by very untoward secondary symptoms, which are likely ultimately to destroy him, and render his life miserable while it lasts. How much of these symptoms he derives from his birth, and how much from his own excesses, is uncertain.'[29] From the Resident's guarded comments it seems that the king was suffering from gonorrhoea, which he had admitted catching from Qaisar Begam, one of his wives.[30] This illness could produce secondary symptoms, including pelvic inflammation and pain in the joints. It was treated at the time by silver nitrate, which has disinfective properties. By March Wajid 'Ali Shah was still unwell, although Sleeman reported that 'under skilful treatment he might soon get well; but the prescriptions of his best native physicians are little attended to, and he has not yet consented to consult an European doctor'.

Unable to leave the palace for some months, Wajid 'Ali Shah spent his convalescence writing a manual of government for 'Ali Naqi Khan, to whom he had deputed the running of the kingdom during his illness. This document, entitled *Dastur-i-Wajidi* (or the Regulations of Wajid), was not printed until a quarter of a century later,[31] and Sleeman was clearly not aware of it when he complained that 'the King ... is utterly unfit to have anything to do with the administration, since he has never taken, or shown any disposition to take any heed of what is done or suffered in the country'.[32] The Regulations, sixty-six in number, show that, contrary to Sleeman's statement, Wajid 'Ali Shah had a very clear idea of what was going on in his kingdom.[33] He knew that his soldiers stole livestock and goods from peasants in the countryside, and ordered them to stop on pain of punishment. Regular soldiers were to be disciplined for their bad behaviour during Holi, particularly the singing of lewd songs and the molestation of women. The king wanted an investigation into the prison population, with details of prisoners confined under his predecessors. He knew that illegal tolls were being levied on travellers, and ordered that 'every effort should be made to secure public peace on the highways'. *Sati*, widow-burning, which had been outlawed in Company territories in 1832, was to be forbidden in Awadh too. The Rajput practice of female infanticide was to cease and notices be posted to this effect on public highways. Private houses in Lucknow were not to remain empty, and if they were rented out, the owner was to take a deposit in advance. There was much sensible advice in this wish list, covering every aspect of urban and rural administration, and had these regulations been put into practice Awadh would have become a model kingdom and attracted praise, not condemnation, from the Company.

Sleeman spent his first year in office drawing up a plan of action, compiling tables of revenue and expenditure and wading 'through vast volumes of correspondence to ascertain what has been said and done ... and to become acquainted with the people in my new field, European and native'.[34] By 20 March 1849, with Wajid 'Ali Shah still on his sickbed, Sleeman was already suggesting that a new treaty should be drawn up 'in case of the King's decease'. He suggested a regency until the heir apparent came of age, which would consist of two or three honest nobles, answerable to the Resident. Janab-i 'Aliyyah was to be consulted on nominating members, though no women were allowed to serve on it.[35] The idea of a regency was to be the theme that ran through all of Sleeman's correspondence as Resident. There were variations as time progressed. The king stubbornly refused to die, indeed, 'he is said to be better', Sleeman noted, adding hopefully 'but the hot season may be too much for him'.[36] An early check to these plans came with the sad news of the death from smallpox of the heir apparent, the ten-year-old Prince Falak Qadr. 'I have seldom seen a more pleasing or promising youth, and certainly never one in whom after so short an acquaintance I felt a warmer interest', Sleeman reported. 'I tried all in my power to prevail upon his mother and father to allow the young Prince to be treated by the Residency Surgeon, but in vain.'[37] The Resident did get permission for the two Residency doctors, Leckie and Bell, to visit the prince, but they were not allowed to treat him.

By the beginning of May the king was well enough to meet the two British doctors and Robert Bird at the palace. 'They found him much better in bodily health than they expected, and in the course of conversation found no signs of any confusion of ideas, and are of opinion that in the hands of a skilful European physician he would soon be quite well. His Majesty is hypochondriac, and frequently under the influence of the absurd delusions common to such persons; but he is quite sane during long intervals, and on all subjects not connected with such delusions.'[38] The idea of a regency was dropped and Sleeman now suggested 'the formation of a Board, consisting of president and three members nominated by the King, subject to the conformation of the Governor General'. One board member would deal with land revenue and the police, the second would have the judicial courts and control of the royal household, while the third would be in charge of the army. Sikandar Hashmat was suggested as a possible candidate—'a most worthy and respectable, though not able man', was Sleeman's judgement. He added blithely, 'The King will probably object to members of his family forming the Board, but I dare say I shall be able to persuade him of the advantage of it.'[39]

Sleeman has been criticised by a modern historian for his obsessional behaviour, verging in his last years on paranoia.[40] Certainly he exhibited symptoms that indicate things were not right during the Lucknow period. Irrational dislikes of Britons living there, particularly the 'three Bs' as he called them—John Rose Brandon, Dr Adam Bell and Captain Robert Bird—took up a large amount of his time and correspondence. While Brandon did have an almost unlimited capacity for annoying British Residents, the doctor and the captain did not. Sleeman thought the three had ganged up on him, and all of them left Lucknow during his tenure. He believed, with little evidence, that he had been the victim of an attempted assassination at the Residency. But the idea that his constant complaints about Wajid 'Ali Shah's behaviour were also irrational has not previously been explored, because so many other people were there to snipe at the king too. When Wajid 'Ali Shah sent some items from Awadh to be shown at the Great Exhibition of 1851 in London, Dalhousie commented outrageously that 'the wretch at Lucknow, who sent his crown to the exhibition, would have done his people and us a good service if he had sent his head in it, and he never would have missed it'.[41] The fact that this was a private letter, and that Dalhousie put a fifty-year restriction on the publication of his letters, does not detract from the venom behind this remark.

With Wajid 'Ali Shah being damned even before he became king, and damned afterwards, it was thus assumed that Sleeman had got it right when he described him as 'a crazy imbecile',[42] 'utterly unfit to have anything to do with the administration',[43] 'no longer in a sound state of mind'[44] and a man who spent all his time with singers, eunuchs and women. But Sleeman constantly misinterpreted the information he was getting from his spies at Court, who were euphemistically described as newswriters. A palace *mush'aira* (a gathering of poets) was described in sarcastic tones, with the remark that it did not finish until the early hours of the morning, which is of course entirely normal for this kind of event. Then the king was criticised for taking part in a Muharram procession, which most rational people, certainly in India, would have seen as an act of faith. There was a gulf of misunderstanding between Sleeman and the king, which could not be solved by inviting the Resident to further events, like the Basant celebrations. Soon after his arrival in Lucknow Sleeman had the misfortune to break a bone in his thigh, in a fall from his horse, and the subsequent pain and medication, which would have been opiate-based, cannot have improved his outlook or his judgement.

An early public rift between Resident and king came with the news that Wajid 'Ali Shah had abruptly closed down the Taronwali Kothi, or Star House, the local name given to the Lucknow Observatory. It had been sanctioned in 1832 and building had begun that year, but it was not functional until 1841, when Colonel Richard Wilcox was appointed as astronomer. The project had been strongly supported by the Company as one of a number of meteorological observatories established in India. The fact that the nawabs bore all the expenditure, including the importation of valuable astronomical equipment from England and the staff's wages, made it even more attractive. Colonel Wilcox, who had accompanied the king to Cawnpore in 1847, had died there the following year, and it became clear to Sleeman that the king was disinclined to appoint a successor. Work had continued at the Observatory under Wilcox's two principal assistants, Kala Churn and Ganga Persaud, but when Sleeman raised the question of pensions for the two men, the establishment was closed down on 8 August 1849 and everyone working there was sacked. Cost was cited as the reason for its closure, an excuse which was scornfully dismissed by Sleeman in a letter to Henry Elliot: 'He [the king] has lavished every month more than enough to support a dozen such observatories among persons who had no claim whatever upon his bounty ... there is strong desire on the part of the court generally to exclude European Gentlemen of respectability from employment under the King.'[45] It was also learned that 'Ali Naqi Khan had his eye on the building and its gardens which 'are among the best, and best situated at Lucknow'. After Sleeman applied pressure and told Dalhousie what had happened, the king changed his mind and the staff received their pensions.

At the same time as the Observatory was shut, the king ordered the closure of all private and lithographic presses in Lucknow, because Kamal-ud-Din Haider, who had been employed by Colonel Wilcox, had written an amusing biography of Wajid 'Ali Shah called *Qaisar-ut-Tawarikh*. The author had unwisely presented a copy to the king 'to flatter his own vanity', but had 'forgot to flatter the King'.[46] He had also related the story of the patent leather shoes, which the king had been told to wear on meeting the governor general, an indication both of how seemingly private matters quickly got into public circulation, and Wajid 'Ali Shah's own sensitivities on the subject.

On 1 December 1849 Sleeman set off on a long-planned tour of Awadh. Having familiarised himself with the urban milieu, he needed to visit the rural areas in order to present a complete picture of the kingdom to Dalhousie. Not surprisingly he did not have much positive to say about life outside Lucknow. His diary, written up daily, was published posthumously in 1858 as *A Journey through the Kingdom of Oude 1849–1850*; it is a readable book, but one that owes more to Urdu or Persian histories of India than Sleeman would have cared to admit. It is discursive, breaking off into long, rambling stories about the people he met and places he visited. Correspondence that he had found in the Residency archives is quoted at length, as well as extracts from books by visitors to Lucknow, like Fanny Parks. All this considerably slows down the narrative, so that it becomes less of a diary and more of a scrapbook. On his return to Lucknow at the beginning of March 1850, Sleeman bought a small printing press which he set up in the Residency and printed off a few copies of *A Journey*, one of which went to Dalhousie and one to the Court of Directors in London. Sleeman admitted to the deputy chairman of the Court, Sir James Hogg, that 'the untoward war with Burmah prevents our present Governor-General from doing what he and I believe the Honorable Court both wish'.[47]

Sleeman pursued the idea of a Board of Management and claimed backing for it from the royal family itself.[48] In a series of long, well-argued letters to the Court of Directors, he said he believed that a treaty of 1837 between the Company and the present king's grandfather, Muhammad 'Ali Shah, 'gives our Government ample authority to take the whole administration on ourselves, in order to secure what we have often pledged to ourselves to secure to the people; but if we do this we must, in order to stand well with the rest of India, honestly and distinctly disclaim all interested motives, and appropriate the whole of the revenues for the benefit of the people and royal family of Oude'.[49] He imagined the time when 'Oude would be covered with a network of fine macadamised roads, over [which] the produce of Oude and our own districts would pass freely to the benefit of the people of both'. Rivers would be made navigable for steamers, a railway would be laid down between Faizabad and Cawnpore via Lucknow, and 'useful public works' would be constructed. The revenue monies that had stuck to the fingers of corrupt officials and Court favourites would become available to fund these improvements. Sleeman correctly identified the disjuncture between the urban and the rural population, describing Lucknow as 'an overgrown city, surrounding an overgrown Court' which had so alienated the great body of people that the king and his officers regarded each other as irreconcilable enemies. 'Between the city, the pampered Court and its functionaries and the people of the country beyond, there is not the slightest feeling of sympathy...'[50]

It is worth examining the Resident's writings in depth because they were to form an important part of the Court of Directors' decision to annex the kingdom in 1856, even though Sleeman himself was against annexation. If the Court had followed his advice and established a Board of Management, while retaining Wajid 'Ali Shah as a nominal, but powerless, king, it is just possible that the Great Revolt of 1857 could have been avoided. There were many other grievances throughout India at the time,[51] but it was the seizure of the kingdom that provided the spark that fired the Uprising. What Sleeman, Dalhousie and the Court of Directors all failed to realise was that the people of Awadh preferred to be ruled by their own king, whatever his failings, rather than by foreigners, however well-intentioned the latter may have been.

Personal hostility between the Residency and the Court of Lucknow did not however deter Wajid 'Ali Shah from carrying out at least some of his kingly duties in a gracious manner. He responded to a plea from Sleeman for a contribution to a fund in memory of the Duke of Wellington, who had died in September 1852. Dalhousie had proposed the building of a college as a testimonial to the old soldier, who had served in India half a century earlier. The king sent 3,000 rupees and 'Ali Naqi Khan another 2,000 rupees, not a huge amount in the scale of things, but nevertheless an altruistic gesture for which they did not expect, nor receive, any thanks.[52] When news of the victory over Russian troops by the allied forces on the banks of the river Alma in Crimea was received in Lucknow, the king remarked that 'This intelligence has afforded me great pleasure and I ordered a salute of 21 guns to be fired immediately on receiving the first official Note. Pray communicate to the Most Noble the Governor General of India my congratulations on this victory.'[53] It was a moment of light relief in the ongoing struggle for possession of Awadh.

Because the government of India did not make good on its threat of action in 1849 promised by Viscount Hardinge, it was gradually assumed that nothing would happen. 'Our Government has cried "wolf" so often that no one now listens to it', Sleeman said, reporting that Captain Bird 'had been trying hard to persuade the King and his minister that our Government could not interfere and that all the threats of the Governor General might be disregarded'.[54] Dalhousie rejected a number of opportunities to meet Wajid 'Ali Shah face to face. In April 1850, on his way to the summer capital of Shimla, he was too busy to meet either the king or the new heir apparent at Cawnpore. A year later he decided against visiting Lucknow and refused to meet anyone from the Court. 'I feel it to be my duty to withhold those usual manifestations of respect and goodwill, which the public conduct and measures of the King have rendered it impossible for the Government of India any longer to entertain.'[55] Wajid 'Ali Shah was deeply hurt by this public snub and responded by saying that he wanted Dalhousie to see how much the administration of Awadh had been improved. But the governor general had stubbornly set his face against any contact, and in 1853 he rudely turned away an envoy sent from the king to Calcutta, declaring pompously that he would only receive communications through 'the proper channel, the Resident at Lucknow'. Since Sleeman continued to report negatively, complaining that Wajid 'Ali Shah devoted his time entirely to the pursuit of 'personal gratifications; he associates with none but those who can contribute to such gratification, women, singers and Eunuchs, and he never, I believe, reads or hears a report of complaint or public document of any kind',[56] the view from Lucknow was distinctly one-sided.

Dr Joseph Fayrer, who took the place of ill-fated Residency surgeon Adam Bell, backed up Sleeman's reports, describing the king as 'apathetic', as well as 'very fat and short-winded' and absorbed in his musicians, harem, *nautch* girls and other amusements. It was Dr Fayrer's job to précis the news of the Court for Sleeman's weekly reports to Calcutta. On a typical day the king would watch animal fights, recite a new poem, watch a wrestling match and enjoy flying kites, a favourite sport at which he excelled. There were further clashes with the Resident when the king appointed a favourite singer, Musahib 'Ali, to investigate delays in the judicial court that dealt with registering house sales and purchases. Another singer, so Sleeman believed, was put in charge of the newly created department for settling loan disputes. This man, Asad Beg, was described inaccurately by the Resident as a *dom*, or Hindu untouchable (despite his Muslim surname). Wajid 'Ali Shah indignantly rejected this slur and pointed out sharply that Asad Beg was in fact of Mughal descent and had been employed by the British government in various supervisory roles with a certificate of good conduct from the government too. Sleeman had to back down, but huffed that it would not be prudent to entrust such unlimited power 'to any individual however high in character' and claimed that Asad Beg must owe his appointment to the 'influence of some friend at Court'. Another long complaint went to Dalhousie.[57]

It became clear to the governor general that the hoped-for reforms which Sleeman had been charged with making in Awadh were not going to happen. There was by now far too much antipathy between king and Resident for the two men ever to work together. Sleeman's constant complaints against everyone, including his own staff, had a negative effect, and Wajid 'Ali Shah reacted by simply withdrawing from public affairs, sensing that whatever he did would be condemned and reported to Dalhousie. By the summer of 1854 Sleeman was talking about retiring. His health was not good, he could make no headway in Awadh, his grand plan of heading a Board of Management or a regency had not been taken up, and he suspected that the chief minister, 'Ali Naqi Khan, wanted to get him out of the way. He was delighted with Dalhousie's choice of successor, Colonel James Outram, but added disparagingly that as none of his own assistants at the Residency knew anything whatever about Awadh, Outram would therefore be at a great disadvantage. He also forecast that 'as soon as I go, some of the most atrocious villains whom I have kept out of office will try to purchase their way back...' It was a grim picture painted as Sleeman left Lucknow early in October.

James Outram arrived to take up his new position early in December, entering the city in a formal procession with elephants and a camel-train, accompanied by cavalry and infantry units. He was met by the heir apparent, Prince Hamid 'Ali, because the king was ill again, a strange echo of the illness on the former Resident's arrival. Outram was allowed a short interview with the invalid in the palace and was struck by how seriously ill he appeared. Daily bulletins on the king's health were 'far from satisfactory', but his own doctors thought there was no immediate danger. Dr Fayrer, who was present at the first interview, said that Wajid 'Ali Shah looked worse than he had done a couple of weeks earlier, although he thought it was 'very possible' that the king 'may temporarily recover from his present illness'.[58] Annoyingly, the cause of the illness is not given. Almost immediately, Outram was sucked into Lucknow politics when he learned that 'certain persons' employed by the British government were boasting that they possessed influence with the new Resident and could, for a financial consideration, get specific benefits bestowed on individuals. Outram stamped on this immediately by saying that if he found anyone defrauding the king or trying to bribe the Residency staff, as had happened in the past, they would be severely punished.

In his briefing from the governor general, Outram was instructed to set up his own enquiry into the state of the kingdom of Awadh and to see if things had improved since Sleeman's journey through it four years earlier. Outram's report was ready by 15 March 1855, and his covering letter to Dalhousie reiterated that 'the condition of Oude is, as I have shown, most deplorable ... caused by the very culpable apathy and gross misrule of the Sovereign and his Durbar'.[59] So there was to be no change in attitude or outlook towards the king. Outram's detailed report looked impressive at first glance, divided into seven sections covering 'The Sovereign and his Minister', revenue and finance, judicial courts and police, the 'Army of Oudh', roads and public works, statistics on crime and outrage, and 'Oppression and Cruelties'. But in fact this report was based largely on Sleeman's own observations, and Outram admitted as much: 'In the absence of any personal experience in this country [Awadh], I am of course entirely dependent for my information on what I find in the Residency records and can ascertain through the channels which supplied my predecessor.'[60] Not surprisingly, the conclusion was that things had not improved, and Dalhousie was being drawn, despite his reservations, towards the idea of intervention before his term of office expired in March 1856. 'I should not mind doing it as a parting coup', he admitted privately, but doubted whether the people 'at home [the Court of Directors] have the pluck to sanction it, and I can't find a pretext for doing it without sanction. The King won't offend or quarrel with us, and will take any amount of kicking without being rebellious.'[61]

While the king was recovering from his unspecified illness, he received a letter from Outram written on 8 February warning him that a Sunni troublemaker, Shah Ghulam Husain, had assembled a 'large force' of Muslims near Faizabad, and was 'determined to destroy and ruin the Hunuman Ghurrie which is inhabited by Hindoos and is peculiarly sacred in their estimation, his lieutenant (or assistant) called the Moulavee Saheb is even still more diabolically inclined and ready for strife...' To defend themselves, and their temple, large groups of armed Hindus had gathered. The Resident foresaw bloodshed and urged the king to send a 'very swift Camel Messenger with all possible speed' to have Shah Ghulam Husain immediately arrested in order to defuse the situation.[62] The Hanumangarhi, a temple built on the conjectured site of the birth of the Hindu god Rama, was at Ayodhya and near a mosque built during the reign of the Mughal emperor, Babur. The mosque, which only became known as Babri Masjid (Babur's mosque) at the beginning of the twentieth century, was built over a Hindu temple, part of a much larger complex that was quite possibly of Buddhist origin.[63] A site with so much history behind it unfortunately attracted fervent supporters from both the Sunni and the Hindu communities. As a Shi'a, Wajid 'Ali Shah could afford to stand aside from the theological disputes; but as a ruler, he had to do his best to prevent loss of life among all his subjects, regardless of their faith.

For some unknown reason the king did not act on Outram's urgent request and the clash predicted by the Resident duly took place. It was followed five months later by a much more serious encounter, which left about 70 Muslims dead, overwhelmed by a force of some 8,000 Hindus, who lost about the same number of men. A detachment of 150 men from the Awadh Army under Captains Weston, Orr and Hearsay was present, but was too small in numbers to act. Outram was summoned, unusually, to an emergency meeting with Wajid 'Ali Shah at the beginning of

August. The king told him that 'no occurrence had ever given him more intense pain or had caused deeper anxiety; that he grieved to find that so much blood has been thus unnecessarily shed and declared with much emphasis, that the whole of this lamentable loss of life was solely to be ascribed to that arch villain the Shah Gholam Hussain who had for a long period led a very vagabond life with a company of disreputable followers, still more vile, if possible, than Gholam Hussain himself'.[64] Outram reminded the king, as if he needed reminding, that two-thirds of his subjects were Hindus, and that there were influential chieftains at Faizabad who would not remain neutral if there was another clash. At the Resident's suggestion, a three-man commission was set up to enquire into the disturbances, consisting of a Muslim, Agha 'Ali Khan; a Hindu, Raja Man Singh; and, as Outram put it, 'a Christian umpire', Captain Alexander Orr—but this only seemed to make things worse. It was not, after all, a game of cricket. The chief mujtahid, Sayyid Muhammad Nasirabadi—the man who had placed the crown on the first king's head—got involved but, while seeming to condemn mob violence, did nothing to calm the situation.

A new and more dangerous leader emerged, a charismatic Sunni maulawi called Amir 'Ali, who collected around him a number of working men, labourers and small shopkeepers, who had given up their businesses in order to follow him. The conflict took on wider dimensions, upper class against lower class, Sunni against Shi'a, Muslim against Hindu. Wajid 'Ali Shah was actively involved, calling Amir 'Ali to the palace for peace talks and proposing that a small mosque could be attached to the temple, a suggestion that was immediately rejected by the Hindus. A truce took place during Muharram, which fell in September that year, but as soon as it was over hostilities recommenced, not least between the Resident and the king. The latter was warned that he would be held personally responsible if a new mosque was erected, or if violence broke out. Amir 'Ali called for an armed protest and Hindu leaders outside Awadh started to ferry in financial aid for their co-religionists. Outram exacerbated the situation by threatening to withdraw British troops from the kingdom, which he anticipated would lead to the collapse of the Awadh government and thus open the way for annexation. But Wajid 'Ali Shah stood firm. By the middle of October Amir 'Ali was losing support, the Awadh Army was in a position to deflect the jihadists in their planned march to Faizabad, and powerful Shi'a landholders like Raja Mahmudabad sent their own forces as back-up for the king. As the maulawi's marchers neared Faizabad they were shot down by the king's troops, and an estimated three to four hundred men were killed.[65] It was the end of the conflict during nawabi times, but not of course the end of the dispute, which erupted in 1992 with far greater loss of life, and the destruction of the Babri Masjid.

The king got no credit for the way he had dealt with the disturbance. On the contrary, Dalhousie said that the Resident's reports only gave further proof, 'if further proof were necessary, of the unfitness of the King of Oude and of his Durbar to hold the powers of government in that country and fortify the opinion which I lately submitted to the Honorable Court [of Directors] that the administration should be entirely taken out of their hands'.[66] A groundswell of opinion in Britain in favour of annexation was now strengthened by the publication of a racy new book by William Knighton called *The Private Life of an Eastern King*. Published in May 1855, it was an immediate success, going into a second edition in the same month, and being quoted in Parliament during debates on Awadh. It told the story of King Nasir ud-Din Haider's reign and was based on eye-witness accounts supplied by the king's ex-librarian, Edward Cropley. Two of the leading characters in the book were George Harris Derusett, the 'Barber of Lucknow', and his companion John Rose Brandon, the latter now a supporter and confidante of Wajid 'Ali Shah. Nothing could have been more timely (indeed, almost suspiciously timely) for those who believed it was the duty of the British government to rescue Awadh and its suffering people from the present king's regime. While Sleeman's indictment (which was not published in book form until 1858) dealt with the miseries of the countryside, Knighton's book detailed corruption and debauchery in the capital. The fact that the 'eastern king' was Wajid 'Ali Shah's uncle, and had been dead for nearly twenty years, hardly mattered to the majority of Knighton's readers. For those who knew something of Awadh, it simply confirmed their belief that little had changed during the last two decades. For others it was an indictment of their own government, which had allowed the situation to continue for so long. The Court of Directors' approval for annexation was sent to Dalhousie in November 1855. In the same month Wajid 'Ali Shah sent a letter to the governor general congratulating him on the allies' victory at Sebastopol. He commented that the friendship between the government of Awadh and the British government was 'manifest and evident' and ordered another 21-gun salute to be fired in celebration.[67]

James Outram travelled to Calcutta early in the new year to say farewell to the outgoing governor general and to receive his instructions on how to proceed with the annexation. Dalhousie told him that extra troops would be assembled at Cawnpore by the end of January, which would be 'sufficient to meet every contingency which could arise at present'. The troops were commanded by three British officers, but Outram, an experienced soldier, had overall control to deploy them as necessary. Conveying the actual news of the British takeover of Awadh to its king was obviously going to be difficult. Outram was advised to tell 'Ali Naqi Khan first, so that the minister could inform the king, 'in order that the King may not be taken by surprise, and that the unwelcome communication he is to receive may not appear to be made to him in a manner unnecessarily abrupt'. As a sweetener, or a threat for 'Ali Naqi Khan, Dalhousie added that 'the degree of favor and consideration with which the Minister will be regarded by the British Government will depend on his giving his hearty aid to the conclusion of a new Treaty' and providing all the information he could to facilitate the new administration.[68]

The treaty, carried by Outram back to Lucknow, was to confirm that the king was signing away his rights to the revenues of Awadh and that he agreed 'the sole and exclusive administration of the Civil and Military Government of the territories of Oude shall be henceforth vested *for ever*, in the Honorable East India Company'. If the king refused to sign it, then Outram was to take over the government of Awadh anyway.[69] The Resident was told that he could offer the king a life pension of 15 lakhs per annum (£150,000), and if Wajid 'Ali Shah thought this was not enough, then the offer could be increased to 18 lakhs a year, 'rather than lose the Treaty which the Government desire to obtain'. How much would it cost to buy a king and his kingdom? 'Ali Naqi Khan and others had already been alerted by newspaper reports that something terrible was about to happen, but when he met Outram on his return at the end of January, the Resident lied and said that the extra British troops at Cawnpore had probably been brought up to quell a disturbance on the Nepalese border.

Wajid 'Ali Shah's response to the minister's announcement of annexation was disbelief. He wrote to the Resident early on the morning of 1 February saying he was astonished and distressed, particularly as he had done everything possible to comply with whatever instructions had been received from the governor general. Outram's immediate response was that the decision was final and irreversible, as he told Janab-i 'Aliyyah later the same day. The final meeting between Outram and the king took place three days later on the morning of 4 February. As he entered the palace, accompanied by two British officers, the Resident noted that the palace guards were disarmed and that none of the courtiers or officials were carrying their usual weapons, an indication that the king still hoped to resolve the situation by peaceful negotiations and not a show of force.

Inside the palace, Wajid 'Ali Shah was supported by his chief minister, his brother Sikandar Hashmat, the finance minister Raja Balkrishan and two other officials. Wajid 'Ali Shah turned to Outram and said, 'Why have I deserved this? What have I committed?' After the Resident's stilted explanation, the treaty was handed to the king who read it carefully and then burst out, 'Treaties are necessary between equals only; who am I now, that the British Government should enter into Treaties with?' His honour and his country were gone, he continued. He did not want a pension from the British, but would go to England and throw himself at the foot of the throne to beg for reconsideration of the orders, and for mercy. His brother backed him up, saying that because the king was no longer independent (and had not been for a long time, he could have added), there was no need for a fresh treaty. Tactlessly, the king's personal seal had already been attached to the treaty in the belief that he would sign it without argument.

Wajid 'Ali Shah, by now in tears, took off his turban and placed it in Outram's hands as a sign of submission. The Resident, no doubt hugely embarrassed by this show of oriental grief, told the king he had three days to reconsider his position, and left the palace.[70] On 7 February Outram received an official letter from the king stating that the treaty would not be signed. At midday it was therefore publicly announced that the kingdom had been made over to the British government, and that James Outram was its new chief commissioner. There was no longer a royal Court, and thus no need for a British Resident.

The story of the journey to Calcutta has already been told, together with the unsuccessful mission to England. But how did the great revolt that broke out the following May affect Wajid 'Ali Shah? Just over a year after the king had arrived in Calcutta, and while his mother, brother and son were still at Harley House in Marylebone, a curious event took place outside the hospital sortie gate at Fort William. The military headquarters of the East India Company was on full alert as the mutiny spread across northern India, and on 13 June 1857 a man called Abdul Subhan approached the sentry on duty at the Gate and told him, 'We have conquered the country as far as Benares. On the festival of Eed, about a month and a half hence, we have made arrangements to take this Fort.' The sentry, Hanuman Dubey, was a Hindu, but Subhan told him that although the two men were of different faiths, their cause was the same (*'Hindu aur Mussulman do deen rahi, magar ek hai.'*)[71]

Dubey reported the incident to his superiors and was questioned by Colonel Cavenagh, the town-major. Subhan was captured the following night and claimed to have come from Garden Reach and 'the King of Lucknow' who, he said, had 300 followers ready to seize Fort William. The man's grasp of what was actually happening as the Uprising unrolled across the plains was shaky, but he insisted that he came on behalf of Wajid 'Ali Shah and his armed retainers. Abdul Subhan was found guilty of 'seducing' the sentry from his allegiance to the British government and of inciting him to commit an act of mutiny. He was sentenced to be hanged on 15 June, in accordance with Act XIV of 1857, hastily passed as the extent of the rebellion became clear. With no evidence other than Subhan's statement to support the idea that the king was planning his own uprising against the British, the governor general, Lord Canning, issued arrest warrants for Wajid 'Ali Shah and his chief minister.

Canning's justification for the arrests reads strangely. There had been, he wrote in a minute of 18 June,[72] a number of rumours that the king 'and those about him were fomenting ... mistrust and disaffection' which had been noted by government, but not acted on for lack of hard evidence. Now the rumours were supported by significant facts, and as a result of Subhan's actions it had become 'necessary that decisive action should at once be taken to put a stop to the use of His Majesty's name, whether used with, or without his authority'. The governor general was anxious that the king's name 'should not be made a rallying point for disaffected soldiers',[73] although he had no evidence that Wajid 'Ali Shah or his courtiers were in fact involved in any conspiracy. He added that the king's detention would not last long if matters settled down, but could give no guarantee of how long he and his party would be detained. A statement by the king that he had no intention of supporting the mutineers could have been published in the vernacular and English press, but this was not done. And somehow, the night before he was due to be hanged, Abdul Subhan managed to escape both from the iron handcuffs placed on him and from his prison cell, and was never heard of again. Had he been planted by British intelligence to discredit the king? The suspicion remains, particularly when the Secret Consultations of the Foreign Department reveal a message sent by electric telegraph from Canning to Sir Henry Lawrence, who had succeeded Outram as chief commissioner of Awadh. Dated 1 June 1857, it reads: 'Will it embarrass you if I lay hands upon your people here? What do you think would be the effect at Delhie? It can be postponed if advisable.'[74]

Following the decision on 14 June to arrest the king, Canning wrote to him the next day: 'Sir—it is with pain that I find myself compelled to require that your Majesty's person should for a season be removed to within the precincts of the Fort William', and promised that he would be treated with respect and made as comfortable as possible. Wajid 'Ali Shah was to be housed in what had been the governor general's house before the grandiose Government House was built outside the Fort. It is a pleasant two-storeyed building that was used to accommodate visiting dignitaries including Bishop Reginald Heber, who described it as a 'large and very handsome building in the centre of the Fort', with lofty and well-proportioned rooms on the first floor and smaller offices at ground level, a typical eighteenth-century Calcutta mansion, in fact.[75]

The king and his minister did not go alone into Fort William. Among the twelve courtiers who volunteered to share their indefinite confinement was the Paymaster General and commander of the Ja'fari platoon, Fateh-ud-daulah, who was to die in prison. The prisoners were allowed their own servants, including the troublesome female servant Karbala'i, who had to be sent back to Garden Reach after causing a disturbance in the king's apartments. 'So wicked, like poison in a snake', wrote the king; 'extremely quarrelsome, excessively argumentative, fighting everyone in all directions'. The prisoners were visited daily by Cavenagh and Major Herbert, who had been appointed 'Agent to the Governor-General with the King of Oude', and who submitted a weekly diary to the Secretary to the Foreign Department. Particular emphasis was placed on the prisoners' physical well-being, and so that there could be no accusations of mistreatment, they were also visited by the garrison surgeon, Mr Macnamara. The news that the king was in prison was known to the inhabitants of Lucknow almost as soon as it happened. The situation there was desperate for the British who were besieged in the Residency, with little chance of escape during the summer. Had there been the slightest hint that the king was being humiliated, or physically threatened, then those in the Residency would have been in even more peril than they already were.

In September 1857 the surgeon found the king 'complaining of palpitation of the heart and also from other symptoms of dyspepsia and general depression. His pulse indicates that he is weak but of the many other symptoms from which he says he suffers I can form no opinion … he refuses to take medicine, stating that his mind is diseased and that drugs cannot relieve it. His attendants tell me that he has seldom risen from his bed during the last three months which fact will account for the attack of indigestion from which he suffers; they also assert and the

THE SORROWS OF AKHTAR

Ex-King confirms the statement that his illness and distress is principally caused by his long absence from his Harem.'[76]

Wajid 'Ali Shah continued to complain of real or imagined symptoms during his confinement. He suffered at times from depression, vomiting, rheumatic pains in his back, 'sickness, stomach pains and sleeplessness', restlessness, nervous excitement, and pain in the head and shoulders. 'Ali Naqi Khan was also ill with what was probably tuberculosis, and was reported coughing and spitting up blood. He was moved to the adjoining Royal Barracks and seemed to improve when he was allowed to walk on the flat roof in the evenings and be taken out for carriage rides by Major Herbert. In January 1858, seven months into his imprisonment, the king wrote to the governor general about the 'affliction and distress' he was enduring which he attributed to the fact that Canning suspected him and that 'evildoers' had made use of his name. 'Owing to the grief and sorrow my indisposition has daily increased', he continued. 'Your Lordship is aware that I have always suffered from palpitations of the heart and nervous debility. Now, although my innocence and my duty as a subject demand that until Your Lordship is fully convinced of the former, I should not make any allusion to my being liberated yet owing to the very violent nature of my disease, debility and afflictions is it certain that I cannot live and it would cause me great anguish to die ere had I had seen my innocence established. I trust under these circumstances that your Lordship will grant me permission to rejoin my family and devote myself to the cure of my disorder ... it is clear that I cannot here obtain, especially in the hot season, any relief from the disease under which I am suffering.'[77] Canning remained unmoved by this plea, and the king remained in custody.

'The Sorrows of Akhtar' is the translation of *Huzn-i-Akhtar*, a long narrative poem or *masnavi*, written by Wajid 'Ali Shah while in prison. In it he describes events and feelings that were not always recorded in the official British accounts. In particular he mentions an incident where he was verbally assaulted by a prison guard who was drunk. The king's sleeping quarters were regularly inspected and 'one night, in particular, I dozed, it was not sleep, but drowsiness. A "gentleman" came and spoke, (Oh God, let not those words be repeated!) He barked at me whatever occurred to him, ranting so much he finished only when tired, occasionally exclaiming "This is the king, bravo! Let us all destroy him together! My father and mother were killed, my dear relatives have left this world—kill this king in the same manner! Rid us of this nuisance".' Wajid 'Ali Shah reported the event the following morning to Colonel Cavenagh, and asked plaintively what he had done to deserve such treatment. Cavenagh, no doubt alarmed, promised the king that there would be no further inspections of his bedchamber and added that the guard 'spoke without cause while intoxicated'. But the poem goes on to relate that the guard's sons then approached the king asking him what had happened. 'I do not know anything', he told them. 'I obey the Colonel's orders.'[78]

There are verses commenting on the king's prison companions, including Diyanat ud-Daulah, who was desperate to be allowed to go on a pilgrimage, 'but the Council's permission was not granted'. Later the eunuch offended the king in some way, and 'having disappointed me, he was removed'. The death in custody, from illness, of Fateh-ud-daulah was described as the 'dimming like a lamp at dawn'. The loyalty of his companions, who voluntarily shared his imprisonment, was emphasised. Zulfiqar ud-Daulah—brother to one of the king's favourite wives,[79] and thus the king's brother-in-law—was praised, together with the younger brother of Fateh-ud-Daulah. 'Accompanying me to prison [they] prepared to die for me like moths. Their hearts never succumbed to animosity. They are prepared to die for my name, they care for me like their own lives. In the same way, all the others are eager. By God! Nothing I say is untrue, my friend! Both women and men are loyal unto death. What great courage! What courage!'

THE SORROWS OF AKHTAR

The governor general's letters to the king were commented on: 'the Lord-Sahib has a letter delivered, very attractive and well-styled. I shall describe the letter's subject, as composed by Lord-Sahib.' Wajid 'Ali Shah then goes on to interpret Canning's letter in a novel way, claiming that the governor general wrote: 'although you never deserved incarceration, Your Highness's honour will not alter. Like lightening, it will retain its brilliance. My officers and I will absolutely not breach your honour.' The king further claimed that Canning admitted he had been 'entirely coerced' by his Council into imprisoning Wajid 'Ali Shah, who was 'blameless' and 'never deserved incarceration'. Although it happened to be true, in this case, it does reinforce the king's attitude throughout his later life, that he was the hapless and innocent victim of a series of misfortunes, inflicted not only by the government, but by his own family members and friends too.

It is not clear how much the king knew of events outside Fort William as the Uprising drew to a bloody conclusion, particularly in Lucknow. He does not refer to them in his poem. The prisoners were allowed to write and receive letters but the correspondence was examined before delivery, and requests for reading material had to be approved in advance. Communication between people at Garden Reach and the prisoners was prohibited, although the servants were allowed to bring home-cooked food for the prisoners twice a day. The various dishes were placed on a stand outside the building before being examined by a guard, who would then signal to the indoor staff that they could be taken inside.

By the beginning of March 1858, Wajid 'Ali Shah was worrying that he had not heard anything from his mother, who he believed was still in England.[80] The news of Janab-i 'Aliyyah's death in Paris on 23 January had arrived in Calcutta by electric telegraph shortly after the event, but had been kept from the king because of his fragile state of health, both mental and physical. Major Herbert reported the king's anxiety and had tried to quell it by explaining that the queen mother had gone to Paris for a change of air, as she was dangerously ill, but he held off from saying that she had actually died. Cavenagh was ordered to tell the king what had happened, but even he ducked out of this unpleasant task and instead told one of the king's fellow prisoners, Mujahid-ud-Daulah. The latter agreed to deliver the news while expressing his own fears that the result would be too much of a shock for the invalid. But even a week later the king had still not been told. Mujahid-ud-Daulah explained that he had delayed breaking the news in the hope that the king would shortly be released and would be better able to bear the bereavement if he was surrounded by his family at Garden Reach. In the end Cavenagh had to tell the king, and this sad news was followed shortly afterwards by the report of Sikandar Hashmat's death in London.

Not surprisingly, the king's thoughts turned towards his son, Prince Hamid 'Ali, the only one of his three relatives to have survived the ill-fated visit to England. He wrote pleadingly at the end of 1858 for the young man to return home to India. This was not the first such letter either, and it is clear that the Prince was enjoying European life too much to heed his father's wishes. 'Though I am a prisoner', wrote the king, 'your mother [Khas Mahal] is at liberty. This will be better than our present separation and my heart even in the Fort William will be consoled by the knowledge that you are with your mother.'[81] Another letter went to Bubu Jan, an old family servant, asking her to persuade the prince to come home because 'he is in a foreign country and perfectly inexperienced'. A third letter went to Masih-ud-Din, asking him to make sure that the furniture and household articles purchased in England were carefully packed and sent to Calcutta for the Garden Reach home. When the prince did finally write to his father, he claimed not to have received Wajid 'Ali Shah's earlier letters, a fairly standard excuse for a teenager abroad even in those days.[82]

THE SORROWS OF AKHTAR

The weary months of imprisonment dragged by as peace was restored throughout the country and Queen Victoria announced by proclamation that the government of India had been formally transferred from the East India Company to the Crown. Lord Canning was to become its first viceroy, while still holding the title of governor general.[83] The end of the Uprising is usually reckoned to date from this proclamation, read out on 1 November 1858 in every major town in India. There were minor pockets of resistance, but there seemed no reason now why the prisoners should still be locked up in Fort William.

Canning had the delicate task of explaining to the king the reason for his continued detention. He acknowledged Wajid 'Ali Shah's previous letters begging for release and told him, 'It would have been very agreeable to me to comply with this request long ago but the condition of Hindostan, and specially, of the province of Oudh, has made it impossible. Your Majesty may not be fully aware of the use which has been made of your name in fomenting disaffection and treason; but you are perhaps informed of the fact that for more than fifteen months one of the most active Enemies of the State has been the Begum Huzrat Mahal, who, assuming in her own person and in that from Your Majesty's son Birjis Khader to represent Your Majesty's House, has supported the pretence by means of the bitterest hostility to the British Government.'[84] Canning explained that when the Begam fled to Nepal after Lucknow was retaken by the Company's troops, she had been offered the chance to surrender and would have received 'gracious treatment and an honorable position for the rest of her life'. But she had refused. 'I regret that it has been so', Canning went on, 'not only for Your Majesty's sake, but also for the sake of many who have been misled into following her hopeless cause and who, had she accepted the offer, might long ere this have returned to their homes in peace and security. But the Begum and those about her are now powerless against the British Government and I am unwilling that Your Majesty should suffer longer restraint on account of their impotent enmity. Your Majesty is free to leave Fort William whensoever it may please you to do so.'[85] Seldom can a divorced wife's revenge have had such dramatic consequences for her former spouse. The governor general added, 'I desire to acknowledge the courtesy which has marked Your Majesty's communications to myself—I have the honor to be, Sir, Your Majesty's faithful servant.'

Cavenagh was instructed to present this letter to the king, and to find out when and how he wanted to leave the Fort. On reading the Persian translation, Wajid 'Ali Shah responded by saying that he had always been 'the servant and well-wisher of the British Government', and that he was unaware of the use that had been made of his name by Begam Hazrat Mahal. He added that 'henceforth he dismissed both her and her son Birjis Kudder'.[86] So sudden was the news of the king's release that his servants had arrived as usual at Fort William with his afternoon meal. They were told to go straight back to Garden Reach and prepare for his return. Wajid 'Ali Shah left the Fort at 5.30 p.m. on 9 July 1859 and drove home accompanied by Major Herbert, who reported that 'His Majesty seemed much affected on leaving the Fort and expressed himself as deeply sensible of the act of grace which restored him to liberty.' As Herbert and the king approached Garden Reach, 'his people came out to meet him, some few in carriages and on horseback and others on foot and enthusiastically welcomed his return. Some of those on foot clung to the door of the carriage and running by its side endeavoured to touch His Majesty's feet with their heads as in the act of obeisance. They formed a crowd of persons round the door of the house where His Majesty, standing in the carriage, silently pressed my hand and alighting immediately, entered the house.'[87]

It was a joyous homecoming to the start of Wajid 'Ali Shah's new life in Bengal. The traumatic events of the past three and a half years were behind him. He had lost his kingdom to the East India Company, in spite of his attempts at reform and his commendable efforts to deal with the Ayodhya crisis. He had been humbled by two years in prison, and saddened by the deaths of his mother and brother in Europe. His palaces in Lucknow were gone, and his prized menagerie had been sold. Loyally, his wives and courtiers seemed prepared to support him in his comfortable exile.

4

THE HOUSE OF FAIRIES

The king as romantic hero and subject of his own youthful autobiography, the Ishqnamah *or* Chronicle of Passion. *He marries numerous women, but after the move to Bengal there are bitter domestic quarrels as they settle into new premises at Garden Reach. British officials become increasingly critical of the king's treatment of his wives, and although he argues for divorce on religious grounds, he is reluctantly forced into providing for them. His role as a great lover is severely tarnished.*

One of the few things for which Wajid 'Ali Shah was not criticised by the British, unless it came under the general heading of debauchery, was his extravagant number of wives. By the end of his life he had married approximately 375 women, more than one for every day of the year. The first question is 'why?' and the second must surely be 'how?' According to one of his numerous descendants living in Kolkata, the king was such a pious man that he could not allow any females to serve him unless he had contracted a temporary marriage with them. It would not have been decent for him to be alone with them.[1] It is an attractive rationalisation and may explain some of the marriages, but certainly not all.

There is no doubt that Wajid 'Ali Shah was a sensuous man who enjoyed being surrounded by women, as we have seen, with his bodyguard of female African soldiers to accompany him when he went out. As a young man he was not unattractive, with long, luxuriant hair flowing over his shoulders in ringlets, a style he had adopted by 1855. The first existing photographs, which were taken when he was in his thirties, show a stout, probably tall, man with a double chin, prominent breasts and sturdy arms. These were pictures taken by Ahmad 'Ali Khan, photographer and reputedly the architect of Qaisarbagh. One of the photographs is an intimate family portrait of the king seated on an elaborately carved wooden couch dandling a little daughter on his lap. Next to him sits a dignified young woman, her eyes modestly downcast, but clearly wrapped up in her own thoughts, which do not seem particularly happy ones. This is likely to be Akhtar Mahal, the king's second official wife, who was married to him when she was eleven years old and was a daughter of the chief minister, 'Ali Naqi Khan. She would have been about fifteen years old when this photograph was taken.[2]

The image most closely associated with Wajid 'Ali Shah and used in books and on websites about him shows the same plump figure, almost bursting out of his richly embroidered tunic and wearing a sash of four rows of large pearls, with his hand on his sword hilt. His left breast and nipple are artfully exposed between the gold-embroidered borders of his dress. Much debate has taken place over the significance of this, but no satisfactory explanation has been found. Traditionally, Muslims buttoned their jackets on the left and Hindus on the right, but whether the king was making an exaggerated point about his religious affiliation or simply wanted to be portrayed as a sensual man, is not now known. This portrait, which hangs today in the Hussainabad Picture Gallery in Lucknow, is a copy from a lost painting, possibly by the last English artist at the Court of Awadh, George Duncan Beechey.

However, it was not the king's physical appearance that determined his frequent marriages. Had he been twice as fat, he would still have been husband to many women, from descendants of the Mughals to Abyssinian slave girls. It was both his authority (and wealth) as king as well as his own priapic nature that led to so many encounters, which inevitably ended in matrimony. The fact that he was prepared to justify and describe this behaviour in writing adds colour to the idea that he wanted to be portrayed, both literally and metaphorically, as a great romantic figure, a lover who was irresistible to women, and who could not resist them either.

One of the frankest autobiographies of nineteenth-century India is popularly known as the *Pari Khana* or 'House of Fairies'.[3] It was begun by Wajid 'Ali Shah in 1847, the year he became king, and was completed two years later. The king was only twenty-six when he decided to write 'the story of my romances from the earliest years until the present', but he claimed to have already experienced heartache from his earliest days. Every human being had been granted 'the taste for love' by God, he wrote, but what should have been an earthly garden of eternal spring had already become for him an 'expansive wilderness'. How this happened is described in the first chapter. When he was eight years old, a middle-aged woman servant called Rahiman was hired to look after the young prince. 'One day, she overpowered me while I slept and began to touch me up. Being a child, I tried escaping out of fear. However, she stopped me and threatened to have me punished by my tutor and guardian. I was upset by the trouble that had entangled me. From that day onwards, it became her habit to fondle me.' What we would describe today as child abuse continued for two years, until Rahiman was dismissed. She was followed by Ameeran, another maid-servant, whom Wajid 'Ali Shah described as between thirty-five to forty years old, and always wearing 'colourful clothes'. Finding him alone in bed one night, she lay down beside him, and this time there was no element of fear or coercion in the unnatural relationship.

But something had happened that was to have a lasting effect. From then on, wrote Wajid 'Ali Shah, 'I have had an attachment to the affairs of love'; and in poetic terms he claimed to be 'often saddened by the condition of true lovers' and to condemn the 'cruel beloved', who showed no mercy to a young man's feelings. The image of a heartless woman toying with male affections is very common in Persian and Urdu poetry, and is sometimes given religious overtones in the search for spiritual understanding. But here it seems a straightforward case of a child who was sexualised at an early age and spent the rest of his life seeking fulfilment by marrying vast numbers of women, but not finding much real satisfaction.

The *Pari Khana* continues with the young prince falling frequently in love with women he met in and around his father's palace, the Chattar Manzil on the bank of the river. His teenage passion was for Haji Khanum, a married woman who lived in Faizabad, which meant that meetings were not as frequent as the lovers would have wished. Sometimes she would upset him by mentioning her husband, but neither thought this an impediment to their relationship. Then there was a brief flirtation with another married woman, whose husband appears to have been, from his name, one of the African servants or soldiers employed by the prince's father, Amjad 'Ali Shah.

At the age of fifteen Wajid 'Ali Shah's first marriage was arranged. For some reason, which he does not explain, the first girl chosen 'after considerable deliberation' did not suit him. (She was later married to his younger brother, Sikandar Hashmat, in a face-saving arrangement.) Another girl was found, and terms for the marriage—that is, the dowry arrangements—had been agreed, but again 'some problems arose' and the wedding did not take place. A third girl, selected by an aunt, was proposed and accepted, but it was then discovered that she had leprosy, a fact that her family had tried to conceal.[4]

Finally, and by this time probably in some desperation, a suitable girl was found, and although, unusually, she was five years older than her intended husband, the marriage went ahead. It was customary for brides to receive honorific titles on marriage, and so she became Malika Muqqadara-i-Azma Nawab Alam Ara. Later, when she had given birth to her sons and her husband had become king, further titles of Begam Padshah Mahal Sahiba were added. But for simplicity's sake she was known as Khas Mahal, the 'Special, or Exceptional Queen', and this is how she will be referred to in this book. Khas Mahal was the niece of 'Ali Naqi Khan, whose own daughter was to become Wajid 'Ali Shah's second official wife. The attraction of the minister's niece and then daughter, as first and second wives, was that 'Ali Naqi Khan himself was the great-grandson of the Mughal Emperor Shah Alam II, which gave him enormous status in Awadh. Curiously this is something of which British officials seemed unaware, often referring to him in detrimental terms, and failing to appreciate the importance of the Mughal bloodline and its connectivity with that of the Awadh royal family.

There was something even more curious in Khas Mahal's background. Although of impeccably noble descent, she had an Anglo-Indian grandmother, whose original name was Sally Begam. Sally was the illegitimate daughter of a former British Resident at the Lucknow Court, Gabriel Harper, and an unknown Indian woman. Harper refused to acknowledge the little girl as his own, and it was left to Major General Claude Martin to 'adopt' her when the Resident left Lucknow in 1787. (Both Martin and Harper appear in the well-known painting by Johann Zoffany entitled 'Colonel Mordaunt's Cock Match'.) By the time Sally was thirteen years old, Martin had taken her to bed, as he did with his other 'adopted' girls.[5] On his death in 1800, armed with a generous life-time pension from Martin, Sally took off for Calcutta, where she became pregnant and gave birth to a daughter, who was named Barati. It is not known who Barati's father was, except that it was certainly not Claude Martin, who was infertile due to various medical conditions.

What might have seemed like a huge handicap for Sally—an illegitimate daughter when she herself was still in her teens—proved not to be the case. Perhaps it was that generous pension, but Sally made a very good marriage to Prince Muzaffar Bakht, a grandson of the Emperor Shah Alam II. Barati also married a Muslim nobleman, Sayyid 'Ali Khan, possibly as a secondary wife, and it was their daughter who became the queen of Awadh, Khas Mahal.

His first marriage did not slow Wajid 'Ali Shah down in his quest for romantic love, although there was at first a compatibility between the newly-wedded couple. Khas Mahal herself was a poet, writing under the pen name (*takhallus*) of 'Alam', and there were certainly times of happiness as husband and wife read their poems out to each other.[6] Later Wajid 'Ali Shah was to name one of his garden houses after his first wife—the Alam Bagh. But by the time *Pari Khana* was composed, Wajid 'Ali Shah had already contracted a substantial number of marriages, possibly as many as twenty, including that to Khas Mahal.

How was this possible, when orthodox Islam limited the number of wives to four, with conditions that each wife be treated equally? The differences between the civil law of the Sunnis and the Shi'as were examined at considerable length in nineteenth-century India, not least because British judges and lawyers needed to have this information to administer justice, but also from a sense of curiosity about the country that was rapidly falling, state by state, into British hands. Sir William Jones, the great scholar of ancient India, had supervised the translation of *A Digest of Mohummudan Law* from the Arabic, which laid down the imamiyyah (Shi'a) code of jurisprudence in temporal matters. The *Digest* was published in 1805 and became the standard work of reference, which was still being used and updated a century later.

In ponderous terms John Baillie, Professor of Arabic at Fort William College, Calcutta, who had translated the *Digest*, explained that Shi'as recognised two kinds of marriage: a permanent marriage (*nikah*) that lasted for life, and a temporary marriage (*mut'ah*) 'contracted for a limited period, for a certain sum of money'. No more than four nikah marriages were allowed. Mut'ah marriages were a businesslike arrangement that could last for anything from a day to a year, or longer, but the length of time had to be specified and agreed by both parties, as did the amount of money or goods in kind that went to the mut'ah wife. If she became pregnant during the marriage, the child was considered to have been fathered by the husband and was therefore legitimate. There were various stipulations: mut'ah wives could only be chosen from among Muslim, Christian or Jewish women,[7] although there were allowances for mut'ah relationships with female slaves too—but basically this was what allowed Wajid 'Ali Shah to acquire such a large number of wives. Later on, as we shall see, there were to be fierce ideological battles between the exiled king and British officials over the fate of his mut'ah wives whose contracts had ended.

But for the time being the young Wajid 'Ali Shah was free to marry whom he chose, as frequently as he liked. With his official wife, Khas Mahal, dutifully producing sons at regular intervals, the children of his mut'ah marriages seemed like an additional blessing. In 1845 he learned that Mahak Pari was pregnant or, as he put it, 'the angel of day and night conveyed the good news of an infant flower's arrival'. Wajid 'Ali Shah immediately put Mahak Pari into purdah and gave her the title of Iftikhar-un-nissa, which means 'dignified among women'. She is better known today as Begam Hazrat Mahal, who defied the British during the great Uprising of 1857–8. The prince's joy over the birth is obvious: 'My darling exalted son was born.' The baby's grandfather, King Amjad 'Ali Shah, granted the infant an 11-gun salute and the title of Mirza Birjis Qadr. The proud father prepared a celebratory banquet, with female dancers and musicians who drew admiration from the spectators for their performance.[8]

Shortly after this event, there was another piece of good news: 'Fizzah the Abyssinian' was pregnant. Fizzah may have been one of Wajid 'Ali Shah's African bodyguards. The term 'Abyssinian' was loosely used to cover men, women and children, usually slaves, brought from the African subcontinent to India by Arab traders. After giving thanks in the 'great shrine', Wajid 'Ali Shah put Fizzah into purdah and in due course a baby girl was born. Her grandfather, the king, seemed equally delighted at her arrival and suggested she should be called Jahanara, which means 'world-adorning'.[9]

Not everything was so harmonious in the 'House of Fairies'. Both Yasmin Pari and Sarfaraz Pari claimed to be pregnant and were duly put into purdah. However, after a few days it emerged that this was only a rumour, and they were both brought out again and resumed their dancing and music lessons. When Hur Pari said she was pregnant, Wajid 'Ali Shah was more cautious, having been humiliated over the two previous false claims. 'I did not attribute much credence to it', he wrote, and it was only when Hur Pari was five months pregnant that she was put into purdah, which she hated. Continually tearful, she refused to be shut up behind curtains (the literal meaning of purdah) and told Wajid 'Ali Shah she would abort the child if he did not let her out. At seven months she gave birth to a little boy, who died just after a month.[10] It was unfortunate, too, that Wajid 'Ali Shah contracted gonorrhoea from one of his wives, Qaisar Begam, with whom he was particularly infatuated. 'Day and night', he wrote, 'I would loiter around her like one possessed. Wherever she slept, I would rest there too. Wherever she ate, I would eat there too ... I gave her papers [Promissory Notes] for thousands of rupees in cash. I also presented her with the mansion of the late Jalal-ud-daulah to live in.'[11] He added ruefully that until he discovered he had the disease he was continually prepared to indulge her, but afterwards found himself spending more time with his doctor than his lover.

Visual material from Lucknow during this period is sparse.[12] The infamous sack of Qaisarbagh by the triumphant British and Gurkha troops in March 1858, which lasted for three days and during which *The Times* reporter William Russell reported that he saw men 'drunk with plunder', is clearly the reason. Paintings, miniatures, illustrated manuscripts and personal photograph albums either disappeared as loot or were simply destroyed. But one important royal treasure survived, rescued from destruction by Sikh soldiers fighting alongside the British. It is the illustrated version of the king's youthful autobiography that we know as the *Pari Khana*, an Indo-Persian manuscript with 103 painted miniatures, produced in 1849/50, shortly after he had completed the original prose version. The Sikh soldiers presented it to Sir John Lawrence, the former chief commissioner of the Punjab, who in turn presented it to Queen Victoria on his return to England in 1859. It has been at Windsor Castle ever since.

The Windsor manuscript is called the *Ishqnamah*, a difficult word to translate. 'Chronicle of Passion' is probably the nearest we can get to it, but is still an imprecise rendition of the subtle Persian title. Its connection with the Urdu version, the *Pari Khana*, has not previously been recognised. The English title of the manuscript, *Customs of the Court of Oudh*, is an imprecise description of the riches contained in this large leather-bound volume. The majority of the illustrations show a succession of women parading, one by one, in front of Wajid 'Ali Shah, who is seated on a gilt chair, or a velvet sofa, under a canopy in the courtyard of his palace. Typically, the young woman enters through a side door, hung with a curtain, and walks across the yard towards the prince. It is both a theatrical performance and an audition, where the courtyard is the stage and Wajid 'Ali Shah the sole audience and casting director. The women are already dressed in the approved court costume of *gharara* (excessively wide, flowing pyjamas), a tight-cropped blouse (*choli*) and a transparent *dupatta*, or veil, across the breast. On their feet they are wearing *ghatelas*, probably one of the most awkward shoes ever invented, where the leather toe is shaped like the trunk of an elephant, curving round towards the wearer. The women's hair is pulled back into a long plait, covered with brocade and looped up to fasten at the back of the head. The faces of the women are beautifully detailed. Each is an individual in her own right, but all look apprehensive, and none are smiling. All the women are named at the top of each painting, and several appear more than once in different scenes.

Safaraz Mahal, one of the fairies who falsely claimed to be pregnant, appears in ten of the paintings and was, for nearly a decade, a favourite mut'ah wife of the prince. In folio 263 she stands hand-in-hand with Wajid 'Ali Shah in a European-style room. A female attendant holding a fan of gilded peacock feathers looks on. An elaborate Victorian couch of gilt and red velvet is the only piece of furniture in the room, placed suggestively behind the couple on a thick and luxurious carpet. Although the scene is painted in daylight, with blue skies beyond the open door at the end of the room, there is an erotic element here in the positioning of husband and wife, which leaves something to the viewer's imagination. The fan-bearer can darken the room by closing the shutters before she leaves. Wajid 'Ali Shah can take off the sword hanging suggestively around his waist, and perhaps the shy young woman can be teased into taking off her dupatta. Sadly, whatever happened in this room in 1845 was not to lead to a lasting relationship. Safaraz Mahal was divorced by the king in 1848 and spent the rest of her life in Lucknow. A catfight between her and another mut'ah wife on the palace terrace was serious enough for Wajid 'Ali Shah to have to wade in and break it up, leading to a lively illustration in a later folio. Many years later, when Safaraz Mahal tried to claim a small pension, she was ungallantly described as 'a common public woman of low origin', who was subsequently found unworthy of the king as she was carrying on an intrigue with another person.[13] Her

1. The queen mother, Janab-i 'Aliyyah, enters the train at Southampton station. From the *Illustrated London News* 6 September 1856. Author's collection.

2. The queen mother and party at Drury Lane Theatre, London. From the *Illustrated London News* 14 March 1857. Author's collection.

3. The Awadh princes, Sikandar Hashmat and Hamid 'Ali at the Art Treasures Exhibition, Manchester, July 1857. Photograph by Leonida Caldesi. Royal Collection Trust © Her Majesty Queen Elizabeth II 2013.

4. Prince Sikandar Hashmat, embellished photograph, i.e. the crown and robes have been painted onto an existing photograph. Private collection.

5. Wajid 'Ali Shah in Qaisarbagh. Painting on cloth, c. 1851. From the collection of Kenneth and Joyce Robbins.

6. Wajid 'Ali Shah celebrates the Basant (Spring) Festival on the river Gomti. Sir William Sleeman, in red coat, sits next to the king. Hussainabad Picture Gallery, Lucknow.

7. The Great Vine and the Lanka, Qaisarbagh, Lucknow. Artist unknown, c. 1862. © Alkazi Collection of Photography, Delhi.

8. Wajid 'Ali Shah is recognised as heir apparent, c.1847. Gouache on paper. Private collection.

9. Prince Mustafa 'Ali Khan, elder brother of Wajid Ali Shah. Photograph by Felice Beato, March/April 1858. © The J. Paul Getty Museum, Los Angeles.

10. Wajid 'Ali Shah greets Viscount Hardinge, the governor general, at Lucknow. c 1847. Gouache on paper. © The British Library, London. Add. Or. 742.

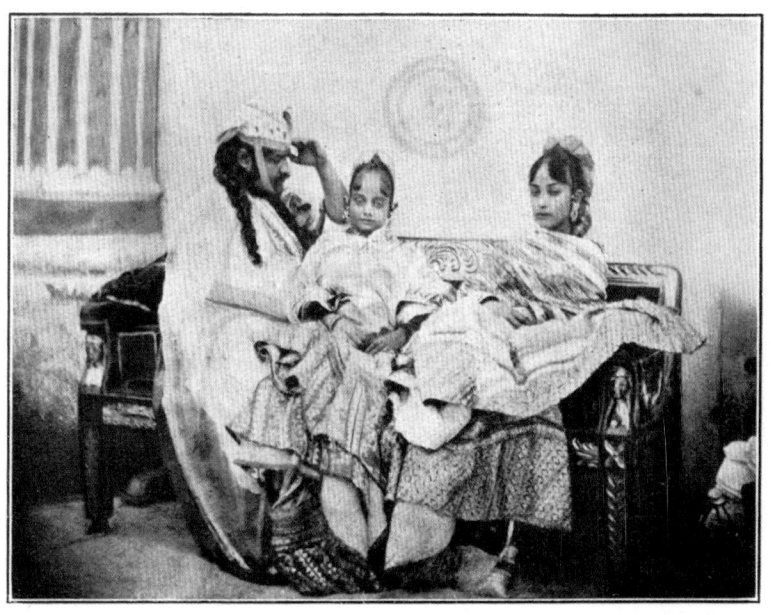

WAJID ALI, KING OF OUDH, HIS QUEEN AND CHILD.
From a photograph found in the Court Photographer's house on the Capture of Lucknow.
See Note, p.xi.

11. Wajid 'Ali Shah with wife (possibly Akhtar Mahal) and child. Photograph by Ahmad 'Ali Khan, early 1850s. From William Low, *Lieutenant-Colonel Gould Hunter-Weston* (1914).

12. Wajid 'Ali Shah, oil painting, possibly from a lost original by George Duncan Beechey. Hussainabad Picture Gallery, Lucknow.

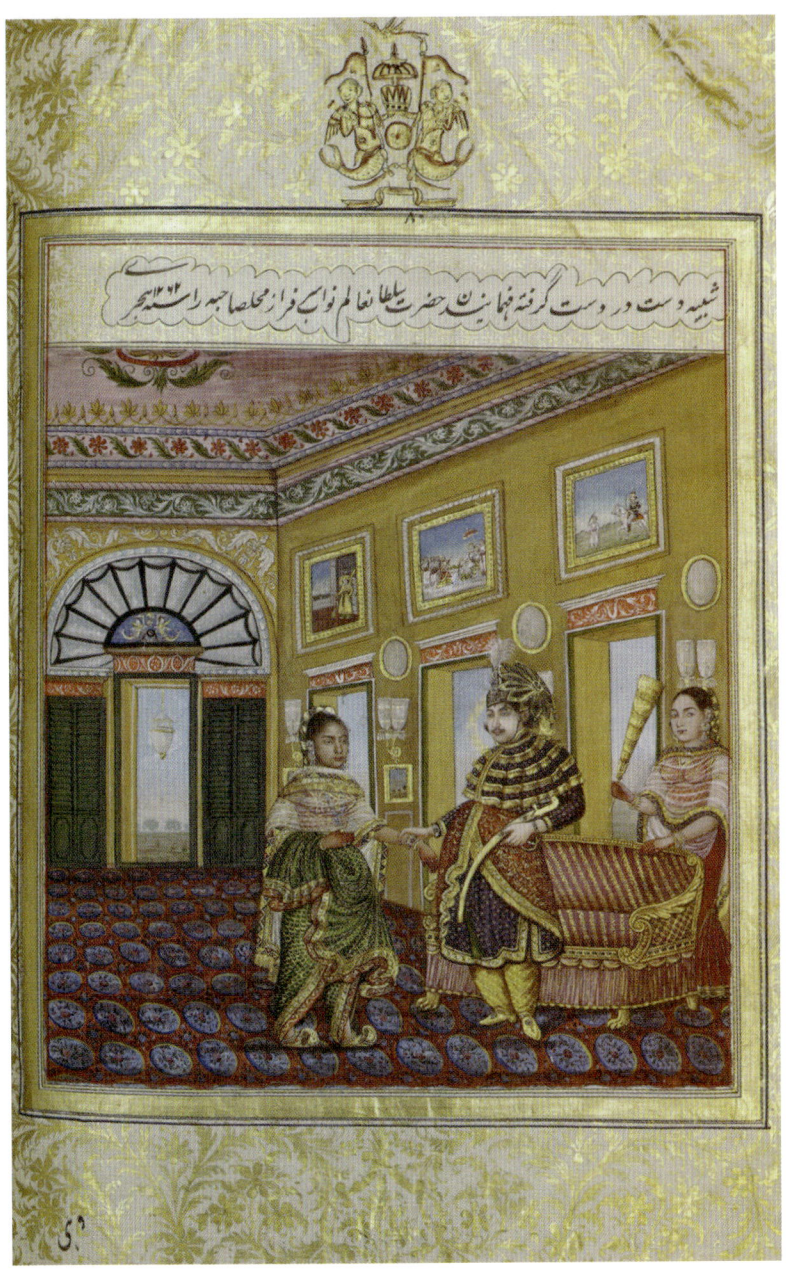

13. Wajid 'Ali Shah and Safaraz Mahal, from the *Ishqnamah*, folio 263, Windsor Castle. Royal Collection Trust © Her Majesty Queen Elizabeth II 2013.

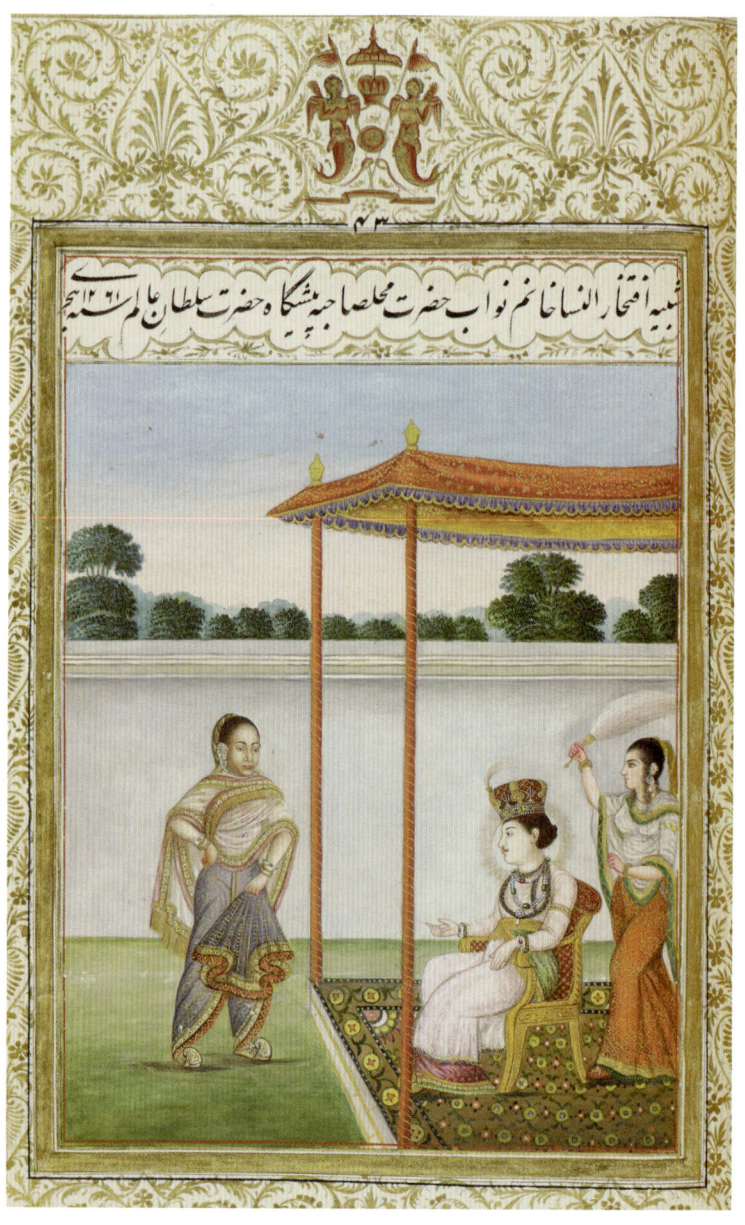

14. Wajid 'Ali Shah and Begam Hazrat Mahal from the *Ishqnamah*, folio 155. The caption reads: The likeness of Iftikharunnisa' Khanum, Lady Hazratmahall, before the Sultan-e 'Alam, year 1261 of the Hijrah. c. 1845. Windsor Castle. Royal Collection Trust © Her Majesty Queen Elizabeth II 2013.

15. Wajid 'Ali Shah in his *zananah* at Lucknow, late 1840s/early 1850s. Gouache on paper. State Museum, Lucknow.

16. The Sultan Khana today, Garden Reach, Kolkata. Author's collection.

17. Wajid 'Ali Shah, date and photographer unknown. Private collection.

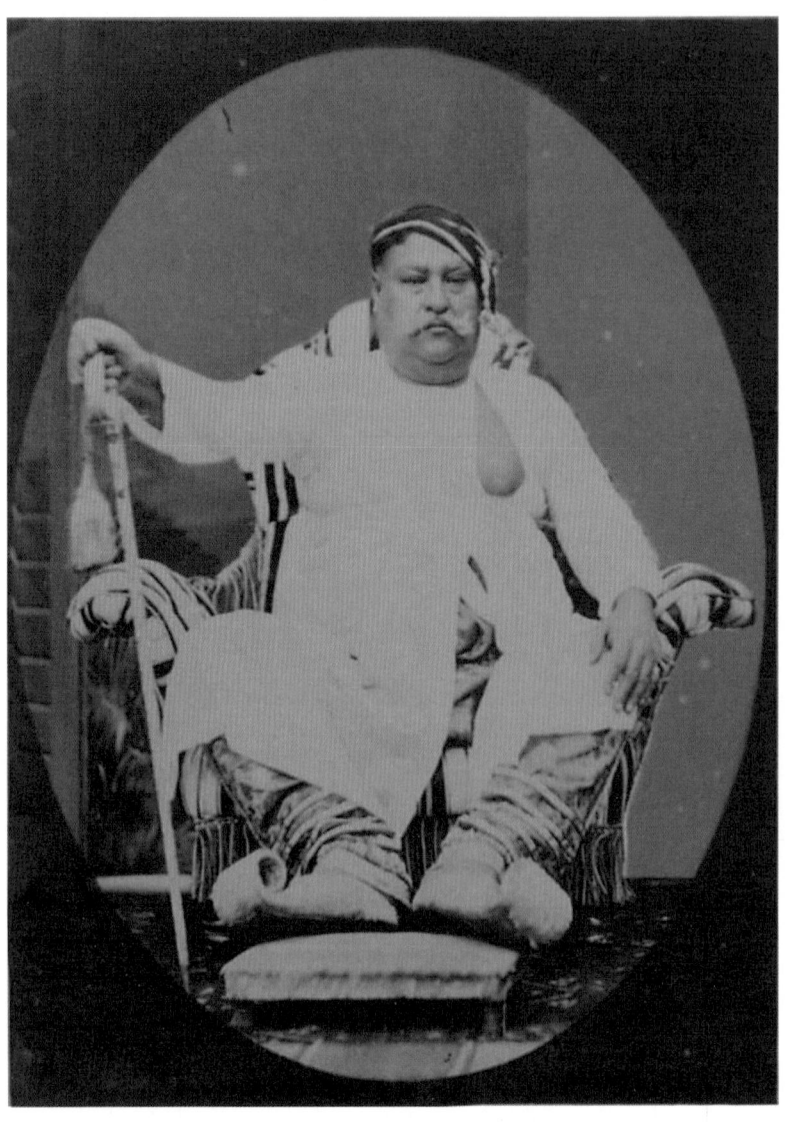

18. Wajid 'Ali Shah in old age, date and photographer unknown. © Alkazi Collection of Photography, Delhi.

original name, before she was elevated on her marriage with the title of nawab Safaraz Mahal Sahiba, was Gana, a Hindu name, so she became a convert to Islam on her mut'ah marriage.

Turning the pages of the *Ishqnamah*, it soon becomes obvious that Wajid 'Ali Shah had a soft spot for dark-skinned brides. Yasmin Mahal, whom he married in 1843, is clearly of African origin with her short black curly hair and un-Indian features. She appears in four paintings, one of which shows her with a group of people seeking permission to make the pilgrimage to Mecca. Another African bride, married about 1845, was named Ajaib Khanum, which translates as 'strange woman', possibly from her foreign appearance. But most intriguingly of all, a recent examination of the old landholding records in Awadh by an Indian scholar has shown that Begam Hazrat Mahal's father was a slave called Umber, who was owned by one Ghulam Hossein 'Ali Khan.[14] Her mother was Maher Afza, Umber's mistress. There is no doubt that for a short time Wajid 'Ali Shah was completely besotted by Hazrat Mahal, writing her many poems. She appears once in the *Ishqnamah*, on folio 155, the only authentic portrait known of her at present. She is a dark-skinned woman, with no obvious African features like Yasmin Mahal, and was clearly highly attractive to the young prince.

Because some of the wives pictured in the *Ishqnamah* chose not to show their faces in public, the artist or artists have found ingenious ways to indicate that they are present, but still in purdah. Some are shown only from the rear, or retreating across the courtyard. Others are coquettishly holding up fans in front of their faces, either the fashionable Victorian bladed fans, or the Indian axe-shaped cloth and card punkahs. When Wajid 'Ali Shah's paternal grandmother, Hazrat Maryam Makani, appears in an early folio, her face is hidden with a golden halo, placed in front of her head rather than behind it (although it is clear that under cover of the halo she is puffing away on a hookah). As the second nikah widow of the King Muhammad 'Ali Shah, she is obviously a purdah woman of high status whose face cannot be revealed, even in an intimate family portrait with her grandson.

The *Ishqnamah* has never been published, although two of its folios, the coronations of Wajid 'Ali Shah (in 1847) and his father Amjad 'Ali Shah (1842), have been copied and used in other manuscripts. It is a unique glimpse into the world of the Lucknow fairies and their restricted lives once they entered the palace. Although written by the prince and illustrated by a (presumed) male artist or artists, it nevertheless unconsciously hints at tensions within the zananah and jostling among the wives for the husband's attention. Wives sometimes invite Wajid 'Ali Shah to a meal in their own quarters in the palace, where dishes are invitingly laid out all together on a tablecloth (*dastarkhwan*) on the floor and the king sits cross-legged to eat. It is clearly a privilege to entertain him, just as it is a privilege to be invited by him to a fireworks party in the palace gardens. In a few curious paintings, a wife shows Wajid 'Ali Shah an injury, usually a burn mark on her inner thigh, which means she has to pull up her skirt to expose it. The captions note that the women receive sympathy from their husband over the injury, which was self-inflicted either as an expression of love's ardour or, to gain attention and sympathy from the king. One atypical painting shows a woman with her hands tied to a tree, while a barber shaves her head, 'on the Prince's order as a warning'. In a happier image, some of the wives are entertained by a dancing *hijra*, dressed in women's clothes apart from masculine headgear and sporting a nascent moustache.[15] The *Ishqnama* was produced for Wajid 'Ali Shah alone and was not for public viewing. It may have been shown to selected friends, and in fact there is nothing indecent in it—no Kama Sutra poses or much that could be considered erotic. But it is the frankness of the whole enterprise, the unsmiling women and the illustrated recital of the king's many passions that make it slightly uncomfortable viewing today in the library of Windsor Castle.

THE HOUSE OF FAIRIES

From outside the Lucknow palace, and particularly from the British Residency up on the hill overlooking the palace, Wajid 'Ali Shah's amours were a private matter. Protocol did not allow the Resident to meet any of the wives when he breakfasted at the palace on official occasions; these were strictly men-only events, where male servants prepared and served the food. It was permissible for British ladies of high status to visit Indian women in purdah, and there are several descriptions of just how embarrassing this was for both parties concerned. Emily Eden, sister of the governor general Lord Auckland, met some of the wives of Sikh ruler Maharaja Ranjit Singh in Lahore in 1838. 'The conversation is always rather stupid', she reported; 'they laughed at our bonnets, and we rather jeered their nose-rings.'[16] But in Lucknow only Mrs Login, wife of the Residency surgeon Dr John Login, seems to have visited the palace at this period, becoming friendly with Janab-i 'Aliyyah, but not with her numerous daughters-in-law.

It was not until 1865, when Major George Malleson, the agent who had replaced Herbert, became involved in a case between the king, now in exile, and one of his mut'ah wives, that the royal domestic arrangements became clear to the British. The 'female establishment', as it was called, was run on business lines, with the eunuch Diyanat ud-Daulah in charge (the same man who had earlier been head of the Customs Department). There were three classes of mut'ah wives, the agent learned: the *mahals*, who had given birth to the king's children, and who were allowed to veil their faces; the *begams*, who had not given birth, and who went unveiled; and the *khilawati*, the lowest class, who did menial jobs around the palace as domestic servants but were nevertheless tied to the king in marriage. In theory, each woman received a monthly allowance, or salary, according to her rank. The mahals, at the top of the scale, could get up to Rs1,600 (about £160) a month; the middle-ranking begams got about Rs100; and the servants got Rs20. But these were nominal wages, and only a very small proportion was paid in actual coin. The begams, for example, got only Rs16 in cash, 'the remainder being withheld to supply food, clothing and accommodation'.[17]

On entering the establishment after a mut'ah marriage, the new wife got a small sum as a dower, a gift from the king, which was hers to keep. She also got 'a uniform of dress and ornaments', including jewellery, but this was only on loan. The king had been in the habit, it was reported, of 'purchasing ornaments from time to time and making temporary grants of them to the ladies of his household for the purpose of being worn in his presence on Muhammadan festivals and other occasions of ceremony'.[18] When the jewels and ornaments were not in use, they were either kept safe by an appointed palace superintendent or if the ladies wanted to retain the jewellery, then each item had to be entered into a register, along with the name of its temporary holder. At the end of the mut'ah marriage, the 'uniform' and jewellery were to be returned to the king. This naturally led to all kinds of 'misunderstandings', where the dismissed women claimed that their jewellery was a gift, not a loan, from the king, which of course was difficult to prove.[19]

Clearly the administration of the female establishment was a responsible and time-consuming job that required good organisational skills, financial acumen and huge amounts of tact. Diyanat ud-Daulah became a wealthy and influential man, and, apart from a period out of favour, he remained a friend of the king. A number of junior eunuchs would have been employed to assist him. Although life in the zananah has been well-documented by the Englishwoman Mrs Meer Hassan Ali, who married a Shi'a and lived in Lucknow for twelve years, she does not touch on the day-to-day running of the establishment. There is also too little evidence to show whether Wajid 'Ali Shah was simply following the customs of his forefathers in the administration of his women's lives, or whether he initiated the rulings on how much each got as a salary and the register recording the deposit of jewellery. The different ranks of *mamtu'at*, the collective noun for mut'ah wives, seems well-established in the Awadh dynasty, and the use of the title 'mahal' for a wife who produced a child was standard among both Shi'as and Sunnis.

However, there was yet another category of women, the *pari* or fairy, who by serving a musical apprenticeship might be taken on as a mut'ah wife if the king found her pleasing and talented. The fairies were certainly an innovation of Wajid 'Ali Shah and were recruited from the lower classes, including the courtesans (*tawa'if*) who lived mainly in Chauk, in the old city. These women were not themselves educated, explained Wajid 'Ali Shah, 'but after instruction some of them acquired knowledge'. Some of the fairies went on to become expert singers or dancers, while others could not even learn the A or B of musical notation. The king employed expert tutors, all of whom had already made names for themselves, to teach the women singing and dancing. He tutored one particular student, Musahib Pari, himself, and having expended 'much effort on her musical education', found that within a few days she had considerably improved in comparison with the other women.[20] Rather like a twenty-first-century talent show, the newly-trained fairies performed at various functions, although Wajid 'Ali Shah was quick to point out that these were 'not organised to satisfy feelings of love and lust' but to provide an ordinary yet interesting entertainment that allowed the women to perform in a supervised setting.

Whether the Pari Khana, the House of Fairies, existed as an actual building is disputed. Some reliable writers like Sharar[21] do not mention it at all, while others place it firmly in the main Qaisarbagh courtyard, where a school of music stands today. Wajid 'Ali Shah himself said that the fairies were taken to a small house called Rashk-e-Iram, 'the Envy of Paradise', which was both a hostel and a school. But there were female African soldiers on guard, to make sure the fairies did not escape, and there was certainly an element of coercion. One way to get out was to catch the king's eye and be summoned to his bedchamber. This could lead to promotion, particularly if the fairy subsequently became pregnant. As we have seen, Mahak Pari became Begam Hazrat Mahal after she gave birth to a son, and others lost their simple names like Piyari (Darling) to become mahals or begams. All the mut'ah wives of the first and second rank were given the title of nawab sahibah[22] in addition to the female title of mahal sahibah or begam sahibah, as well as their personal name. The khilawati servants, the lowest rank, got the simple suffix *pasand* (pleasing) after their personal name, with no additional title.

There was no element of snobbery, as we would understand it today, in the king's choice of female companions. Once his nikah wives had been selected from good families and had started producing heirs, he was free to choose whom he wanted and clearly found lower-class women, maid-servants and African women perfectly acceptable, as long as they were pretty. Some of these women were introduced to Wajid 'Ali Shah by intermediaries, for the king did not often go roaming the streets of the old city in person. Money certainly changed hands, and in at least one case it was the girl's mother who brought her daughter to the palace. Others were promoted by his first mut'ah wives, who gave him young women as 'gifts' in order to please him, and Khas Mahal supplied eight of the fairies with extravagant outfits and jewellery. Sexual desire among princes for lower-class women has been named the Cophetua syndrome, after the legendary king who fell in love with a beautiful beggar woman, and this is certainly a recurring theme in Wajid 'Ali Shah's love life. It may be that his feelings of superiority and power in such a relationship added to the sexual frisson.

His father, the saintly Amjad 'Ali Shah, had not been immune either, falling in love with a greengrocer's daughter in middle age. Sultan Mahal, who came from 'the humblest class of society and in very poor circumstances', was spotted delivering vegetables to the palace when Amjad 'Ali Shah 'conceived for her that passion which led to her becoming his wife'. Sadly both king and queen died within a few months of each other in 1847. Wajid 'Ali Shah then tried to claim the £10,000 which his father had willed to Sultan Mahal, but her mother and brother boldly put in a counterclaim as her heirs. The case went all the way up to the governor general, who ruled that the greengrocer's family was entitled to the money, a decision that Wajid 'Ali Shah accepted fairly gracefully.[23] This story shows that there was not only social mobility for a lucky few, but that wealth could trickle down too. The financial gain for a mut'ah wife was not great, particularly if, or when, the marriage ended, but it was better than remaining among Lucknow's poor. And of course it did widen the gene pool in a society where cousin marriage, or marriage between relatives, was common.

There were fundamental changes after the move to Calcutta, which affected the 'female establishment' perhaps even more deeply than it did the king. The zananah was recreated at Garden Reach, and we know more about its many inhabitants there than in their Qaisarbagh days. This is because the bulk of the money that supported the wives now came from the British government, not the land revenues of Awadh. This gave British officials more authority to interfere in Wajid 'Ali Shah's domestic arrangements (while appearing not to do so), and also led to a few of the wives complaining directly to the British agents about their husband's behaviour towards them.

When the king left Lucknow on 13 March 1856, he took with him, as well as his mother, three of his wives, including Khas Mahal and Akhtar Mahal, the first two nikah or official wives. The fourth woman may have been Mashuq Mahal, the first mut'ah wife and one of the king's early passions. An unknown number of wives were left behind in Lucknow, as well as nine divorced women, including Hazrat Mahal and her young son.

Although a considerable amount of work has been done on the Awadh family tree, the exact number of wives and children will probably never be fully known. In part this may be because mut'ah marriages do not always require witnesses, and secondly because no records appear to have been retained in public ownership when the Garden Reach establishment was broken up.

When it became known in Lucknow that the king was not going to travel to England to plead his case, and had in fact rented a large compound at Garden Reach, a number of wives and children travelled to Calcutta to join him. The local District Magistrate, Mr Ferguson, decided to find out how many of the king's people were already established at Garden Reach in June 1858, by which time Wajid 'Ali Shah himself had spent a year in prison. Apart from the king's personal assistants and servants, who numbered nearly six hundred, there were also twenty 'nobles and favourites' with their own households, and Ferguson found '183 Begums and other females, including servants and slaves girls'. He was also told that 170 houses in the compound had been put aside for the king's women, although it was not possible for his staff to examine them, as the men were not permitted to approach these female quarters.[24]

Ferguson describes the zananah buildings both as 'houses' and as 'thatched huts', or bungalows. In the confusion and disruption of the flight from Lucknow, the ensuing Uprising and the imprisonment of the king, there had been little time to plan the new settlement in Calcutta. There was an ad hoc nature to the establishment, a kind of refugee camp atmosphere which persisted for years, even after proper houses had been built. This initial impression was to colour the views of British officials dealing with the king and his numerous dependants and staff, particularly as the area was not under their control, although only a few miles distant from the seat of British government in India. As many as 250 bungalows and houses were counted during the first survey, and the magistrate promised to watch 'most carefully' the retainers of the ex-king, although he thought 'The presence of the Begams and other females is, to my mind, a pledge for good conduct...'

Not surprisingly during the Uprising, when Lucknow had suffered first from the influx of supporters besieging the Residency, then from the dreadful revenge of the British, many inhabitants had indeed been refugees, some seeking safety in the East India Company's territory. It has been estimated that the city's population fell by around 50,000 people following the king's departure and the events of the following year. Many of these had been notionally connected to the Court—soldiers in the king's regiments, tradespeople, craftsmen, builders and animal keepers, to name only a few who found their livelihood gone when the king left. The position of the wives was different. They had been taken into the sheltered palace life, usually as girls or very young women. Some had been 'bought' by the king, and could not return to their parents, who themselves benefited financially from their daughters' royal marriages. Even with Wajid 'Ali Shah imprisoned, and the date of his release unknown, the wives continued to arrive in Calcutta, including at least two who had been divorced but had children by the king.

Between April and September 1859 more wives and courtiers made the journey from Lucknow, some in groups and some alone, travelling with their servants. Only one wife, Nawab Zaib Mahal Sahibah, who arrived on 13 July, went back to Lucknow in September 'on account of bad health, the climate not agreeing with her'.[25] The others settled down in their new quarters and made the best they could of their altered lives. The Pari Khana must have seemed to them now like a distant fairyland. There were financial difficulties too. The king had had to borrow money from the British government during his imprisonment, and his generous pension of 12 lakhs per annum was not finally agreed until his release in July 1859. When the payments began in the autumn he went into an orgy of spending, but mainly on himself, making up for all those months of deprivation. Major Herbert reported that at a time when Wajid 'Ali Shah's 'considerable resources are ... required for the purpose of providing accommodation for the ladies and others who are with the King', his wives were living in 'thatched mat huts, which it is desirable should be replaced so far as is possible with brick houses'.[26]

Khas Mahal, the first and senior official wife, was outraged at the situation, and wrote to Lord Canning requesting a separate pension for herself, independent of what her husband was receiving. Her own expenses were 'thousands of rupees a month' and were impossible to reduce. She claimed that as she and her son were heirs of 'His Majesty the King [Wajid 'Ali Shah] it was incumbent and fitting for the British Government in consideration of the connexion between the two Courts, in every way to protect the family'. The implication that the court of the ex-king in exile was in any way comparable with the court of Queen Victoria was not well received. Major Herbert was instructed to tell Khas Mahal that her request was rejected, and to remind her that her husband's allowance, equivalent then to about £10,000 per month, had been given to him during his lifetime for his own support and the support of his family.[27]

However, Khas Mahal's hopes were raised when she learned that the crown jewels were to be restored to the king early in January 1860. With considerable foresight on the part of Sir Henry Lawrence, the chief commissioner of Awadh, the jewels had been forcibly taken from the Qaisarbagh treasury and into the Residency for safe keeping, shortly before the siege began. They had been buried in barrels under the lawn in front of the Resident's house, and remained there for nearly five months while the British and their Indian supporters faced death and near starvation as the Residency was bombarded daily by its besiegers. When rescue came at last in November 1857, the jewels were disinterred and somehow got to safety together with those people who survived the siege. On their way down to the treasury at Fort William, the jewels and ornaments, including several tinsel crowns, had been catalogued and repacked into thirteen 'strong timber boxes'.[28] Their arrival was an unexpected bonus for the king, when so much had been looted. Khas Mahal immediately put in a written claim for 'certain articles' of her own among the treasures, but submitted it to Major Herbert, who was now in the unfortunate and embarrassing position of intermediary between husband and wife. What should have been a domestic matter became the subject of government correspondence. Herbert was told that the queen could have her articles 'provided the King does not refute the claim of [Khas Mahal]. Should he do so as respects any of the jewels she claims it will be necessary to put the disputed articles aside, in safe custody, until the dispute is settled.'[29] Whether the queen's claims were accepted is not clear, because the jewels were soon put up by Wajid 'Ali Shah for auction in Calcutta at Hamilton & Co., the well-known jewellers. They fetched 5 lakhs (about £50,000), a sum which went only a small way towards his enormous annual expenditure.[30]

This unhappy incident demonstrates the final breakdown of the relationship between the king and his first wife, to be followed by bitter accusations. On 10 April 1860 a devastating fire swept through Garden Reach. At this time of the year, when everything was bone dry before the monsoon, the thatched bungalows with their bamboo supports and coconut matting partitions would have gone up like fireworks. Major Herbert, visiting Wajid 'Ali Shah a couple of days later, could not resist pointing out that had his advice on replacing the thatched huts with brick houses been followed, 'the fire and its disastrous consequences could not have occurred'.[31] The king's reaction was impassive, and he appeared to the agent to be unable to reflect on what to do for the best. Herbert then visited Khas Mahal, after an urgent request the previous evening by her diwan, Mahdi Quli Khan.

He found the queen, her son the prince, her daughter-in-law and their attendants crammed into four rooms in her fire-damaged bungalow. Two further rooms were unusable. The queen was deeply distressed, not only because of the fire, but by the subsequent behaviour of her husband. Immediately after the conflagration she had sought shelter in her husband's brick-built house, but when she returned to her own bungalow to see what had been salvaged, she was told by the king to stay there. Khas Mahal immediately sent a note to her husband begging him to provide her with suitable accommodation, and to increase her allowance from the Rs900 a month which was so inadequate for her needs that she had refused to accept it.

Later that same evening, the king sent round to her ravaged bungalow what sounds like a group of bully-boys, led by munshi Safdar 'Ali, a dubious and deceitful man, as we shall see. He and a 'concourse of men' surrounded her house and in the name of the king demanded entrance to examine some boxes that had been saved from the fire, and to find out if any valuables were among them. Khas Mahal refused to admit him, and her son indignantly pointed out that it was improper for the munshi even to think of entering a zananah dwelling. A crowd of the prince's supporters quickly gathered and violence would have broken out had Safdar 'Ali not had the wisdom to withdraw. An answer to the queen's letter came the next day from her husband. Wajid 'Ali Shah said that he had given her as much allowance as he could afford, and as for new accommodation, he had just given orders 'to all members of his suite to disperse and find lodgings where they could and that she may go and live where she likes'. Tearfully Khas Mahal told Major Herbert she took this to mean that she was being ordered to leave the damaged bungalow, that she was an invalid without any means, and that to live apart from the king would be a disgrace to her.[32]

In his weekly diary report, which was sent regularly to the Foreign Department, Herbert can be seen struggling to remain sympathetic, but at the same time trying to distance himself from these distressing domestic disputes. He advised the queen and her son to remain put, but they insisted that if nothing was done, Wajid 'Ali Shah would have them forcibly thrown out. This was unlikely, replied Herbert, because the king would certainly not want to bring such disgrace upon himself and his own family. But of course he could not interfere in the king's private affairs. Was not Herbert, as a government official and agent to the king, there to protect the family and look after their affairs, demanded the prince? No, that was a mistaken assumption, Herbert replied; but he did promise 'to bring their statement to the knowledge of the Government'. His diplomatic skills were being painfully stretched in trying to adopt a neutral position in the royal family's disputes, yet at the same time acting as advisor and critic to the king. He concluded his report by stating that Khas Mahal and her household were embarrassed for want of money, and the king seemed to have given up. His own affairs were in 'great disorder. He does not seem to take any serious thought of the real wants of his dependents and it appears hopeless...'

Wajid 'Ali Shah may have suffered some kind of breakdown at this point, which paralysed him into inaction. The previous year had seen life-changing events for him—his release from Fort William after two years of imprisonment, the realisation that his pension was a fixed sum for the remainder of his life, the shabby conditions of his new, permanent home and now the fire. But like a shopaholic suffering from compulsive buying disorder, he could not stop spending money he did not have. He had wanted to purchase a further estate at Garden Reach that lay between the two houses he had already bought. Major Herbert reported in a diary entry that after the dreadful fire Wajid 'Ali Shah would have been able to buy the estate for much less. Presumably it was fire-damaged too, but the king was so impatient to have it that his staff made ridiculous offers to the owner, who naturally held out for more. Prepared to offer the equivalent of £9,500 for the property, nearly a month's pension, the king was neatly forestalled by Khas Mahal, who moved into the property herself.[33] After her plea of poverty to Herbert, money had obviously been found or borrowed by the queen from somewhere. Less fortunate and less wealthy wives were forced to move out of Garden Reach and 'are now dispersed about the neighbourhood living wherever they have been able to find lodgings'.

Major Herbert's reports, and those of subsequent agents, show that although the chief wives were unseen, they were certainly not unheard. Protocol meant that the agents did not meet the women face to face but through intermediaries, sometimes a son or a diwan. *Purdah-nishin* women, that is those who were concealed behind a veil, could only meet a very limited number of close male relatives; to men outside this small circle they were *haram*, or forbidden. All their servants were female, apart from the eunuchs, who appropriately inhabited a kind of no-man's-land between the zananah and the masculine, or public, part of the palace. But this did not prevent the wives from running their own, often influential, power-bases. The establishment of Khas Mahal, as chief wife, was a smaller, female version of the king's, with tailors, washerwomen, nursery maids, bedchamber assistants, sweepers, hookahberdars (women who prepared the hookah), storytellers and punkahwalis, who operated the large cloth fans. Other women prepared *paan*, the addictive betel leaf and areca nut delicacy, and sherbet drinks. The male diwans dealt with matters outside the zananah, negotiating loans with the Calcutta moneylenders on behalf of the queens, who ran up respectable debts on their own account (though not on the scale of their husband), and carrying messages to and from their lawyers. There was no need to go shopping, because everything the women wished to purchase was brought to them for their approval and displayed on the floor in front of them.

THE HOUSE OF FAIRIES

Inevitably there was rivalry, intrigue, tale-bearing and back-biting between the establishments of the different queens, and this was sometimes exacerbated by mischievous male interference. A number of mut'ah wives had decided to return to Lucknow, despite the loss in status that this would involve. Choti Begam was the first to go, in the autumn of 1859,[34] and her departure led to others asking to leave, perhaps not permanently, but certainly until the problem of accommodation had been sorted out. As a result, Wajid 'Ali Shah was advised by Safdar 'Ali (the man who had tried to enter Khas Mahal's bungalow) that the king should get all his wives to sign an affidavit promising to obey all his wishes, and admitting that if they failed to do so, they would forfeit all legal claims on the king. This was undoubtedly in response to the fear that if enough wives left, the king would have to pay out large sums as leaving presents. When a copy of the affidavit was presented to Khas Mahal, she flew into another rage and refused to sign it.

Indignantly she stated that although it might be reasonable to require a written promise from a 'concubine', as she dismissively called the mut'ah wives, it was an insult to demand a signature from her, who could not be cast aside. She wished to please the king in what she did, but was not going to sign the affadavit. The second official wife, Akhtar Mahal, similarly refused to sign, which made Wajid 'Ali Shah 'much displeased' with them. But male relatives of the two queens defended them robustly, and were extremely indignant that they had ever been asked to sign such a document.

The truth, or at least a plausible explanation, behind the affidavit story came from the diwan of Khas Mahal. He said that his employer, the queen, had tried to persuade her husband to cut back his expenditure, particularly as he owed nearly 4 lakhs to the unpleasant Safdar 'Ali and also had to pay back the loan made to him by the British government while he was in prison. The munshi had been overcharging the king outrageously for

151

items supplied, and was now afraid that the two queens would demand an enquiry into his accounts. The affidavit was a ploy to alienate the husband from his wives and deprive them 'of any influence' with him.[35] Admittedly it sounds far-fetched, but it is a further illustration of Wajid 'Ali Shah's gullibility, not to mention his ability to fall for tall stories spun by those who wished to manipulate him for their own ends.

Another case of wife-bullying was reported in 1865 when Begam Khanum Sahibah, a second-class mut'ah wife, reported that she had been robbed of jewellery worth half a lakh of rupees (£5,000) by the superintendent of the king's mahals, Nawab Julus ud-daulah, and three male 'companions'. The begam said she had been tricked into entering a carriage with all her belongings 'on the pretext of changing her residence'.[36] She was driven to a house in Calcutta, told to get out, and immediately had her property and jewellery seized by the four men 'who stated that they had the authority of their master [Wajid 'Ali Shah] for so acting. The house where she was left proved to be a house of ill-fame.' The agent, Malleson, carried out a thorough investigation, which included interviewing Wajid 'Ali Shah, several members of his household, and the ex-minister who had formerly been in charge of the wives. In the end the case failed because the king denied giving the begam any jewellery at all. He said she would not have been able to purchase half a lakh's worth from the low wage she was on, which was only Rs16 a month. She had been dismissed 'on account of her quarrelsome disposition by order of the King'.[37] Although there was insufficient evidence to prove the theft, Malleson said he wanted to make it clear to the king 'and those who surrounded him, that no act of tyranny or oppression towards his dependants should pass unnoticed, and that the pretext of his authority would be no protection to those who might violate the laws of the land'. The outcome was unsatisfactory for Khanum Sahibah, but another marker had been put down by the British government showing that its attitude was hardening towards the king's treatment of his women. This was to lead to confrontation in the next decade between two opposing ideologies, when changing British views collided with the traditional mindset of the king.

A word needs to be said about the agents appointed to the king, because it is through their eyes and their reports that we see Wajid 'Ali Shah's women and chart the deterioration in his relationships with his chief wives. Their official title was 'Agents of the Governor General with the King', and these men, all army officers, were the link between the deposed king and the governor general. Their role was a diminished version of the post that the British Residents to the Court of Awadh had previously undertaken, with the difference that while the Residents had had the task of reporting and monitoring all pertinent events in Awadh before its annexation, the agents now had the limited task of reporting only on the king's actions in exile. Wajid 'Ali Shah had no choice over who was appointed as his agent, any more than he had had over the Residents at his Court.

George Bruce Malleson, the third agent, had served in the Bengal infantry and fought during the Second Burmese War. He was a scholarly, somewhat pedantic man, best known for the six-volume *History of the Indian Mutiny*. His fellow author, John Kaye, had published the first volume in 1864, a year before Malleson took up his post. It contains the standard British description of Wajid 'Ali Shah before his deposition: 'Sunk in the uttermost abysses of enfeebling debauchery, the King pushed aside business, which he felt himself incapable of transacting, and went in search of new pleasures. Stimulated to the utmost by unnatural excitements his appetites were satiated by the debaucheries of the Zenana.'[38] Although Malleson's report on the Khanum Sahibah case is factual and unemotive, he must nevertheless have relished the opportunity to lay down the law to this debased character, as he saw him.

In the summer of 1874, Major Mowbray Thomson was appointed as the seventh agent to the king. If Wajid 'Ali Shah was not aware of Thomson's past, then everyone else in British India was. As a young man, Thomson had joined the 53rd Bengal Native Infantry at Cawnpore during the Uprising. (He had previously been an officer with the Cawnpore police.) Fired on by the Nana Sahib's troops at Satichaura Ghat (known to the British as Massacre Ghat) on the river Ganges, Thomson was one of only four survivors, out of hundreds of British civilians and soldiers, to escape downriver. After reaching the safety of Allahabad, he followed General Havelock back into Cawnpore where the massacre of women and children was discovered, their mutilated bodies thrust down the infamous well. One of the photographs of Wheeler's Entrenchment, after its recapture by Havelock in 1857, shows Thomson standing in front of the barracks with his arms folded, and the single word 'mad' written on the photographer's notes.[39] Thomson was subsequently wounded and invalided home to England, where he was feted as an outstanding hero of the mutiny. On his return to India he was given a civilian post as political agent in Manipur, and then, in an inspired moment at the India Office, was allocated as agent to Wajid 'Ali Shah, the man whose deposition had been a major cause of the mutiny. Thomson was not a man to be trifled with, and Wajid 'Ali Shah found much to complain about. In a series of letters, misleadingly called *mohubutnamahs* (friendly addresses), the king said he had lived in Calcutta 'with greatest comforts and ease, under the shade of Kindness of the Hon'ble Government and the favours of Political Agents', but from 1877 things had changed and his 'religious necessities' had been interfered with.[40]

During the twenty odd years that the king had been in Calcutta he claimed to have 'released and dismissed' about forty or fifty of his mut'ah wives with no objection from the earlier agents assigned to him. But when he decided in 1878 to dispense with twenty-seven wives all at once, Thomson protested; and not only that, the new agent insisted that the king continue to pay them maintenance after their 'contracts' had ended. It was to be a long and bitterly fought battle between the two men: the king citing Shi'a religious custom and usage for his part, and Thomson retaliating in the language of the Victorian gentleman he was, reminding the king of his 'moral obligations' towards the women and accusing him of 'unmanly behaviour' and of acting like a spoilt child. Had he wished, Wajid 'Ali Shah could have put up a much better fight than he actually did. He did not employ lawyers or religious leaders to argue his case, but relied on direct appeals to Thomson; and when these failed, he sent expensive but futile telegrams to the governor general Lord Lytton, who was then in Lahore monitoring British progress in the Second Afghan War.

The king complained of interference with his religious practices. The taking of mut'ah wives, he said, was done 'in accordance with the Holy Koran, and the universally accepted customs of the Shia sect'. Women could be married for a 'limited time and in payment of a limited sum', and when the contract was over that was that and the former wife became 'forbidden'. 'It is repugnant to the religion of the Mohammedans of the Shia sect for such wives to claim maintenance from the husband', he blustered.[41] The religious argument in Wajid 'Ali Shah's refusal to pay maintenance to his divorced wives was soon abandoned, although it would have carried the most weight in a country that was still using *A Digest of Mohummudan Law* as the basis for legal decisions. Instead the king cited lack of money, misrepresentations from his wives and general ingratitude all round from his numerous family. The story of the king's children is told in the following chapter, but in summary, trouble started when two of his adult sons, by different mothers, requested an increase in their pitiably small monthly allowances. They were supported by Thomson and the temporary agents appointed when Thomson was on leave. Wajid 'Ali Shah saw this as an unwarranted interference in his own affairs. 'It is a recognised rule in domestic circles', he told Thomson, 'that the owner of the house alone should have uncontrolled authority over the disposal of his income and over the destinies of his children and wives.'[42] This applied to everyone, he added, not just ex-kings, but 'rich or poor' alike. Of course had the king been an ordinary individual, and not in receipt of a British pension of 1 lakh of rupees every month, then Thomson's intervention would have been intrusive, but this was not the case. Wajid 'Ali Shah was the highest paid pensioner in India, and the British government naturally felt it should have a say in how the pension was spent.

When the king got his pension for February 1878, which was delayed until the 13th of that month, he found that 2,500 rupees had been deducted from it at source by the government. He took the remaining 97,500 rupees but refused to sign the treasury receipt. The deducted money was paid directly to Prince Farid-ud-din Qadr, now the eldest of the king's surviving sons,[43] who had been struggling along on 90 rupees a month. In spite of further protests from Wajid 'Ali Shah, the government declined to alter its mind and in fact threatened that if the king did not voluntarily increase the pensions to his dependants, then Mowbray Thomson would be put in charge of all his financial affairs. Instead of agreeing to the government's not unreasonable order, the king chose a novel form of protest. Thomson was startled to learn at the end of April that Wajid 'Ali Shah had divorced two of his wives: Mashuq Mahal, the mother of Farid-ud-din Qadr, and Wajid Mahal, whose son had also requested an enhanced pension. It was a spiteful act, punishing two of his oldest wives because their sons, the king's children, had dared to ask for more money.

Both women subsequently wrote dignified letters to Thomson describing how their lives had deteriorated during the long years that they shared their husband's exile.[44] Mashuq Mahal described a lost paradise in Lucknow where she was ranked 'as the Sovereign Queen and proprietress of the whole Kingdom' and 'the jewel in the crowns of all the ladies of His Majesty's household'. She recalled sitting on a golden throne when the king held an open durbar for the women attached to his house. Those attending the durbar brought presents for her and Khas Mahal, and there were salutes and soldiers presenting arms. Both women wore crowns during festivals like Eid. Now she had been divorced on a matter of principle outside her control. 'I ought not to be sacrificed at the shrine of my husband's whims', she wrote, adding that she was now 'Alone in a foreign place and deserted by a husband for whose sake I flew away from the arms of loving parents, my only hope now lies in the kind promise of Government that all families of His Majesty should be provided for out of the ample and kingly stipend fixed for His Majesty.'

This moving letter prompted Thomson to write to Alfred Lyall, Secretary to the government of India. He told Lyall that Mashuq Mahal was the king's first mut'ah wife, who used to get 3,000 rupees a month, 'but now she has become aged and suffers only because her son prayed for an adequate allowance'. Mashuq Mahal, whose original name had been Piyari Sahib, was about the same age as her husband, that is, fifty-eight years old, at the time of her divorce. Thomson added that 'she has, unlike the other ladies in the Ex-King's household, been always a great favourite of His Majesty and up to the present time I have heard nothing against her character'.

Wajid Mahal, who was married in 1845 and had an apartment in Qaisarbagh Palace, used to get a monthly salary of 1,000 rupees, which was gradually whittled down to 100 rupees a month. She did not complain but commented that she had received the king's favours for thirty-three years. Now, 'if it pleased him to withdraw his favour and subject me to distress and discomfort in my declining years, I could not do better than silently submit to his will'. Immediately following her son's request, the king had ordered a sepoy guard to be withdrawn from the gate of her house in Kidderpore, which she saw as a public disgrace, indicating that she was no longer worth protecting. 'What grievous fault had I committed?' she asked pathetically. 'In the midst of my grief and anxiety, I cannot but feel amazed as to how His Majesty could have persuaded himself to inflict such a serious indignity on me in my old age, and I would fain believe this to be not the acts of his own unbiased will and judgement, but the work of evil advisors and secret enemies.' She added, 'Compared with my position, I am indeed poor.'[45]

Wajid Mahal was singled out by Thomson as a particular example of the king's callousness, even though she had by now moved out of Garden Reach and was 'known to be in the keeping of' Maulawi Mir Fazl Ahmad, a former Inspector of the Oude Police Force. She had been 'a respectable woman in Lucknow' before the king took up with her, Thomson said, but now she was not only dismissed from the Court, but was in debt too. Wajid 'Ali Shah angrily refuted this charge, claiming that Wajid Mahal was a female tailor, who worked for one of his 'official' wives. She was also a married woman when he first spotted her, but 'faithlessly leaving off her husband [she] became my mota wife'. He then added with astonishing insouciancy that 'the said lady was [only] a respectable woman at Lucknow because I increased her respectability; and she has been involved in debt here by her own act ... the allegation of her being a woman of respectability and position is quite untrue'.[46] What was even worse, he had had to remove her from one house to another in Garden Reach 'to keep her separate, her selfishness and partiality go to wound my feelings and render my other mota wives bold and refractory'. He added that even one of his official wives (probably Khas Mahal, who comes over as a strong-minded woman) wanted to start interfering with his 'religious and domestic affairs'. This was indeed a palace mutiny and the women were up in arms. Another mut'ah wife 'of a lower order' called Mussamat Wali Begam, on a salary of 48 rupees a month, he claimed 'roves from door to door and spends every day with a paramour and every night with another'.

THE HOUSE OF FAIRIES

Wajid 'Ali Shah seemed completely unaware of how he himself would be seen and judged in his long, ranting letter to the new governor general, Lord Dufferin, who had only been in office for two weeks when this missive landed on his desk. The idea of the king flitting about like some ariel Rubenesque figure, descending at intervals to bestow 'respectability' on poor, working-class women with the touch of a magic wand, is both comical and sad. It is too much of a fairy story. But the crux of the matter is that Wajid 'Ali Shah had not seen that the times were changing. What had seemed to him, if not to others, as romantic and even kingly behaviour thirty years ago in a semi-autonomous kingdom was not acceptable in British India towards the end of the nineteenth century, particularly when the British government was paying his pension. Moved by the plea of Mashuq Mahal, the government ordered the king to pay her a further 2,500 rupees per month. This raised her income and that of her son to 5,000 rupees a month, which Thomson said would enable them to get a house together in Calcutta, to employ guards for the house and 'to live in comfort and peace and remove them altogether from the baneful influence of Garden Reach'. He added, 'Threats were also conveyed to the Prince and his mother that His Majesty would forcibly turn them away' if they did not leave their Garden Reach home within three days. The government order was conveyed to the king on 8 July 1878.

Three weeks later, after Thomson had closed up his Chowringhee office for the day, he received an unexpected visit from nawab Amir 'Ali, the king's accountant and manager. The king, reported Amir 'Ali, had retaliated against the government's order by suddenly divorcing twenty-seven of his mut'ah wives. The divorces had all taken place on 31 July. Thomson found this hard to believe at first, and sought confirmation of it from the king the next morning. Then, rather rashly (for Thomson was not a diplomat, but a retired soldier), instead of waiting for that confirmation, he let fly in a letter for which he subsequently had to apologise. If the news was correct, he said, then 'Your Majesty will be acting most unjustly towards these ladies who are entirely at your mercy, and who at their time of life will find this treatment exceedingly hard and unkindly, having all their lives been accustomed to the luxuries of your zenana ... the driving away of a few old ladies will look more like the pettish anger of a spoilt child at finding itself thwarted in doing that which it should not have done.'[47]

The king, responding immediately by letter, chose to ignore the jibe about a 'spoilt child' for the moment (although he filed it away for future use). It was true, he said, that he had terminated the marriage contracts of twenty-seven mut'ah wives. This had been done for financial reasons, as there was an 'insufficiency of income'. By divorcing them, 'this absolves me from my obligation to support them and takes away all responsibility as to the course of life they may lead in future'. He told Thomson to 'strike out the names from your register' and helpfully added a list of the women's names, with their fathers' names, where known, and the dates of the marriages, which ranged from 1 November 1859 to 25 August 1869. It was evident that Wajid 'Ali Shah had celebrated his release from Fort William in the way he knew best, by taking on yet more wives—three in one day alone, on 16 November 1859.[48] Not surprisingly, given the king's strong sentimental attachment to his place of birth, a number of the new wives had come from Lucknow.

Faced with this fait accompli, Thomson could only express his regret that the news of the mass divorce was true and that he considered it an 'unmanly, and at the same time, useless measure of economy'. The sharp exchanges of August 1878 between the king and Thomson read as though the two men were engaged in a bitter personal game of chess, and to some extent they were. Thomson had a fair measure of autonomy, as long as he kept the government of India informed about what was going on by writing to the Secretary to the Foreign Department. Guidance and comments on his reports came back down to Thomson from the governor general and council, via the secretary. The agent could also make recommendations to government about future strategies to deal with the king and his vast, chaotic household. This is what Thomson sat down to do in the autumn of 1878, meticulously working out how the king's monthly pension should be expended.[49] Since the government had already threatened earlier in the year to put Thomson in charge of the king's financial affairs if he refused to pay his dependants, this was sensible forward planning.

At some point during his calculations, he realised that a solution to the problem of the newly discarded wives lay in the divorce, earlier that year, of Mashuq Mahal. Because she and her son were ordered out of the rent-free accommodation in Garden Reach, where they had lived for the last twenty years, new living quarters in Calcutta had to be found and paid for. An additional expense was hiring security guards for the new house. If these costs were to be multiplied by twenty-seven, Thomson mused, and then deducted from the king's monthly pension before it reached him, the ex-wives could be provided for at no cost to the government, considerable irritation to the king, and benefit to the women who would be shifted from the 'baneful influence' of Garden Reach. It was an ingenious move, and a chart was compiled showing how much each woman could expect. Because the women had been on different monthly salaries, from 26 to 50 rupees a month, the sums had to be worked out proportionately, calculating an extra one fourth of their allowances to pay for the hire of new houses. The sums involved were not large, but the principle was important. Although adamant that he would not pay maintenance for the divorced wives, the king agreed that he would not turn them out of their Garden Reach homes until the governor general had responded to Thomson's report, thus giving a period of grace to the worried women and their children.

Thomson was urged by the government of India to try to persuade the king to meet his financial obligations. It was estimated that if all the wives, ex-wives and dependants were to get a reasonable, but not over-generous pension, it would cost the king 24,500 rupees a month, just over a quarter of his own monthly pension. This calculation infuriated and alarmed Wajid 'Ali Shah. The realisation that the government could, and would, deduct the money prompted him to make a rare visit to Calcutta to protest in person to Thomson. The agent duly reported the bizarre conversation that took place in his office on 24 February 1879. 'How can a small quantity of oil [be] spread over a large surface?' asked the king, which Thomson interpreted as meaning how could the royal pension provide for so many dependants. When he first started receiving 100,000 rupees a month back in 1859, the king complained, he did not have so many people to provide for. One can imagine Thomson manfully holding back the obvious retort about more wives often leading to more children. Instead, his reported words were, 'Why, Your Majesty would not even cease to provide for any old dog or other animal in your menagerie when it became old and worn-out?' referring 'to his wives who in their old age he wished to dismiss penniless'.

The king's answer was, 'But the women are old and ugly, and can bear no more children; they are no use to me.'
'Then who is to provide for them in their old age?'
'The Government, whose *ryots* [peasants] they are.'[50]

How far Wajid 'Ali Shah had fallen from that self-deceived vision of the passionate lover of Lucknow, forty years earlier! Did he really see women only as providers of children? Had he never realised that to grow old with a loved companion is not to mind the inroads of age into one's partner? Clearly not. By the end of his life he was to sever all links with his long-suffering family.

The king's relationships with his numerous wives and children, although taking up a large part of his time and energy, and that of the agents, were in some ways easier for the government to deal with than other facets of his behaviour. There were certainly flashpoints that called for delicate negotiations, but ultimately these were domestic matters. His wives suffered as much, if not more, in the move to Calcutta and in adjusting to their changed circumstances. Not only did they lose the comfort of palace life in Lucknow, but also in many cases their income. As the king grew older, he became spiteful towards the women he had married thirty years earlier, including some of the 'fairies'. Their plight moved government officials to intercede on the wives' behalf.

5

AT GARDEN REACH

Life in the Bengal palaces, as Wajid 'Ali Shah recreates the vanished world of Lucknow. He is wildly extravagant and continually in debt, which is made worse by his servants, who fleece him shamelessly. British officials try to rescue him from his own folly. They also try, unsuccessfully, to control the royal estate through policing and improved sanitation.

When the Chief Justice of Calcutta, Sir Lawrence Peel, retired to England in 1855, he settled down on the Isle of Wight and built himself a pleasant house, which he named 'Garden Reach'. This was a tribute to the area that lay south-west of Calcutta where Peel had lived during the latter years of his Indian career. Wealthy British officials had begun building country or 'garden' houses in the 1770s along a two-mile stretch on the southern bank of the Hugli. Although referred to as 'bungalows', these were substantial two- or three-storeyed houses, often Palladian in style, with fashionable bow-fronted facades. A decade later, when the artist William Hodges travelled upriver, he wrote in his journal: 'As the ship approaches Calcutta the river narrows; that which is called the Garden Reach, presents a view of handsome buildings, on a flat surrounded by gardens; these are villas belonging to the opulent inhabitants of Calcutta.' They were indeed very handsome buildings, and well able to rival the large houses along Chowringhee that gave Calcutta its proud name, 'City of Palaces'. At Garden Reach there were no constraints on space, so each villa stood in its own large garden compound, with separate buildings for stables, kitchens and servants' quarters. The area was known locally as Matiya Burj, which means a clay or earthen tower, as an old watchtower of unbaked bricks had stood somewhere here to guard the bend in the river that led up-country.

William Hickey, the Calcutta lawyer more famous for his entertaining memoirs than his career at the Bar, hired a garden house here for the three 'horridly dusty and disagreeable months of March, April and May' in 1791.[1] It was a 'very large and commodious residence in Garden Reach, the last in that line, about seven miles and a half from Calcutta, beautifully situated within a few yards of the river, affording us the advantage of water as well as land carriage'. Hickey's rented house, which he shared with a friend, had nine large apartments, with four smaller ones on the ground floor. There were 'six very spacious ones above stairs', two of which had their own private staircase. There was a noble dining room, a similar breakfast room, a spacious sitting or drawing-room and an adjoining billiard room. Such luxury had a price too, and Hickey found his share of the hire, at the end of three months, was over 7,000 rupees. A similar house at Garden Reach was sold for 35,000 rupees a few years later to Lord Wellesley, who intended to set up a college here for junior East India Company staff. Wellesley imagined something along the lines of an Oxford or Cambridge college with professors, and in fact he purchased another four houses along the riverbank for this purpose. The Court of Directors in London was horrified by the potential expense involved, and the idea of the college at Garden Reach was dropped, leaving the Company with a number of large houses to rent or sell. However, it remained a popular place among the legal profession, and apart from Sir Lawrence Peel it was also home to two Chief Justices, Sir Edward Ryan and Sir Charles Grey. In the late 1830s the road from Chandpal Ghat (in central Calcutta) to Garden Reach was built and opened 'to the public' on payment of a toll. By 1855 the road was made over to the East India Company, who now took on its maintenance.

A recent history of the area cites a map of the 1840s, where the grand houses along the southern riverbank were prosaically named Bungalow No. 1, Bungalow No. 2 and so on.[2] (There were thirteen 'bungalows' in all.) Peel's former house was Bungalow No. 11, which now belonged to Chand Mehtab Bahadur, Raja of Burdwan. Following the hurried flight from Lucknow and preparations for the journey onwards to England, Wajid 'Ali Shah was installed in No. 11 early in June 1856, less than two weeks after his arrival in Calcutta.[3] The king's new home was a smaller version of an existing building in the centre of Calcutta called Metcalfe Hall. Constructed in 1844 and named after the acting governor general of the time, it was considered one of the finest examples of classical Grecian architecture in the East, with its thirty graceful Corinthian columns supporting the entablature. Peel's house was a cosier, more domestic building, and not intended as a grand imperial statement, but it was still of sufficient pretension to attract Wajid 'Ali Shah.

The building was cruciform in shape, with four wide verandahs behind its twenty-four double-height columns. Inside, a fine central staircase rose to the second storey, with its high-ceilinged rooms, all interconnected with tall doors so that the river breezes could waft through and cool the humid air. Apart from being well removed from the noise and dirt of central Calcutta, No. 11 had its own private *ghat*, or landing stage, onto the Hugli. It was advantageous to have the choice between river or road transport into Calcutta, as William Hickey had found. Even after it had been adopted as a public highway, for many years Garden Reach Road was little more than a narrow track running between the thatched huts of villagers and enveloping trees, so a river journey would certainly have been quicker and more comfortable. Wajid 'Ali Shah could, if he wished, sit on the northern verandah of his new house and look directly across the garden and over the Hugli, a much grander river than the Gomti, which ran beside his first home in Lucknow. Bungalow No. 11 was renamed Sultan Khana, or King's House. Little is known about how it was adapted from an English gentleman's residence into a palace for a king in exile, except that a private mosque was built adjoining the house for daily worship, equivalent to the private chapel of grand country houses in England. Unusually, the mosque had no domes or minarets, and was a flat-roofed building. Several rooms inside the Sultan Khana were decorated with chandeliers and 'set apart as imambarahs' for private worship. It was reported that the king's sons were not allowed into their father's house at all, and that his wives were only allowed into the imambarahs 'on certain special days'.[4]

Two adjoining garden houses were also rented. The king had been followed from the Lucknow Court by many of his 'principal officers' whom he wanted to have near him. It was discovered after his death that, although only a tenant at first, the king immediately issued *firmans* (official written orders) to these men and their families, granting them specific plots of ground as building sites within the compounds. 'In addition to these occupiers of houses who are in possession of firmans from the King, there are a large number of persons who either on the verbal sanction of His Majesty or probably in many cases, with no sanction at all, but with the connivance of his officers have squatted on the land and built tenements for which they now exact rent.'[5] And in some cases tenants refused to pay rent, claiming that they were occupying the land on a *mu'afi* tenure, that is, a rent-free agreement. It was a recipe for chaos and, as we have seen, within two years of the king's arrival there were already an estimated 250 thatched bungalows and houses on the site in June 1858, all tucked into three large compounds. The king's long imprisonment in Fort William meant that nobody was in charge of the Garden Reach area, and the Burdwan raja, who owned the site, did not choose to intervene.

At the time of Wajid 'Ali Shah's release in July 1859, he was paying the raja a rent of 1,000 rupees a month. However, he was anxious to buy the Sultan Khana, because he said that as a tenant he could not get proper repairs made to the house. He also wanted to purchase the neighbouring two houses and compounds, where his staff and courtiers were already squatting.[6] Major Herbert, the agent, was sympathetic to the king's request, passing it on to government for approval. A sum of 3 lakhs of rupees was allocated for the purchase of the Sultan Khana and the two neighbouring houses, which were promptly named Asad Manzil and Murassa Manzil. Knowing the king's financial habits, not to mention his debts, the purchase money for the properties went straight from the government treasury to the vendors. (Many years later, government officials queried whether the 3 lakhs had been a loan to Wajid 'Ali Shah or an outright gift, but at the time it seems to have been considered as compensation for his palaces in Lucknow, which had been seized by the British.)[7] The king paid the annual land tax on the houses from his own purse. Once in full possession of the three houses, and with his pension backdated to 9 July 1859, Wajid 'Ali Shah's extravagance knew no bounds. Major Herbert now reported that he had heard 'from various quarters that a wasteful expenditure is going on'.

Herbert had been approached by Babu Ramprasad Roy, a government-appointed official of the civil court, who was trying to get some outstanding accounts paid by the king. When Herbert said he had no control over the king's financial affairs, Roy replied that some form of control should be established and warned that the government would find itself in 'considerable trouble' over the king's debts if nothing was done. Roy said that some up-country bankers had consulted him professionally as to whether they should accept 'certain negotiations for considerable pecuniary transactions' that the king's courtiers were proposing. This was potentially alarming. The 'up-country' bankers were likely to be established at Lucknow, and although the flow of people from Lucknow to Calcutta could not be halted, unless everyone was arrested, the less communication Wajid 'Ali Shah had with his old haunts the better. And what could these 'certain negotiations' entail?[8]

The agent had no reason to doubt what he was hearing, because he knew 'it is the drift of the King to deny himself nothing and to incur debt' in order to demonstrate that his pension, generous as it was, would not meet his needs. It was a risky game and 'a course which cannot fail eventually to produce a great deal of trouble'. Lord Canning stepped in to say that if Wajid 'Ali Shah continued like this it would 'infalliably lead him into embarrassment and distress from which he will look in vain to the Government of India to extricate him'. 'Ample provision' had been made for him, and under no circumstances would the government intervene to relieve him from the 'embarrassment of debt'.[9] Years later, Wajid 'Ali Shah justified money spent on the buildings by claiming that 'the three houses that were given me were from their fashion and style and their then existing accommodation fit for habitation of no more than twelve Europeans. I have had to spend lakhs of rupees to alter and convert them into Hindoostani fashion and style.' He added, somewhat unbelievably, that he had even 'had to curtail his daily expenses'.[10] Just how unlimited expenditure was to transform three large European houses into a huge new palace complex we shall see later. For the moment there was considerable anxiety among British officials about the king's indebtedness.

Canning learned that Wajid 'Ali Shah had been 'trying to raise money in the bazaar' to cover his expenses, which was certainly embarrassing for the ex-king, but also as embarrassing for the

British government, which faced continuing criticism of its treatment of the deposed monarch. Any suggestion that the richest princely house in India had been deliberately impoverished by the government could have had dangerous consequences in a country so recently emerging from the Uprising. And yet the government could not be seen to bail out a man who was receiving the equivalent of £10,000 a month. The king had to be saved from himself and his extravagant ways; that was the clear message from government. But in fact for the remainder of his life Wajid 'Ali Shah made constant pleas for more funds, and there were a series of 'one-off' face-saving financial concessions by the government. The words Garden Reach and 'extravagance' became synonymous.

While the king was in prison, life had to go on for his wives, his children and the numerous courtiers and servants who had followed him from Lucknow and were now cramped together in the three compounds. Some were wealthy people in their own right, if they had managed to realise their assets before leaving Awadh. Numerous restrictions had been put in place by the British, particularly on property, and if the courtiers' wealth was in land, then they now had to rely on the king to support them. Others learned that their houses had been looted, either by rebel soldiers opposing the British or by the British themselves. The chief minister, 'Ali Naqi Khan, lost 72 lakhs in cash, gold and jewellery before the city was recaptured in 1858. Servants whose wages were paid by the king were wholly dependent on him. These included 50 African slaves, 245 'special guards', 120 sentinels armed with swords, 20 mace-bearers and 18 eunuchs. There were also various tradesmen attached to the Court, including butchers, confectioners, bakers and potters, and domestic servants like sweepers, grooms, barbers and 'gunta pandies', men who marked the passing hours by striking bells. Two of the 'Abyssinians', or African slaves, said that they had not been paid for eighteen months, and on reaching Calcutta were told rather sharply they could leave again 'if so inclined'.[11] The king had been forced to borrow money to maintain his family and staff at Garden Reach, before accepting the pension offered by government. Once the pension was in place there was an orgy of spending, which clearly did not have repaying the moneylenders as its first priority. But there was still an urgent need for money.

Were there any remaining nawabi assets that could be realised? Two years after his release, Wajid 'Ali Shah learned with 'great surprise' from the Delhi newspapers that the tomb and gardens of his ancestor, the second nawab Safdar Jang, had been put up for sale by the British authorities. Grand tombs, like that of Safdar Jang, were maintained by renting out small houses and shops in the surrounding areas, the rent paying for the tomb's upkeep. Through his agent, the king laid claim to this and other property in and around Delhi worth £10,000, including a house near the Lahore Gate. This was a large and ancient property, known as haveli Sa'adat Khan, and dated back to the time of the first nawab. The government's response to the claims was confused, but not unexpected. Firstly, it had not realised that Wajid 'Ali Shah owned any property in Delhi, and if he did, then he should have spoken up sooner. 'Whatever rights he had, he has compromised himself by his long silence.'[12] Secondly, a man called Amir-ud-daulah claimed that the king himself had given him the old haveli shortly before the Uprising, and the 'deeds of gift' appeared genuine. The lucky recipient was believed to be a man 'of very low extraction of the "doom" caste'. Thirdly, it was supposed that all the king's property throughout India had been confiscated, and the three Garden Reach houses given in lieu of all other claims, public or private, although this had not been stated explicitly to Wajid 'Ali Shah. Lastly, did the Safdar Jang tomb and its garden private property belong to the king? British lawyers were not certain about this, but thought it unlikely, and in any case the king should not get it back.

Much more worrying was the news in January 1862 that the king had been forced to mortgage his recently purchased house, Sultan Khana. A Hindu moneylender, Manohar Das, had obtained a High Court decree against Wajid 'Ali Shah over loans which had not been repaid. It was another embarrassment. The deeds of the house were made over to three men, including Safdar 'Ali, who was to cause the king endless trouble, and Zulfiqar-ud-daulah, one of the king's 'most intimate and trusted retainers' and his brother-in-law, who had shared imprisonment with him. A 'stay of execution' was granted for the moment. Could the king actually mortgage a house bought for him by the British government? Apparently he could. Lord Canning, in the last months of his governorship, confirmed, 'however painful it may be to see him [Wajid 'Ali Shah] squandering the property granted to him as a residence by the State, it is absolutely at His Majesty's disposal'. Canning also cautioned the king against allowing himself to be bound by the acts of his servants, and regretted that, in spite of the liberal provisions of his government pension, he was deep in 'pecuniary difficulties which must prove ruinous to him and his family' and that the government would not extricate him from these.[13] But in fact it did—not by paying off his debts, but by something more subtle.

Within a week of his arrival, the new governor general, the Earl of Elgin, was to give his assent to 'The King of Oude Act No. VIII of 1862'. This was one of five 'King of Oude' Acts passed during Wajid 'Ali Shah's lifetime (the sixth and final Act was passed posthumously). The Act passed on 27 March 1862 was to set out the 'expediency of partially exempting the King of Oude from the jurisdiction of the Courts of Law'. It meant that Wajid 'Ali Shah could not be summoned to a criminal or a civil court and that he could not be served with a warrant, or arrested in his own house. If he had to be interrogated, then Major Herbert, or subsequent agents, would show him a list of written questions and take down the royal answers. There were various clauses and caveats, of course. If the king committed an offence that was punishable by death under the Indian Penal Code, then he would not be exempted. If anyone attempted to serve a writ concerning civil, revenue or criminal matters, it had to be approved first by the governor general and signed by the Secretary to the government of India. Although this was unfair to the king's existing creditors, the hope was, as Herbert admitted, that it would in future 'prevent persons from granting His Majesty unlimited credit and producing eventual troubles'. There was a constant emphasis on avoiding the trouble that would ensue if the king's expenditure was not reined in. Since he had so far given every indication that he was not going to live within his means, it seemed sensible to warn off potential creditors. There was also the faint hope that by preserving the king's dignity and not allowing him to be sued, he might turn over a new leaf and actually cut down on his expenses. This hope was not to be realised.

In November 1863 the Earl of Elgin died suddenly from a heart attack while on tour in the Kulu Valley. Sir John Lawrence was appointed to succeed him and was in Calcutta by the beginning of the following year. Unlike many of his predecessors, Lawrence knew India well and was highly respected for having kept the volatile Punjab under control during the Uprising. It was his elder brother, the saintly Sir Henry, who had been killed at the beginning of the siege of the Lucknow Residency. Sir John was briefed on the situation at Garden Reach by the Secretary to the Foreign Department, Henry Marion Durand, who tried (and failed) to explain away the apparent contradictions in the 1862 Act.

It was true, Durand wrote, that the governor general had the legal authority to prevent Wajid 'Ali Shah from being sued by his creditors for debt, but the 'exercise of this power in favour of the King of Oude might assume a very dubious and unpopular aspect if His Majesty, building on such anticipated immunity, were to run riot in extravagance'. Durand went on: 'It would seem but fair to warn tradesmen in Calcutta that all credit granted to His Majesty must be on their own risk ... it would be exceedingly inexpedient to expose the King to the humiliation and distress which if he live, and no check be given to the extravagance, is sure to over take him.'[14] (It was not the first time that the king's health had been discussed in this way, with the implication that he was not long for this world.)

Sir John, bringing a fresh mind to bear on the dilemma, dashed off a note in response. While agreeing with the Secretary, he thought that the Act did not 'absolutely exempt' the king from jurisdiction and believed that some leeway was allowed to the civil courts. He ordered that a third opinion should be sought, that of the clever Henry Maine, a member of Council, Vice-Chancellor of Calcutta University and an expert in law and legal history. Like all good lawyers, Maine refused to commit himself. 'I agree with His Excellency [the Governor General] that the King is not intended to have perfect immunity for the consequences of his imprudence, but some responsibility is cast on the Government which, on the one hand could not sanction all process against the King as a mere matter of form and on the other hand could not systematically refuse its consent to the King's being sued.' Maine thought, however, that the idea of a written warning to Calcutta tradesmen was the best way forward.[15]

Major Herbert was closer to the situation, not least because he was enduring a Calcutta monsoon while the government enjoyed the summer in Shimla, and thought there would be difficulties in issuing a circular to tradesmen because 'it would be extremely difficult, if not impossible to get a complete list of the entire native trades-people of Calcutta with whom His Majesty is supposed to have dealings through his people. And if they left any out, as is probable, from the circular, they could probably say when it suited them, that they had not been warned.'[16] There was also the fact that a government circular might be 'misunderstood particularly among the native dealers in the bazaar', because it would imply that the government felt that there *was* a danger of its being held responsible for the king's debts, and might therefore put ideas into the heads of tradesmen and moneylenders which had not been there before. Although everyone knew that the king's pension came direct from the government, the responsibility for his own financial misconduct was entirely his own.

Wajid 'Ali Shah blithely ignored the bankers, merchants and tradesmen to whom he owed money. He 'only deals with his own followers from whom he purchases whatever he may require without reference to how or where they may obtain the articles and understanding that they make a profit on each transaction'.[17] Herbert had his own suggestions about how the king might be reined in. 'The root of the mischief lies in the character of certain persons about His Majesty's person, who pamper his fancies and passions in order to enrich themselves at the cost of His Majesty's extravagance.' Referring to Safdar 'Ali and Zulfiqar-ud-daulah, Herbert thought that if they could be removed, the situation would improve. It was Herbert's unpleasant task to question Wajid 'Ali Shah during the High Court case between the moneylender Manohar Das and Zulfiqar-ud-daulah. Because Wajid 'Ali Shah could not be called to appear in court, Herbert was instructed by the High Court to ask a series of 'cross interrogatories', which were all the more distressing as the king was fond of Zulfiqar-ud-daulah. But it became clear that his 'trusted retainer' was charged with making large sums of money from his transactions, using the king's name. At the end of a two-hour session of writing answers to the interrogatories, the king was left so exhausted that Herbert discreetly left, with other important business unfinished.[18]

Instructions came down from Shimla that Herbert was to issue the warning to Calcutta tradesmen in spite of his misgivings, 'as it may have the effect of deterring merchants and tradesmen from trusting the King'. As for complaints about 'certain persons' at Garden Reach, he was told that the government of India had 'no power' to remove such people. But this was at the heart of the problem. Wajid 'Ali Shah had often exhibited a credulous, over-trusting nature, and coupled with his undoubted selfishness and disregard for petty financial problems, he was naturally a victim for those wishing to exploit him for their own benefit. In this he was doing no more than following the example of his forebearers, who simply could not say no to anyone who suggested something excitingly new and expensive on which to spend money. Wajid 'Ali Shah had cleverly circumvented the intentions of the 1862 Act. If the idea had been to deter people from lending him money or allowing him goods on credit because they could not sue him if he defaulted, then why not get his courtiers to act for him? Safdar 'Ali, the chief *karindah* or agent, would purchase goods and negotiate loans in his own name, then sell them on to the king. At a profit, of course.

How and when munshi Safdar 'Ali first inveigled himself into the king's confidence is not known, nor where he came from. It was later claimed that he had begun supplying Wajid 'Ali Shah with goods in December 1859. The first mention of him is in April 1860 when, as we have seen, he was sent by the king to threaten Khas Mahal. The title of 'munshi' means a scribe or writer, and it may be that he had originally been employed as a clerk in one of the offices, but like employees before him he quickly realised the opportunities to make considerable sums of money, far more than could be earned at his original trade. The fact that Wajid 'Ali Shah trusted him sufficiently to intimidate the chief wife meant that Safdar 'Ali had wormed his way into the king's circle shortly after Wajid 'Ali Shah had left prison. He was the king's new best friend, and one of the three men who now held the title deeds to the Sultan Khana.

The agent's warnings about the munshi and his gang went unheeded, and for six years Wajid 'Ali Shah was extravagantly overcharged for goods and services provided by Safdar 'Ali and his cronies. What did the king get for his money? One supplier, Lisan-us-Sultan, who was later to petition Wajid 'Ali Shah, listed what he had 'presented, furbished and prepared, in compliance with Your Majesty's order'. There were 'utensils studded with jewels, glass wares, pictures or portraits, looking glass, tables, chairs, a kind of sofa, *almirah* [cupboards], articles to furnish the tables and dresses of every description', carpetings, screens, pillows, glass, lime, brick-powder, bricks, [wooden] beams, rafters and colours [wall paint], *nawar* [thick tape for tying up blinds], cut *seetulpati* [fine canes for woven matting], iron, copper, fancy silver laces, and articles for the erection and decoration of new buildings at Garden Reach. Lisan-us-Sultan had started working for the king immediately on the latter's release from prison in the summer of 1859. In just under two years, he had spent, on the king's orders, the equivalent of £130,000, a long way over Wajid 'Ali Shah's total annual pension of £120,000.[19] Another petitioner had supplied 'goods of all kinds, shawls, wearing apparel and money in cash to supply the urgent wants of the King'.

In December 1865 a petition to Sir John Lawrence was received from Gajadhar Lal, an accountant in the service of Wajid 'Ali Shah. Lal had gone to some trouble to get his petition printed, on blue paper.[20] After a polite preamble, he stated that since the governor general had custody of the 'ex-king of Oude', he supposed that Lawrence 'would take an interest in the proper management of his pecuniary affairs'; otherwise the governor general would, in future, have to provide for a numerous family of wives and princes. Lal reported that dishonest officers employed by the king 'have introduced here a greater degree of mismanagement and fraud than they dared practise at Lucknow'. Now these same officers were demanding payment of more than 50 lakhs, equivalent to about half a million sterling. It was in pursuit of a small part of this enormous sum that a civil court writ had already been served on the king, which had led to the hastily devised Act of 1862, disallowing such writs to be served, except with the governor general's approval. Not only was the 50 lakhs debt looming, but the king was being pestered by petty claims 'even for labourers for amounts which His Excellency paid, but [which were] appropriated to themselves by the aforesaid officers'.

Gajadhar Lal added that, as one of the king's accountants, he 'knew all the secrets of that Department' and that if Lawrence was 'graciously pleased to arm your petitioner with power, he will be able to detect and bring to light all the fraudulent items in the accounts, and thereby extricate the ex-King from the liability of more than 50 lakhs of rupees'. Lal sensed that as a whistle-blower his job was under threat, because in his next petition, of January 1866, he reported that he had been dismissed by Safdar 'Ali immediately after the December petition had become known, and this had produced a 'sensation' at Garden Reach. Major Herbert had written to the king with a polite request that the royal accounts be inspected, following Lal's accusations. Citing the privacy of his palace accounts the king had refused, 'on the advice of those whose interest was at stake', claimed Lal. Was it just a palace squabble with a Hindu working in a Muslim court, or something more serious?

Lal also added, reasonably enough, that if Safdar 'Ali did not have anything to hide, then he should agree to an inspection of the books.[21] The excuse that the palace accounts were private was groundless. These accounts 'are the daily *jumma khurruch* [accumulated balance] in the hands of several accountants under Moonshee Sufdar and others'. But Wajid 'Ali Shah knew nothing about these accounts, because they were never put in front of him. They showed the actual amounts paid to the traders, not the inflated figures that the king was being charged. No further action was taken at the time. Less than six months later, in June 1866, Safdar 'Ali was dead and the whole sorry mess of cheating and false accounting began to unravel.

Safdar 'Ali had built up a little empire of his own, outsourcing the king's requests through various contacts, so that Wajid 'Ali Shah never appeared as the purchaser of goods and services and therefore could not be accused of debt when he did not pay up. It had been Safdar 'Ali's custom to make monthly repayments to the middlemen who had supplied him with goods that he then sold on to the king at vastly inflated prices. With the munshi's death, these payments of course stopped, leaving a number of people considerably out of pocket; they complained loudly and threatened to sue the king. Safdar 'Ali was 'a notorious scoundrel and robbed the King whenever he had a chance', claimed a number of creditors, with hindsight. An unidentified vernacular newspaper expanded on this: 'The management of the King's affairs was in the hands of one Munshi Sufdar, who acted in defiance of all judgement; for one rupee [he] took ten, and cheated in all directions. But even with this knowledge the King treated him kindly, and this gave courage to others who were inclined to be dishonest, and they took every opportunity of robbing and clearing out the house—making away with all they could lay hands on.'[22]

The government was unsympathetic to the creditors' pleas. In many cases, it said, they were 'great friends of Sufdar Ali [and] their dealings were so large and profitable that they could afford to run a considerable risk'.[23] It was suggested that Safdar 'Ali's property, at the old Faujdari Bala Khana, should be sold and the proceeds divided among his creditors and heirs. But this would not have met the huge debts run up which were now estimated at nearly £450,000. Eyes were turned towards Wajid 'Ali Shah, who had, after all, employed Safdar 'Ali as his agent and who had accepted the goods and services offered to him. With pressure mounting on the king, Major Herbert, who seems to have developed a certain sympathy for his royal charge, introduced to him the man who was to become his financial saviour over the next decade.

AT GARDEN REACH

Amir 'Ali Khan Bahadur was some twelve years older than the king and came from a small town in the Patna District of Bihar. He had had a varied and highly respectable career, with a connection to Lucknow, and was clearly well thought of in official British circles. He had been an assistant superintendent in the Special Commissioner's Court at Calcutta, and later a government pleader (equivalent to a state prosecutor) in the Sadr Diwani Court. During the Uprising he was hastily sent to Patna as special assistant to the new Commissioner, Mr Samuells, who was trying to control the volatile situation there. Amir 'Ali managed to keep the Muslim majority inhabitants 'quiescent if not actively loyal to the British'.[24] He received the title of Khan Bahadur in 1864, when he became a member of the Bengal Legislative Council. By the time he was introduced to Wajid 'Ali Shah late in 1866, as legal advisor, he carried with him a solid reputation as a man who was prepared to take on the king, and whose attempts to lead him back into financial stability would be respected by government officials. Although Amir 'Ali's experience and contacts meant that he was able to negotiate on the king's behalf with the government and the law courts, there was still a very difficult period ahead for both men. The voices of those owed money by the late Safdar 'Ali grew louder and shriller until they reached Government House, where Lawrence had been alerted by Gajadhar Lal to what he must already have suspected. It was mischievously pointed out by a newspaper that Wajid 'Ali Shah, on a yearly pension of £120,000, was actually receiving twice the amount that Queen Victoria got in her privy purse.[25]

Although the Act of 1862 seemed, at first reading, to exempt the king from the jurisdiction of the law courts, there were certain clauses in it that were open to interpretation. In particular, there was nothing in the Act to stop an individual or a group of people from suing the king, although he could not be called to appear in person in court. What would now be called a 'class action' was launched by three of the late munshi's female relatives, Begam Bibi, Bismillah Khanum and Zainab Khanum, who, with other creditors, were represented by the Hindu lawyer Babu Dwarkanath Mitter. The group was known collectively as the 'Heirs of Safdar 'Ali'. The initial hearing was in October 1866 and took place in the Court of the 24 Parganas, whose curious name derived from the grant of lands to the East India Company in the middle of the eighteenth century. The heirs filed a suit against the king for nearly 40 lakhs, equivalent to about £400,000. Lawrence duly informed the District Judge, Mr F. L. Beaumont, that as he declined to let the king be sued, the case should be struck off. But there was too much at stake to accept this initial defeat. The plaintiffs, led by their lawyer Mitter, appealed to the Calcutta High Court, which decided that while it could not issue a writ against the king without government agreement, there was nothing to stop it from accepting the suit, or case, from his creditors.[26]

The case was heard in the High Court on 16 February 1867, and to Lawrence's dismay it was allowed to proceed. By error there was no counsel to represent the government, although its official solicitor, Mr Stack, had been told to liaise with the advocate general to make sure that the government's view was heard. When Stack was reprimanded, he replied quite reasonably that a case could not be tried until the defendant had been summoned, and since the king had not been summoned, there was no point in a government lawyer attending. The new English-language newspaper *The Pioneer* reported on 18 March 1867 that 'The case of the heirs of Moonshee Sufdur against the ex-King of Oude seems beset with mishaps. It came on for trial, and it was expected that it would prove of no ordinary difficulty. Instead, however, of an exciting legal contest, the ex-King was unrepresented and the case was therefore, decreed against him.' The advocate general was told to apply for a review of the judgement, and a week later it was reported that Amir 'Ali had applied on behalf of the king for a postponement of the case, which was subsequently permanently withdrawn while bargaining went on behind the scenes.

Although it is gratifying to note the independence of the judiciary, the problem of the king's creditors remained. The High Court decision was 'fraught with serious consequence', wrote Lawrence. Although any decree the 'Heirs of Safdar 'Ali' might obtain would be ineffective, 'yet the existence and perhaps the accumulation of unsatisfied decrees against the King will obviously be a public scandal, bringing odium upon the Government'. It was a measure of his continuing significance that Wajid 'Ali Shah was capable of causing almost as much trouble as a deposed monarch as he had when a ruling king. Lawrence admitted that his officials had not foreseen the full extent of the difficulties facing them when tackling the problem. Safdar 'Ali was blamed 'as the ex-King's principal parasite', but Wajid 'Ali Shah, though certainly naïve, was not blameless either, as it was his 'custom to make all purchases at second-hand from his own attendants, the great majority are parasites of the lowest repute, who enrich themselves at his expense. All of them have allowed the King credit as a speculation, demanding enormous interest for their risk.'[27] The 'parasites' had deliberately traded on the assumption that their accumulated demands against the king would ultimately create such a public scandal that the government would be forced to bail him out. It was a dangerous game and played for high stakes. Would the creditors get their inflated bills met by the government, or would the government face them down and risk more public criticism over its treatment of the king, wrenched abruptly from his throne under the old Company regime?

A solution was proposed by John Lawrence and his Council, but not without a further mention of the king's supposedly delicate health. 'Though not an old man', wrote Lawrence, he 'has exhausted his constitution by his habits of life, and is not likely to live very much longer', although 'on the other hand the ex-King may live much longer than his present physical constitution leads us to expect, and the longer he lives, the heavier and more complicated will his debts become'.[28] Even Major Herbert, who knew the king better than most, 'thought [his life] may be cut short at any time'. (The king's premature death, long anticipated by British officials, would have solved a number of problems. In fact Wajid 'Ali Shah was forty-six years old at the time and, in spite of his hypochondria, was to live for a further twenty in reasonably good health.) Assuming that the king did not die immediately, Lawrence suggested further legislation that would place him in the same position as 'minors and others incapable of contracting debt'. The king would be given another 'final warning', and six months to resolve his financial problems. If he did not do so by 1 March 1868, then a government-appointed commission would take charge of his affairs.

The governor general's warning letter was written from Shimla on 9 August and ten days later it was given to the king, who expressed 'immediate annoyance' at its contents. Major Herbert was pretty upset too, because it seemed to him as if a senior government official was going to take over his job. 'I can't think', he wrote in a pained letter, 'that the Government would so injure me after I have worked gratuitously in the office of Agent to the governor general as to nominate some other person over my head to perform a duty that would naturally fall to me, and I trust that such would not be the case.'[29] Lawrence's letter to Wajid 'Ali Shah was called a *kharitah*, the Persian term for 'a letter between two great personages', and one would think that such a sensitive matter would be highly confidential. Instead the kharitah was leaked to the press and appeared in full in *Allen's Indian Mail*, showing that the governor general had addressed the king as 'My Royal and Illustrious Friend'. The leak was almost certainly deliberate, by a government official. Publication of the letter would stave off criticism from Wajid 'Ali Shah's numerous creditors that nothing was being done; it would, hopefully, warn off anyone else who might feel inclined to lend him money; and it would embarrass him, the very thing that government claimed it was trying to avoid.

Once he got over his annoyance, Wajid 'Ali Shah appointed Amir 'Ali to audit and adjust all his accounts; and after a three-month scrutiny, the king explained to Herbert what had happened. 'The rumours of my indebtednesss which have been generally circulated, and especially reported to His Excellency [the governor general] and yourself, are nothing but the ingratitude of my own dependents. I only employed my own dependants and advanced and paid to them, pending and after their own work, lacks [lakhs] and thousands of rupees; but being in the power of Moonshee Sufder, they agreed among themselves and deceived me and obtained my signature to papers and formed the evil design of embarrassing me.' As soon as the lawsuit against him began, he 'understood their rascality' and was in fact actually in the process of 'arranging his affairs' when the kharitah from Shimla arrived.[30] So once again, as in the quarrels with his wives, it was not the king's fault, but the faithlessness of those around him.

Herbert had by now seen off the proposed challenge to his own position, and began work with Amir 'Ali on 9 November 1867, sifting through the ridiculous claims by the creditors. A list of fourteen chief creditors, men who were employed by Wajid 'Ali Shah to provide goods and services, was compiled. Safdar 'Ali had been the 'chief authority' and the other thirteen were appointed to specific duties, receiving cash and goods: 'and, in my opinion', wrote the king, 'each has received more than his due'. Statements were taken from eight of the men. Aluf-ud-daulah admitted that he 'could not explain the accounts and prove all items', so his claim was reduced. Amanat-ud-daulah, who lived in Garden Reach, confessed that he did not have all his 'papers of accounts with him', and in fact when he questioned his clerks again, it turned out that all his bills had been paid by instalment 'and not a pice remains due to me'. 'I cannot prove every item' and 'I cannot explain the accounts and give proof of all items', said the others. Those accounts that were produced, wrote Herbert, were 'simply diaries, without any system and unsupported by vouchers'. Defending his royal burden, Herbert gallantly explained that 'His Majesty's necessary ignorance of the world and unfortunate aversion to advice, or to anything like interference, rendered him an easy victim.' At the same time, Herbert praised Amir 'Ali, who had 'exhibited great shrewdness and untiring industry and [who] deserves the greatest credit'. By the end of the 1867 calendar year, Herbert and Amir 'Ali had managed to reduce the king's debts from nearly half a million sterling to a more reasonable £71,000, and the king agreed to pay off the revised figure by monthly instalments.

By the end of the British financial year, 5 April 1868, all claims had been settled, except for the 'Heirs' case, which was still pending in the civil court. This was dealt with in an adroit move by Lawrence, who on 11 April gave his assent to The King of Oudh's Act No. XIII of 1868. The new act contained two important clauses: it made the king incapable of entering into any financial obligations through contract; and it also exempted the Secretary of State and the government of India from any liability for the king's debts which had already been run up. It seemed that both the king and the government had been saved from further embarrassment, particularly as the civil court case could not proceed. But the tenacity of the 'Heirs' had been underestimated, and they now petitioned Lawrence himself, as any Indian or British national had the right to do. The patient Major Herbert had retired in July. He had been with Wajid 'Ali Shah since 1857, after the murder of the first agent, Captain Fletcher Hayes.[31] An officiating or temporary agent was appointed, Captain Henry Phipson Peacock, who as a twenty-year-old officer had been present at the recapture of Lucknow in March 1858.

Peacock was soon initiated into the claims and counterclaims still flying around Garden Reach. The fact that agreements had been reached with the king's major creditors gave the 'Heirs' new hope that, even if they could not now bring a court case, by sheer persistence they might be able to wear down the king and his new agent. Wajid 'Ali Shah admitted that he had employed two of the seven petitioners, and their evidence was further proof of the king's financial gullibility. Muhammad Beg had been introduced by the late Safdar 'Ali and got a job as a *sowar*, or cavalryman. His starting salary was 25 rupees a month, later increased to 30 rupees, which included the cost of fodder and stabling for his horse. He was dismissed in August 1867 when the king claimed to have realised the full extent of the 'imposition played upon me' by Safdar 'Ali's 'creatures, relations and connections'.[32] In his statement, dictated to a clerk, Muhammad Beg said he could neither read nor write, with the exception of writing his own name. Nevertheless, he claimed he was owed £30,000 for 'merchandize and money' supplied through Safdar 'Ali to the king. 'I don't consider my claim really against the King', he said, but admitted that he was petitioning the governor general in the hope of getting some of the money due to him.

Like others before him, Muhammad Beg was unable to produce account books and, when challenged, slammed out of Peacock's office 'in a most insolent manner'. Peacock's robust response was that if Beg did have the account books hidden away, they would show that his financial dealings were with Safdar 'Ali and not the king. Wajid 'Ali Shah seemed bemused by how members of his menial staff could run up such enormous bills against him. Ali Raza, a brother-in-law of Safdar 'Ali, got 20 rupees a month for his job as caretaker of the Badami Kothi, but claimed he was owed £12,500. 'How could such persons, indigent, needy, and living on such small salaries as they are, amass vast amounts enabling them to prefer such large claims?'[33] the king asked. The sad fact was that anyone who came into contact with the corrupt Safdar 'Ali could hope to make a small fortune at the king's expense, and many clearly did.

An ingenious excuse was proposed by three higher-ranking servants who had written agreements from the king, and therefore stood a better chance as petitioners. One claimed it was out of 'sheer kindness' that Wajid 'Ali Shah ordered goods from them. The servants bought goods in the bazaar, on credit, in their own names, then sold them on to the king as a dealer would do, making a profit of course, but one which the king accepted as a way of boosting their salaries. The old eunuch, Diyanat ud-Daulah, reiterated this. The king had given him a written order, a *hukumnamah*, to supply him with money to pay day-to-day expenses, and even to erect buildings for him. It was an honour to deal with the traders on the king's behalf, he said, and of course the accounts were kept in his (Diyanat ud-Daulah's) name. Any traders trying to claim direct from the king would be quite wrong. 'How can their such false claim be admitted by the British Court?'[34] he demanded indignantly.

There was much more. Endless petitions in highly flowery language passed in front of Peacock's bewildered eyes. It seemed that even those servants with written agreements from the king were to be disappointed, for Peacock discovered that they 'distinctly declare that His Majesty was in no way to be held liable for the transactions of his servants, and clearly show, I think, that the present petitioners have no just grounds'. The governor general agreed and issued his verdict in November 1868. The majority of petitioners admitted that they had no orders from the king to furnish the goods and money for which they now demanded compensation. Their transactions were entirely with Safdar 'Ali, and therefore they could not claim against the king. They had taken the risk 'on their own shoulders in dealing with the King's servants as principals, if they knew of the Agreements. If not, they have fallen victim to the dishonesty of the King's servants.' Although there were some mutterings, Lawrence's statement signalled the end of the matter. It had exposed the king's naïvety and his vulnerability in what was to him a new world, full of unforgiving Bengali creditors.

AT GARDEN REACH

Major Herbert had left Calcutta before the end of the Safdar 'Ali affair. One of his last tasks at Garden Reach was an unpleasant one. On the morning of Tuesday, 23 June he was informed that Diyanat ud-Daulah had died, shortly after defending his master's financial dealings. As a eunuch, of course, there could be no descendants, and as an African slave imported into Lucknow, there were no relatives either. But Diyanat ud-Daulah had adopted a young boy, Fida Hossein, as his son. The garden house in which the eunuch died was within the Garden Reach boundary, and thus outside Herbert's jurisdiction. Nevertheless, Amir 'Ali called Herbert and reported that Promissory Notes, or bonds, to the value of 67,000 rupees (about £6,700) were missing from the eunuch's house. Jewellery and cash had also been taken. Herbert grumbled that the police should have secured the house immediately after the death was reported, and he got the Bank of Bengal to put a stop on the Notes. Although Diyanat ud-Daulah's origins in India were unpropitious (he may have been among the eighteen African slaves sold to Nasir-ud-Din Haider in 1831), his subsequent career was spectacular, as we have seen. He died a wealthy man. He left his house and its land to Wajid 'Ali Shah, who claimed it anyway, saying it was customary on the grounds that the deceased 'had been of his household'. The king had also borrowed 34,000 rupees (about £3,400) from the eunuch, which the latter had graciously cancelled in his Will.

It was quickly established that the thief was none other than Fida Hossein, abetted by Mirza Hossein 'Ali. Both boys were employed as armed guards at the *karbala* (shrine) in Lucknow—built by Diyanat ud-Daulah in 1852—and both claimed, although it could not be proven, that they had sent the Promissory Notes to Lucknow to stop Wajid 'Ali Shah getting his hands on them. The eunuch's body was taken to Howrah Station, from where it travelled by train to Lucknow to be interred in his karbala.[35]

If Amir 'Ali had not called in Herbert to investigate the theft, then the agent would have been none the wiser. In spite of being a familiar face at Garden Reach and trusted by Wajid 'Ali Shah, insofar as any British officer could be trusted, Herbert said that he had no way of knowing what was going on behind the high boundary walls of the estate. 'In case of anything happening to the King of Oudh himself, the Agent might be hours, or even a day or two, before he heard of it, for all would be interested to keep him in the dark as long as possible to carry out their own purposes.' Herbert imagined that looting on a grand scale would take place on the king's death. There was a police superintendent at Garden Reach who was supposed to keep the agent informed of 'police occurrences', but his salary was paid by the king, and he was 'as much his servant as other retainers'.[36] The whole question of law, order and security at the palaces needed to be examined.

On Wajid 'Ali Shah's release from Fort William in July 1859, it was made clear to him that he would not have the right to 'exercise jurisdiction or administer justice within the limits of his residence'. As ruler of Awadh he had had ultimate authority over all the kingdom's administrative departments, including those that dealt with criminal and civil cases. Now it seemed that he was not even to be master in his own house. The governor general admitted that the king had been promised the right to keep order and dispense justice within his palace when Awadh was annexed. But this promise had been made in another world and today, post-mutiny, 'this privilege can now no longer be conceded to any person, however high his position, who is resident within British territory'.[37]

This ruling may have seemed clear enough when the king, grateful to have been released, returned home, but it began to unravel in less than a year. There was an inherent paradox in the treatment of the king by the British, which was never really resolved. While the government needed to demonstrate, in India and abroad, that its behaviour towards the ex-monarch was fair, at the same time it wrestled with the problems of a traditional native court now transplanted to British India. Herbert, on his official appointment as agent, was instructed that 'as concerns the personal dignity of the King, you will assure His Majesty that he will not cease to be respected and protected by the Governor General in Council and that no suitable mark of the honor due to his rank will be wanting'.[38] This grandiose but vague statement needed constant redefinition as events occurred concerning the king and his property. The boundaries of the king's estate were clear—a mile on both sides of Garden Reach and as far south as the Circular Road. There were 'privileges and rights of private property which the Ex-King has purchased'. There were thirty-six Calcutta policemen stationed on the roads around the estate, although they could not enter it. But if the king could not exercise jurisdiction or administer justice inside his own premises, then who could? Clearly the question of law and order had not been thought through.

At the heart of Garden Reach a princely court was being developed based on that of Lucknow, which in turn had its roots in Mughal times. There was both a need for privacy for the king and his many wives, but also the need to house a substantial number of dependants and followers. Samuel Wauchope, the first commissioner of Calcutta Police, was told that there were an estimated 5,000 people at Garden Reach (this was in 1862), but Wauchope reckoned it was nearer 7,000 or 8,000—the size of a small town. It was as if a private gentleman had allowed his servants and their relatives to build huts on his premises, he told the government—the king 'has merely done this on a gigantic scale'. It was not only the king's immediate followers either, but thieves, prostitutes, gamblers and other disreputable characters. They were annoying the neighbours by 'the constant discharge of guns and fireworks' and there was every reason to believe they had committed a series of thefts which had taken place in the neighbourhood. And was anyone paying the *chowkidari* tax, the municipal tax that funded night watchmen patrolling the streets? Wauchope knew that the king was heavily in debt. Everyone knew, but the commissioner's fear was that if the king's credit dried up, and he could no longer support this riff-raff, they would be loosed onto the streets of Calcutta.[39] He had already spoken to Major Herbert, who, he said, 'was in charge of the King'. While agreeing about the noise and nuisances, Herbert pointed out that he was certainly not 'in charge of the King' and could only act as advisor, and that his advice went unheeded.

The Calcutta Police had been established by Lord Canning only a year before the Uprising, but had come through it in commendable fashion, thanks to Wauchope, who was later knighted for his work. He was not therefore prepared to have a large and seemingly lawless enclave that threatened the urban stability of his own patch. He argued that his men should have access to Garden Reach, and its inhabitants should be taxed to pay for the additional police required to look after them. Clearly a forceful man and somewhat lacking in tact, he told Herbert to inform Wajid 'Ali Shah that the police *did* have the right to go into Garden Reach in pursuit of thieves. Tell the king, he threatened, that since he has turned his premises into 'a populous town full of disreputable persons [then] it would be impossible to treat them in any exceptional manner, and the visits of the Police might become so constant as to be very disagreeable and discreditable'. And the governor general could help too, by telling the king to keep better order, and that 'town laws' should apply to the grounds of Garden Reach.

There were many disreputable characters inside Garden Reach. Gambling, drinking, thieving and every kind of debauchery were being carried out within the grounds, 'but being private, the Police have no power to enter them, and can exercise no control over their inmates as long as they remain inside. In fact the lower part of Garden Reach has become a perfect

AT GARDEN REACH

Alsatia [sanctuary] in which any persons escaping from justice may take refuge and set the Police at defiance.'[40]

But the governor general had lost the will to carry on, much less to engage the king in what would clearly be a battle royal in all senses of the word. Canning was a sick man. The sudden death of his much-loved wife had shocked him profoundly and he stepped down from office in March 1862; he left immediately for England, only to die there three months later. One of his last acts was to suggest, without much conviction, that perhaps Major Herbert could be appointed as magistrate to try cases arising within Garden Reach. The area could be limited to the three houses bought for the king by government, but exclude those bought by the king with his own money. Herbert's own suggestion was not much more practical. He thought that Wajid 'Ali Shah should appoint his own police officer and team to register his own retainers and those of the different family members within Garden Reach. Thereafter only registered followers would be allowed inside; the king's officer would hand over to Wauchope's men anyone who looked suspicious and would also assist the Calcutta Police in tracing miscreants. The king could also stop the use of firearms, fireworks and noisy processions on the high road and such other 'amusements' declared to be a public nuisance.[41] Neither scheme was ever going to work. It was the classic dilemma of an over-cautious government, only four years distant from the Uprising, which, although it grumbled furiously in private, found it easier to meet each fresh crisis with a fresh response rather than tackling the whole question of the exiled king once and for all. If government had thought that the award of the huge pension of £120,000 per annum would solve the embarrassing problem of a deposed ruler, whom it anticipated would shortly die due to his 'debased life', it was wrong.

Exactly twenty years later the same problems were being debated, in almost the same language, showing that little had changed except the personnel. Colonel William Francis Prideaux became agent to the king in 1881. Prideaux is best known today for his study of ancient Arabian inscriptions discovered when he was assistant Political Resident in Aden, and his appointment in Bengal must have been in striking contrast to his previous desert posting. Nevertheless, as a career civil servant he was quickly immersed in the seemingly unchanging problems of Garden Reach. An early report from him advised that births and deaths in the estate should be registered, criminals identified, epidemic or contagious diseases notified and the Port Commissioner put on standby to prevent nuisances. The government of Bengal was on the defensive, claiming that it had been trying 'for twenty years past' to induce the ex-king to behave reasonably about his private affairs 'and for twenty years we have steadily failed. The advice of successive Agents to the Governor General is either rudely rejected or runs off the ex-King's back like water off a duck's back, leaving no impression whatsoever.'[42] Could he be coaxed into changing his behaviour, even at this late date?

Prideaux went on to report rather dramatically that 'debauchery and rioting' were going on inside Garden Reach, causing a nuisance in the neighbourhood. He added that 'there is reason to believe that gross oppression is continually exercised by the King's officers over the ladies residing within the premises'. Was it time for another King of Oude Act? Henry Peacock, the former agent to the king, had now been elevated to the position of Secretary to the Foreign Department, so he was sympathetic and knowledgeable about his successor's complaints. But Peacock thought the king should be given an ultimatum 'before we fire a broadside into him from the Legislative Department'.[43]

Since the king could not exercise his jurisdiction in British territory, he had to be made amenable, to some extent, to British law. In a sarcastic vein Peacock told Prideaux that it was proposed to locate 'a new King, represented by a European constable, within the sacred precincts of the King of Oude's walled residence at Garden Reach'. But he urged caution, fearing that if the real king, 'who is isolated within his four walls', was not warned, there could be trouble from a 'cohort of political agitators at Home or in India', who would rake up past promises made to Wajid 'Ali Shah about protecting his privacy. Clearly passions could still be aroused on behalf of the king nearly thirty years after he had been deposed. At the same time the Bengal Legislative Department was trying to push through the highly controversial Ilbert Bill. Introduced by Sir Courtenay Ilbert in 1883, it proposed an amendment to existing legislation that would allow Indian judges and magistrates to try British offenders in criminal cases. A huge and horrible demonstration of anti-Indian feeling by Britons and Anglo-Indians burst out from all quarters, and the Bill, which was passed on 25 January 1884, was considerably watered down. The last thing the government wanted was further protest over its treatment of a former king, though Peacock did not explain how the 'political agitators' opposing the Ilbert Bill might want to support an Indian ex-king.

There was undoubtedly a need for better policing within Garden Reach, although this could not be properly estimated because of the secretive nature of the establishment. Every entrance into the estate was 'grimly guarded', and high walls had been erected defining its limits. Strangely, it was now harder to find out what was going on inside the Court at Garden Reach than when it had been in Qaisarbagh. Then there had been a well-established and acknowledged spy system in Lucknow, operating between the palace and the Residency. Servants were paid for tip-offs by the other side, and letters from the Resident to the king were leaked in advance of receipt. But it did not work in Calcutta. There was a physical distance between Garden Reach and Government House, and a distance of perception too. It was one thing to whisper into the ear of an official in the Lucknow Residency; it was quite another to approach the governor general or even his agent, appointed to liaise with the king. At the same time, it may have been convenient to exaggerate the impenetrability of Garden Reach as a reason for inaction by British officials.

Only rarely did crimes in the great estate come to light. In the autumn of 1883, the body of a woman was found drowned in a tank a short distance outside the boundary wall. The civil surgeon thought she had been violently killed before being dumped in the tank. The deputy commissioner of police and Major Prideaux investigated and learned that the woman had been employed by one of the king's wives and had been accused of theft by 'another inmate of the zenana'. The king's own police had arrested the woman, locked her up and also beaten her up. Although nothing could be proved conclusively, Prideaux concluded that the death 'was attributable to the treatment the woman had received at the hands of those officials. If the tank in which the body was found had not been outside the king's premises, very probably nothing would have been known of the matter, as the police merely report what suits them, and I have no means whatever of exercising supervision over them.'[44] New government proposals were made to employ Calcutta Police patrols inside Garden Reach, with their salaries deducted from the king's pension.

But would this be fair? The secretary to the Bengal government, William Lee-Warner, argued provocatively that the king 'does not object to the smells or the dilapidation inside his four walls. It is the sensitive organs of the Calcutta residents that object. It will be a great blow to the King to see his walled-off enclosure invaded by our police, especially if one is a European, and it adds insult to injury to ask him to pay for the intrusion.'[45] It was agreed that there were sufficient Calcutta Police for a small detachment, without a cost attached. After all, argued Lee-Warner, 'the King cannot live for ever, and this can only be a temporary arrangement'.

The lack of sanitation and general unhealthiness at Garden Reach was almost as worrying as the unreported crimes. Along with the proposal that municipal police should be allowed inside the estate was another that the Sanitary Commission of Bengal should be able to send a qualified medical officer inside to inspect the premises. The junior undersecretary, Henry Durand, thought that 'We have the moral right to provide for the maintenance and health of his family and establishment if the King fails to apply the stipend to that purpose.' There had been a number of complaints over the years from the female relatives and the princes about unhygienic conditions, although no major outbreak of disease like cholera had occurred. The question of vaccination against smallpox had been raised in 1870, when the king was asked if he would allow his numerous children to be vaccinated. Wajid 'Ali Shah replied, 'Myself and my children have been habituated to the treatment of the Oriental Hakeems, who are in constant attendance with various sorts of medicines required under all circumstances.' His personal doctor, Hakeem Ta'ib-ud-daulah, an experienced physician, 'was always prepared with different medicines to afford relief and advice, agreeably to his own system in all kind of diseases whenever they may occur'.[46]

Although the king did not go into detail, he was probably referring to the native practice of variolation, widespread and long established, particularly in Bengal, with a success rate estimated as high as 70 per cent. Unlike vaccination, popularised in England, variolation did not call for skin to be punctured with a needle, but relied on dried and powdered smallpox scabs being ingested, which produced a mild, survivable form of the disease. There were considerable debates among medical practitioners in India about the merits of the two preventatives. Vaccination was seen as a superior Western method, while variolation was easy to obtain and sanctioned by centuries of custom. British officials had no doubt about which method was better, and criticised the king for not ordering his wives to allow the children to be vaccinated. It was Amir 'Ali who took the initiative and persuaded some of the king's dependants to submit their children to Surgeon

Kalidas Bose, the vaccinator. The dependants 'seemed to have feared mortality from its effect', he reported in a letter, but 'when they find their children doing well after the operation the dread with which they appeared to regard vaccination will be removed from their and other's minds, and doubtless all classes of them will avail themselves of the benefit of it generally'.[47]

In spite of this encouraging news, the perception remained among British officials that Garden Reach had become inherently unhealthy ever since the king and his followers settled there. By contrast, the Calcutta municipality was forging ahead with public improvements that disposed of the sewage of a million of its inhabitants, provided them with fresh water, lit their streets with gas, cleaned and improved their bazaars, relocated slaughterhouses to the outskirts, and removed *bustees* (slums) by driving new roads through them. The Municipal Corporation, set up in 1864, wanted to get its hands on Garden Reach, which it perceived as an anachronism in modern Calcutta.

We can see the British officials' wish for cleanliness, law and order in Garden Reach as the manifestation of a wider unease with the whole idea of a deposed king who had set up his own small kingdom just outside the capital of India itself. Political opinion, to which the government of India seemed over-sensitive, meant that the situation had to be tolerated, with legislative measures (the King of Oude Acts) when things got out of hand. They consoled themselves with the mantra, 'the King cannot live for ever'. Garden Reach had fallen short of British expectations of how a king should live in exile. And although it was not put into so many words, there was a lingering memory in Calcutta that Garden Reach had once been an exclusive British enclave, with houses that had been owned, albeit briefly, by the governor general himself. Its decline, as the British saw it, was all the more poignant compared to its former splendour. Because the houses built by the king and all of the additional structures and gardens have been swept away, it is impossible to say today what the estate looked like after Wajid 'Ali Shah had resided there for thirty years. Perhaps it really was as splendid as it seemed to be in the Indian memory?

The writer Abdul Halim Sharar had lived at Garden Reach as a boy for ten years, from the age of nine. His father was employed there by the king, while his maternal grandfather had worked in Qaisarbagh. In his quaintly titled book on Lucknow,[48] Sharar has a short chapter on Matiya Burj, as he called it, which is the fullest account we have. Sharar is seldom less than flattering about the nawabs—Wajid 'Ali Shah in particular—and his account is distorted, seen as it was through the prism of nostalgia, more than thirty years after he left Garden Reach. None of the domestic squabbles between the king and his wives and children were noted, nor the squalor or restrictions that the princes were to complain about as they grew older. Sharar's book lists 'scores' of buildings all beautifully furnished with carpets, pictures and silver bedsteads. 'Surrounding them were gardens and lawns set out in geometrical designs.' The king had established 'a beautiful town of fine houses'. Even the Royal Botanic Garden across the Hugli was 'as nothing compared to the earthly paradise of Matiya Burj and the entrancing wonders it contained. There was a high-walled enclosure surrounding all these houses, lawns and markets.'

Somewhere between these two extremes—of British disappointment and Indian romanticism—lay the real Garden Reach. The area was certainly photographed, but the original images have not been traced and we are left with poorly reproduced copies, which nevertheless hint at the grandeur of its conception. Between Sultan Khana and Garden Reach Road lay a large artificial tank crossed by a double-spanned fancy bridge. Graceful cypress trees lined the edges of the tank. A covered verandah ran behind Sultan Khana, fronting the river, and behind it a staircase led down from the palace roof to the verandah. Small pavilions were dotted around and a substantial building stood to the left of Sultan Khana. In the gardens were cages to house the animals, and these included a large rotunda, ringed from top to bottom with iron bars. Quaint little structures with conical roofs stood in open parkland while flocks of geese gabbled contentedly around. There is no sign here of the wretched thatched huts that the king's wives were complaining about, but it is unlikely that the anonymous photographer was given the freedom to explore every part of the estate.

By the 1870s, the three original houses purchased for the king, each in their own large compound, had been so adapted, added to and joined up that they were no longer free-standing buildings, but a new version of Qaisarbagh—with animals. Sharar listed fifteen separate houses that formed the heart of Garden Reach, but admitted there were 'several other houses' too, the names of which he had forgotten. British officials had counted 'nineteen distinct properties'.[49] Six of these houses had been built on the eastern side of Garden Reach Road, so they had no river frontage. All were given stirring or poetical Persian names more suited to a Mughal estate of the seventeenth century, rather than the suburb of a rapidly industrialising city. There was the Victory House, the Court House, the House of the Sun, the Jewel-studded House, the House of Prosperity and the Asmani and Badami Kothis, a pair of houses, painted pale blue and almond-hued respectively. More prosaically, and in order to collect ground rent and house rates, the Calcutta Municipality numbered them 63 Garden Reach Road (Tahniyat Manzil), 64 Garden Reach Road (Shams Manzil) and so on.

Quite apart from questions of jurisdiction and lawlessness, the estate was not without other problems too. The disastrous fire of 1860 has already been mentioned, and four years later there was another, smaller outbreak that luckily did not cause so much damage. The real calamity came on 5 October 1864 when Calcutta was struck by a devastating cyclone, which is estimated to have killed 60,000 people in and around the city. Many of the king's Garden Reach houses were damaged, and valuable furnishings lost, although there is no report of loss of life on the estate. Another cyclone three years later was less traumatic. These were physical events, over which Wajid 'Ali Shah had no control, but Mowbray Thomson thought that even more damage had been done by the king's own staff. Former 'faithless servants having practised fraud by constructing buildings with bad and inadequate materials', the roofs of the houses simply collapsed within six or seven years of construction.[50] This meant that while new houses were being built, others were under repair, or being expensively refurbished.

A six-year rebuilding programme began in 1868, a year after the second cyclone had struck. Amir 'Ali had negotiated a government loan of 3 lakhs for the work, which was deposited in the Bank of Bengal. Although the original loan agreement has not been found, an 'Abstract of Works' does exist which adds considerably to our knowledge of what the estate looked like.[51] Marble fountains erected on masonry bases played in front of the houses and each fountain was named in fanciful fashion as 'Fairy Spring', 'Example of the Sun', 'Specially noted' and so on. A small creek flowing by the newly constructed Shahinshah Manzil had been elaborately bridged with gate-pillars at either end. Sultan Khana, as the principal house, had an iron gate, an outdoor sitting platform, an adjoining bungalow and, importantly, proper brick-built drains. Within the 'Verdant Garden' were numerous 'flower tube pillars', dovecotes, fountains, two small pavilions named the 'Diamond' and the 'Special', as well as two tiger enclosures. Nearly every house seemed to have a dovecote or pigeon-house attached to it. The House of the Crescent Moon had four pigeon-houses, as well as a large marble fountain and a brick-walled garden. There was a vine-trellis (in imitation of the Great Vine at Qaisarbagh), a parrot-house, a splendid brass gate for the Shining House (Taban Manzil) and iron railings around nearly everything else.

Proper roads had been laid between the houses, and were lined at intervals with black pillar bases for statues and white marble pillars for gas lamps. It may seem strange that someone so firmly wedded to the past as the king was should employ modern technology for lighting the estate, but the picturesque effect of lights reflected in water and shining through the splashing fountains would have appealed to his theatrical instincts. Gas lamps had first appeared in Calcutta in July 1857, lighting up the main street of Chowringhee, and a year later the first pavements were built to accommodate the lamps. The Oriental Gas Company had supplied the municipality with lighting, and the Garden Reach lamps were 'a reproduction on a smaller scale'. Unfortunately, Wajid 'Ali Shah's imaginative idea of lighting the estate with gas soon ran into problems. The contract was first given to Messrs Hubbard & Co., who went bankrupt after the king had advanced them over £1,000.[52] The work was then taken on by the trader Mr Lackerstein, who left it uncompleted on his death, and it was subsequently handed over to two of the king's servants, each on a very handsome salary. By 1880 the work was 'still far from being finished', although it had been going on for several years at an annual cost of nearly £7,000. Running the fountains was less of a problem because they were powered by steam-engines, as they had been in Lucknow.

The noise levels at Garden Reach were considerable, with the steam-engines chugging away, the thump of the antique printing press and the constant hammering from workmen. Competition came from screeching peacocks roaming through the gardens and the sound of wild animals including monkeys, tigers and bears confined in their iron cages. From the domestic animals came the lowing of cattle kept for their milk, the cackling of the geese and overall the cooing of thousands of pigeons. At night there were firework displays and 'noisy processions', with musicians celebrating marriages or solemn religious festivals. In short, it was a small but exotic town, a miniature Lucknow, which provided a home to the king and a steady irritant to the government of India for thirty years. Relations between Wajid

AT GARDEN REACH

'Ali Shah and British officials have been closely examined in this chapter, but there were other inhabitants of Garden Reach too, both animal and human, whose stories are worth telling.

The king lost no time in adapting the English villas at Garden Reach to his own tastes and convenience. This involved spending huge sums of money on construction and furnishing, with the inevitable result that Wajid 'Ali Shah was soon living way beyond his resources and was also being defrauded by his staff. The government brought in legislation to curb the king's debtors, which had a limited effect. The appointment of Amir 'Ali as accountant and manager proved more beneficial. Questions of jurisdiction within Garden Reach, along with policing and sanitation, were never really settled, and although undoubtedly a handsome estate in parts, it remained an irritant to the government.

6

A TIGRESS ESCAPES FROM THE MENAGERIE

As Wajid 'Ali Shah grew older, his animals became increasingly important to him. The significance of royal menageries is examined, as are the British attempts to manage Wajid 'Ali Shah's collection, and thus to manage the king himself. At the same time, some of the king's wives and children become dissatisfied with the claustrophobic life at Garden Reach. The escape of the tigress is a metaphor for their own unfulfilled dreams.

Early on the morning of 6 January 1879 a large group of *coolies* (labourers) was lined up in the Royal Botanic Garden at Howrah ready to start work.[1] The Botanic Garden had been established nearly a century earlier, under the direction of Colonel Robert Kyd, military secretary to the government of Bengal, and a keen botanist. Over the years the Garden had expanded until it covered 270 acres, slightly less than the Botanic Gardens at Kew, near London. In the lush Bengal climate all kinds of plants and trees flourished, some native and others brought from abroad in experiments to increase profits for the East India Company. Cinnamon trees from Ceylon were found to do well, and tea bushes from China were cultivated. The Garden lay on the north bank of the Hugli, with a river frontage of a mile, and was also exactly opposite Garden Reach. From the king's own gardens and palaces, the Botanic Garden looked like a particularly fertile stretch of jungle, but closer inspection would have shown carefully laid out paths, groves, nurseries, plantations and a herbarium, with a few staff houses dotted among the trees.

As the coolies waited to be detailed off to various parts of the Garden, some of them, standing near the landing steps, 'observed a tiger swimming in the river a few yards from the shore'.[2] Both the Garden's superintendent, Dr George King, and its curator, Herr Adolph Biermann, were standing nearby, and within a minute of the alarm being raised they saw a fully grown tiger bounding across the riverbank path no more than twenty yards ahead of them. The animal ran through the nursery near the curator's house, across the Ribben Walk and through the mango grove towards the teak avenue. 'Guided by the excited chattering of the monkeys in the mango grove', the two men were 'led to infer that the tiger had gone into cover somewhere'. Dr King acted promptly: he sent coolies to warn Mr Scott, the curator of the herbarium; he told Biermann to keep everyone together in the nursery area; he ran to his own house to warn a friend who was staying with him; and he sent a messenger by boat to the Howrah Magistrate asking for help. Dr King also sent an urgent note to the commissioner of police, Mr Soutter.

In spite of his commendable efforts, Dr King was soon to receive the awful message that his deputy, Biermann, had been attacked by the tiger and had suffered severe head wounds, with 'about a fourth part of his scalp hanging in shreds over the left ear—and two less serious wounds in the face'. Biermann, a German citizen working in Calcutta, was attended to by the Civil Surgeon, Dr Pilcher, but for some reason was not admitted to Howrah Hospital until the following day. It was later found that Biermann had not followed the superintendent's careful instructions, but had gone instead to find Mr Scott. The two men, Biermann and Scott, both unarmed, then went looking for the tiger. In this they were successful, for 'the animal, suddenly springing out below a bush, struck Mr Biermann down and quietly returned to the bush from which it had jumped. Mr Biermann was stunned by the blow and remained insensible for a little.' All the coolies had wisely taken themselves off to safety, so it was left to Scott to drag the wounded man to the nearest house, which happened to be that of the superintendent.

A police party arrived, with beaters, who managed to get the animal out of the Garden and into a neighbouring sugarcane field, but there it attacked Lance Corporal Shaik Azeem, wounding him severely. It was not until two days later, and after having killed two cows, that the tiger was shot dead by the Howrah Magistrate, Mr Wace, who stood on the roof of a house in Paddapukur village.

Initially Adolph Biermann had seemed to make good progress in hospital, but then he developed a fever and the Civil Surgeon advised him to return to Europe for at least a year in order to recover. 'There will be', he added, 'permanent disfigurement.'[3] Almost immediately the question of compensation was raised. Biermann was on a modest salary of 375 rupees a month and, as a European, had to pay for a private room and a nurse at the Howrah Hospital. The German Consul thought 15,000 rupees would be a suitable sum. It was quite clear who was to blame. Not the tiger, which turned out to be a tigress, but Wajid 'Ali Shah, his large menagerie and his 'insane ideas'. Members of the German community in Calcutta sent a memorial to the superintendent, Dr King, pressing for compensation and summing up the general feeling: 'We … wish to record our indignation at the criminal carelessness which has obtained within the ex-King of Oudh's enclosure, and which has almost in the centre of a densely populated town, the capital of the empire, exposed the public to dangers otherwise only to be encountered in the wildest jungles.'[4] It was an extreme case of *rus in urbe*, the countryside in the town, and perhaps something more fundamental too—old India in modern Bengal.

A long report of the incident was sent to the government of Bengal because it was deemed to be a local rather than a national matter, which would have been put up to the governor general. Mr Soutter said that the escape of two tigers, a male and a female, from the Garden Reach menagerie had been reported to him early on the morning of 6 January. He sent his superintendent, Mr Hill, to deal with it. Armed with a single-barrelled smooth-bore gun, 'the only weapon to hand', Hill hurried off to Garden Reach 'and brought down the tiger with a single shot as the animal was making its escape out of the enclosure'. But the second animal, 'a large tigress, had taken to the river and made good its way across to the Botanic Garden', with tragic consequences. Unlike most other members of the cat family, the Bengal tiger is a good swimmer, and the short journey of less than half a mile across the Hugli between Garden Reach and the Botanic Garden would not have been difficult, particularly with the tempting jungle-like greenery beckoning the beast.[5] Dr King blamed Wajid 'Ali Shah's servants, both for allowing the animals to escape, and then for not taking any measures to warn the staff in the Garden about the escape. In his report to the lieutenant governor, he wrote:

'The river at the point where the tiger crossed … is sufficiently narrow to allow a voice to be heard distinctly from the opposite bank by simply calling to the *manjees* [the master or steersman of a boat]. The river is nevertheless so wide that it must have taken the tiger a considerable time to swim across.' He added that more than a hundred coolies were on the river bank at the time, together with *durwans* [guards or porters], himself and Biermann. It would have been 'perfectly easy for the ex-King's servants to have attracted our attention to the tiger, while it was still in the water. And had this been done some attempt to kill it, or to prevent it from landing might have been successfully made.'

Mowbray Thomson, the agent, went further with his speculation of what might have happened. If the tigress had not actually been seen entering the Garden, he told the superintendent, then 'she might have lurked about for days in the dense cover in which this Garden abounds'. And had she landed later in the day, and 'at a spot near one of the visitors' pic-nic parties, which are so commonly held in this Garden during the cold season, the consequences might have been very much more serious'.[6] Thomson knew that Wajid 'Ali Shah had twenty-three tigers, lions and leopards in his menagerie, but as Europeans were not allowed into the gardens, he was unable to say whether or not the animals were enclosed in proper cages. He added dryly that it was possible 'there is a defect in some part of the arrangements for their custody', and given the awful scenario he had painted of a Victorian picnic interrupted by a tigress, he demanded that the government either persuade Wajid 'Ali Shah to give up keeping such dangerous animals, or allow his menagerie to be 'regularly inspected by some competent person'.

The commissioner of police asked whether Wajid 'Ali Shah should be keeping animals in the first place, but added a curious caveat: 'I am not sure that I can see that he has any special claim at all to keep dangerous carnivora about him as compared to anyone else, but there may be considerations with which I am unacquainted.' He knew that the number of animals had greatly increased in recent years, and that the increase, as far as Soutter could establish, 'is due more than anything to what may fairly be called the insane ideas of the ex-King'.[7]

In spite of the commissioner's views, Thomson's recommendations and the concerns of Calcutta's German community, the government of Bengal was not at first inclined to take the matter very seriously. In particular, the lieutenant governor, Sir Ashley Eden, seemed quite relaxed about it and thought no action was necessary. He said that the public were admitted to the menagerie 'from time to time' and there had been no reports of animals not being properly secured. On 12 February the government's view was that 'The recent escape of a tigress from the ex-King's gardens was an accidental and quite exceptional occurrence.'

But only five days later, on 17 February, a black leopard escaped from the menagerie and was shot dead in the Botanic Garden. Mr Hill, the police superintendent, perhaps hoping to repeat his success in shooting the tiger, went back to Garden Reach to search the premises, but learned shortly afterwards of the leopard's death. Hill took the opportunity to inspect the menagerie and reported that some of the animals 'are confined in very insecure cages' and that better arrangements were needed. Sir Ashley Eden then had a sudden change of mind, no doubt prompted by concern from the government of India. By the beginning of March he was agreeing that Wajid 'Ali Shah should be prohibited from keeping tigers, lions and leopards and 'so many dangerous carnivores' and that he 'should content himself with harmless animals and animals he can keep under control. It cannot be pretended that the menagerie is maintained for public instruction or for any purpose of public utility, as the public are only admitted on very rare occasions. It is kept up for the mere personal gratification of the ex-King; and though it is not right to interfere in any way with his amusements, so long as they are harmless, the interests of the public should ... receive the first consideration.'[8] And here was the crux of the matter, and the authentic voice of the British civic administrator in late nineteenth-century India. It was another collision between the medieval and the modern, the change from autocratic rule to the public good.

The word 'menagerie' is used loosely today to describe a collection of animals, and is almost interchangeable with 'zoo'. But it had a specific origin from the French word *ménage*, which means 'domestic', and was first used to describe animals about a large household—carriage horses, dairy cattle, hens, working dogs and the like. The term then became associated with royal collections of exotic animals, kept for entertainment and prestige. The menagerie was generally private, to be shown only to favoured guests. If the public were occasionally admitted, it was only to emphasise the royal owner's power, wealth and ability to collect unusual animals. Menageries date from at least the medieval period, the first in England being the royal menagerie in the Tower of London, which was started in the early thirteenth century with a pair of lions. Prestigious gifts of wild animals were exchanged between royal families and rulers throughout Europe, and as trade expanded, between Asia and Europe too. Wajid 'Ali Shah's uncle, the nawab Nasir ud-Din Haidar, had sent two horses, two elephants and a rhinoceros to William IV and Queen Adelaide, who had sensibly gifted them to the newly opened London Zoo.[9]

Initially, Indian rulers kept menageries for similar reasons to their European counterparts, although the elephant is an ancient symbol of Indian royalty and particularly associated with kings and rulers. These malleable animals, together with horses and camels, were kept in purpose-built stables and used on ceremonial occasions. Inspecting the elephants and horses was a pleasant, often daily, task for their kingly owners. Exotic animals, including giraffes and zebras, were imported into India from Africa. Lions, tigers, leopards, panthers and Himalayan bears, the 'dangerous carnivores', were captured in the jungles and the hills and sold to Mughal menageries. The possession of wild animals in the subcontinent came to symbolise the rulers' universal power over the forces of nature, a significantly different concept from the detached, scientific curiosity of European collectors, which developed from Enlightenment ideas in the eighteenth century. But both European and Indian royalty enjoyed watching animal fights, the latter well into the nineteenth century, as we know from numerous descriptions of fights at the Lucknow court of Nasir ud-Din Haidar.[10] An undated report by an eyewitness says that Wajid 'Ali Shah opened his menagerie to the public once a year, and that on one such day he organised a fight between two rams. 'Soon the noise of butting could be heard but it was nothing in comparison with the noise made by the Europeans in the "hurrahs" and shouts of acclamation.'[11] This was the final flicker of an 'entertainment' that dated back for centuries. The place where the animals were kept was called the *wahush khana*, the 'wild beasts' house', a descriptive word with its hint of the wilderness confined between four walls, although the term 'menagerie' was always used in referring to Wajid 'Ali Shah's collection. An aviary was a *chiriya-khana*, the 'bird-house'.

No pre-annexation description of Lucknow was complete without a detailed report of the royal menageries, shown to favoured visitors, as many Europeans were. The animals had been moved around, as new palaces and gardens were built, and ended up in a *ramna* or park on the north bank of the Gomti. An English chaplain, the Reverend William Tennant, had visited the menagerie of the fourth nawab, Asaf-ud-daulah, just after the latter's death in 1797. After describing its inhabitants, which included rhinoceros, porcupines, 'Cabul sheep', serpents, leopards, tigers and flamingoes, the chaplain voiced what many Britons thought, and continued to think for almost a century when contemplating the nawabi passion for animals: 'the food employed in this manner [to feed the menagerie] would remove want from the city, if not from the kingdom of Oude: but the art of government is less understood, or more perverted, by the Indians, than any other science, meanly as we may regard their attainments in them all'.[12] It was a curious juxtaposition to make—the costly menagerie and mis-government—but the idea of something wrong, something almost immoral, in keeping so many animals for private pleasure continued to nag at the official British mind.

After annexation, the new British administration in Lucknow had sold off Wajid 'Ali Shah's prized menagerie by public auction, with almost indecent haste, even before he had reached Calcutta. There were pragmatic reasons, of course, the chief one being the expense of feeding the birds and beasts, but there was also something spiteful in the action, which not only saw a large number of

A TIGRESS ESCAPES FROM THE MENAGERIE

animal attendants immediately thrown out of work, but a deliberate dismantling of the trappings of kingship. It is easier now to see why the Garden Reach menagerie was so important to the king. Like the ram fight, it was the last reminder of the animals collected by his ancestors, and another confirmation of their status as heirs to the great Mughals. Because the Lucknow auction had been widely advertised, with buyers arriving from as far afield as Delhi and Lahore, it was a public humiliation too. The king had been asked before the auction, in a 'peremptory' letter, to select a number of animals from his Lucknow menagerie, but he had declined to do so, saying in a dignified note that since he had never been consulted over *any* of the arrangements on annexation it was 'needless for the Chief Commissioner to refer to His Majesty on the present occasion'.[13]

Even more humiliatingly, shortly after the king's arrival in Calcutta *The Englishman and Military Chronicle* had carried the following advertisement:

24 June 1856 'We are informed that all the finest animals of the King of Oudh's menagerie have arrived in Calcutta and will be publicly exhibited as soon as they can be suitably placed for the reception of visitors. Some of the tigers are the very finest specimens of the kind ever caged. We have no doubt it will be a very interesting exhibition.'

And a few days later:

Advertisement: 'The Great Fighting Tigers of Lucknow. On Exhibition for a few days, from Sunrise to Sunset, at Tiretta Bazaar Godowns, Chitpore Road—these are animals purchased at the late Govt. sale at Lucknow. Entry Rs1 per person.'

Mr Soutter had remarked on the recent increase in the number of animals in the Garden Reach menagerie. When Wajid 'Ali Shah was released from Fort William prison in 1859, he started a new collection of animals, both as a riposte to the British auction of his Lucknow menagerie and also, by his own admission, from a genuine love of animals. (How he squared this with his enjoyment of watching animal fights is never explained.) In the mid-1870s two events occurred which seem to have accelerated the process. The idea of a Zoological Garden in Calcutta had first been suggested in 1842 by Dr John McCleland, curator of the Asiatic Society of Bengal's museum. Nothing came of his proposal, but twenty-five years later the idea was mooted again, by the then-president of the Asiatic Society, Dr Joseph Fayrer, the same man who had been attached to the Lucknow Residency before annexation, and who had visited Wajid 'Ali Shah at Qaisarbagh. By 1867 Dr Fayrer had become a specialist on snakes, snakebites and venom. A zoological garden in Calcutta, richly stocked, would enable him to study numerous specimens *in situ*. But there were arguments over a suitable site, and it was not until 1875 that the decision was taken to demolish a shanty town near the governor general's official residence in Alipore. Once started, work progressed quickly on the site and it was opened to the public on 1 May 1876.

The first superintendent of the Zoological Gardens was a Hindu, Ram Brahma Sanyal, who was a protégé of Dr George King, superintendent of the Royal Botanic Garden, and also a member of the zoo's managing committee. Although men like King, Fayrer and McCleland had different specialities, each had a common interest in promoting institutions that would further research into India's rich natural history, as well as providing education and instruction for the citizens of Calcutta. One of those citizens was Wajid 'Ali Shah, and Ram Sanyal described a meeting with him in the zoo's gardens:

'His Majesty the King', wrote Sanyal, 'was wont to visit the Gardens as he was deeply and scientifically interested in animals and used to go round the gardens in a sort of a Japanese rickshaw, drawn by eight men. One day he remarked "Babu Sahib— you think I consider myself a king and so allow you to walk by my side while I ride in this carriage." The Superintendent replied,

"Jahanpanah [protector of the world], Your Majesty is certainly a King while as a subject it is most proper for me to walk on foot by your side." Wajid 'Ali Shah then said, "You are a *sharifzada* (gentleman) and I should have walked with you, but am old now and weak and incapable of walking even for a short distance."'

Sanyal added that he could no longer believe 'that such a noble soul with such chivalry in his disposition and such kindly and gentlemanly consideration could have ever been guilty of the foul charges brought against him'.[14] It is a touching picture of two animal-lovers together, but the new, scientific approach of keeping animals as something other than a status symbol only seemed to have prompted Wajid 'Ali Shah to increase his collection in a random way.

The Zoological Gardens were formally opened on 1 January 1876 by the Prince of Wales (later Edward VII) during a winter visit to India. Accompanying him was William Howard Russell, the journalist from *The Times* whose reports during the recapture of Lucknow in March 1858 had provided one of the first objective accounts of the resistance put up by its citizens against the British. Now, eighteen years later, Russell was interested to note that: 'As the Prince [of Wales] was passing the gardens of the residences of the King of Oudh, the retainers of his ex-Majesty lined the bank, and stood in crowds on the tops of the houses within, in the enclosure, and in the verandahs, but they did not make any sign of welcome.'[15]

The Prince of Wales and his party stayed at Government House in Calcutta, where a large reception was held for the native 'Chiefs', but this did not include deposed rulers, so neither Wajid 'Ali Shah nor the Mysore princes were invited. The British prince was reputedly fonder of shooting animals than conserving them, and tiger-shooting parties were arranged for him, as they had been for royalty in the past. Grand hunting parties were equally popular among Indian rulers and the British, a place where both could meet on (nearly) equal terms. The Prince of

Wales was, however, also presented with an embarrassingly large number of live animals and birds as gifts, part of the usual tribute to a ruling monarch. These were shipped back to Portsmouth and donated to the London Zoo. Among them were two elephants, the particular signifier of royalty in the East, who had to walk to their new home along the main road.[16] Wajid 'Ali Shah would have reflected on all of this and the fact that he had to buy his own wild animals now instead of receiving them as gifts. Indeed, after the escape of his two tigers and the leopard in the spring of 1879, he had to purchase 'a fresh supply of tigers'.

An inspection of the Garden Reach menagerie was arranged for 24 April. The inspection party was made up of Mowbray Thomson, Mr Soutter, Mr Lambert, the deputy police commissioner, and Amir 'Ali, now manager of the king's household. On arrival they met the three garden superintendents: Rayhan-ud-daulah, Mansur-ud-daulah and Munshi-us-Sultan. Thomson reported that there were seventeen felines, including lions, leopards and black panthers, housed in eleven dens.[17] The dens were constructed of solid masonry with iron railings, and the railings had small doors in them. The doors had previously been padlocked, but since the escape they had been fitted with iron rings, which could only be opened by a blacksmith. Thomson thought that the animals were now reasonably secured against future escapes, but the real question was not so much the custody of the animals as their number.

There was only one old man and three assistants, reporting to the garden superintendents, to look after the animals, and there was no guarantee that the king would not purchase even more tigers or swap them around in the cages. One cage had been constructed on a 'high elevation' in the zananah area of the Zard Kothi. Thomson recommended that the animals were not replaced when they died, and that there should be only one pair of each particular species—a Noah's Ark of two lions, two tigers, two spotted leopards, two black leopards and two pumas. The commissioner of police did not see why Wajid 'Ali Shah should keep *any* dangerous animals. There were always risks involved in keeping wild animals, even at Alipore Zoo, 'which has every conceivable safeguard against danger' and where there was at least the justification of public advantage counterbalancing the risk involved. Soutter repeated that there was no public advantage, or advantage of any kind, in the king's menagerie 'beyond the gratification of a costly individual craze'.

A Menagerie Committee was set up on 1 May 1879 to deal with the question of public safety. Thomson was one of its three members, the others being Colman Macaulay, then undersecretary to the government of Bengal, and Amir 'Ali. Following the inspection of the previous month, Wajid 'Ali Shah had appointed eleven men to feed the animals, keep their dens clean and care for them. It was recognised that the menagerie 'was a constant source of pleasure to the King', but at the same time, it should contain only harmless animals and 'animals under control'. Thomson's proposals for limiting the animals to pairs was accepted. In future the cages were to be 'solidly constructed and properly guarded' and regular inspections by Thompson were to take place. Wajid 'Ali Shah was forced to accept these terms under the government's threat that if he did not, he would not be allowed to keep any carnivores at all. He grumbled that there had only been one tiger escape in the twenty years since he had started his Garden Reach menagerie, and that was purely accidental. By contrast, there had already been an escape from the new Alipore Zoo, within four years of its establishment. Moreover, he added, one had only to look around to see plenty of wild animals being kept in the dealers' shops in Calcutta, or even in their houses. Animals were not only sold from cages that were not secure, but were being transported from one country to another by sea, river and rail. No doubt the king had in mind the two boatloads of animals given to the Prince of Wales during his visit, which had followed him home to England.

'My menagerie is not like the Zoological Gardens', Wajid 'Ali Shah continued, because in Garden Reach there were 'places for my residence, the compound and courtyards of which accommodate the menagerie and the gardens, and which pertain alike to the male and female departments'. Thomson had already noted a tigers' cage on an artificial mound in the middle of the zananah. This can only have added to the misery of the wives, in their wretched, unsanitary accommodation. The smell and the noise of the beasts would have penetrated their quarters and made them fearful about venturing outside to get some fresh air in the gardens. Descriptions of the menagerie are understandably scarce and the best information we have comes again from Sharar, who lived at Garden Reach as a boy.

In front of one of the newly built palaces, the Nur Manzil, he wrote, was a large, open park-like space fenced by iron railings where spotted deer, buck and 'other wild quadrupeds' wandered freely. In the middle of the park was a marble pool which attracted the king's fine collection of partridges, ostriches, turkeys, cranes, geese, herons, ducks, peacocks, flamingoes and the humble tortoise. The tiger cages were noted, as well as 'a row of large wooden cages into which scores of different species of monkeys had been collected from far-flung places'. A pair of giraffes wandered around in the company of a two-humped camel from Baghdad and a couple of donkeys, who were let loose in a meadow. Fish pools scattered throughout the gardens were noted, but the most spectacular site was the serpentarium, a long, deep tank in front of the Shahinshah Manzil. In the middle of the tank, or pool, was an artificial hill pierced by pipes, some of which carried water. 'Thousands of large snakes, six to nine feet long, had been released on this hill and would crawl about it.' There was a 'sort of moat' around the snake hill where the reptiles would come to catch frogs. Apart from the animals there were 'thousands of shining brass bird-cages in the Sultan Khana itself'. Outside, there were scores of large aviaries enclosed with wire netting, all containing birds of various kinds, including some 24,000 pigeons.[18] Sharar was quite precise about the amount of money spent on the menagerie and the financial cost of indulging the king's fancies. Food for the animals alone was almost 9,000 rupees a month, he reported.

By interrogating Amir 'Ali, Thomson learnt just how much money was being set aside for new acquisitions. 'I find one Daroga, Muthur Ali Khan, gets Rs500 per month for purchasing fish. Am I to understand that he gets this sum every month to purchase fish with, and if so, how long has he been getting it?' The sum was paid monthly, confessed Amir 'Ali, adding that he did not recollect how long this had been going on for.[19] Thomson then established that another superintendent, Hyder Ali Beg, got 1,193 rupees a month to purchase 'country animals' from the Indian subcontinent, while Rayhan-ud-daulah was picking up nearly 2,500 rupees a month to buy animals 'imported from foreign countries, such as England and America'.

Although the king had been forced to agree to the menagerie committee's recommendations that the number of 'dangerous animals' be limited to pairs and kept in secure cages, restrictions had not been put on the acquisition of other animals. In a show of defiance, after the committee had been set up, Wajid 'Ali Shah arranged with Mr Rutledge of Jaun Bazar Street, Calcutta, to supply him with imported animals to the value of 1 lakh per year.[20] The previous supplier of foreign animals (and garden superintendent), Rayhan-ud-daulah, had not been paid, and he had become another of the king's many creditors. Under the new arrangement Rutledge was to get 48,000 rupees a year, less than half the value of the animals ordered. 'No man in his senses would take such a contract', retorted the Committee when it learned of this. The inference was that by sleight of hand and through corrupt court servants, 'with or without Rutledge's connivance', the Englishman would indeed buy animals to the value of 48,000 rupees, but that the king would be charged 100,000 rupees or 1 lakh a year for them and the difference would be pocketed by the servants—and Rutledge, if he was in on the deal.

Money was spent 'without restraint' in acquiring one-off purchases of exotic animals and birds, and anyone bringing a new species for sale to Garden Reach was paid whatever was asked. Wajid 'Ali Shah is said to have paid 24,000 rupees for a pair of special pigeons and 11,000 rupees for a pair of white peacocks.[21] There is something reminiscent here of descriptions from nawab Asaf-ud-daulah's time, when foreigners were able to sell the gullible ruler any novelty that momentarily attracted his interest. The fact that Wajid 'Ali Shah thought he was ordering foreign animals from Mr Rutledge worth 1 lakh a year, when in fact they cost less than half that amount, is typical of the regal attitude for things that caught his fancy. The kingly response was not to haggle over the prices asked, but with a wave of the hand to accept what was offered and instruct a clerk to pay the seller. Kings did not concern themselves with rupees, annas and pice—that was the job of the Treasury Department. And this was precisely the point on which Wajid 'Ali Shah and his British agents were never going to agree, simply because neither could step outside the mindsets and rules that bound them. Wajid 'Ali Shah would always behave like the king he had once been, ruling his kingdom as, he believed, the successor to the great Mughals. The British agents would always behave like government officials working far from home, but with an undiminished sense of Victorian propriety and financial acumen. Neither party could compromise, so both were condemned to play out their respective roles.

The king wanted to make it clear that his animals were intimately connected with his own royal status, and he batted away criticism. 'As regards the expenditure on the menagerie, the world knows that I am very fond of the collection, inasmuch as it almost can be said that I am born with it! I am therefore attached to it with a degree of fondness which far exceeds that [which] I entertain towards my sons, daughters, etc.'[22] This outrageous statement naturally infuriated Thomson, who commented that it showed 'pretty plainly what little regard His Majesty has for the welfare of his children'. It was the welfare of these children, and their mothers, to which the government of Bengal now turned its attention.

In March 1879, the government of India formally transferred 'the charge of the Oude and Mysore Princes' from central authority to the lieutenant governor of Bengal, Sir Ashley Eden, who had taken up his post two years earlier. As we have seen, the lieutenant governor had initially seemed supportive of the king, probably regarding him as an eccentric old man living some way outside Calcutta. Eden's credentials for his own powerful position were impeccable. He was a nephew of Lord Auckland, who had formerly been governor general of India for six years. Eden's own career had included the invasion of Sikkim (as political agent) and governor of Burma. 'With these natural advantages', wrote a perceptive journalist, Eden 'was able to champion lost causes and advocate unpopular beliefs without inflicting injury upon his prospects or erecting an obstacle to his advancement'.[23] But support for Wajid 'Ali Shah was a lost cause too far, as Eden found out after a briefing from Thomson on the king's refusal to support his vast family.

Central government had been bothered during the previous year by 'various matters connected with the proceedings of the ex-King of Oude', matters which 'chiefly concern the arrangements to be made for the maintenance of the ex-King's wives and children, the marriage of his daughters'[24] and his personal expenditure (or extravagance, to put it less politely). There was also the problem of the menagerie, which throughout this period seems curiously bound in with the king's own household arrangements. Indeed, one domestic account scrutinised was for the 'rhinocerous enclosure, repairs of the Sultan Kothi and articles of dress for His Majesty's wardrobe', which totalled one and a half lakhs, with no breakdown or explanation.

The governor general thought that a better settlement of the king's affairs, 'which frequently involve local interests', would be if Thomson and future agents submitted correspondence and reports about Wajid 'Ali Shah to the lieutenant governor of Bengal, who would act as a filter, before sending selected material on to central Government. Apart from Thomson's role as agent to the ex-king, he was also appointed agent to the Mysore princes, the descendants of Tipu Sultan. The Mysore princes were a trouble-free family in Calcutta, who might almost have been placed there solely as an exemplar of how deposed royalty ought to behave in exile.

Ashley Eden was charged with setting up a three-man committee to report on the 'arrangements necessary for proper superintendence' of the king's affairs. Naturally, Thomson was one of its members, together with Amir 'Ali and Henry Peacock (a former agent), who was appointed president. The committee was formed on 1 May 1879, and by March 1880 its report was ready.[25] Its brief had been to determine the nature and extent of the provision to be made for the family of the ex-king, that is, how much it was going to cost, and who should be included in the payment of pensions and allowances.

Wajid 'Ali Shah was consulted by the committee during its investigations, and it was reported that a 'large number' of the committee's recommendations came from the king himself. It was an adroit move to work with Wajid 'Ali Shah rather than simply telling him what he should do, as had been done so many times in the past, with so little result.

Payment for the wives was tackled first. Both the nikah wives, Khas Mahal and Akhtar Mahal, got small increases, bringing their monthly pensions to 600 rupees and 500 rupees respectively. These were not large sums, commented the committee, but both queens had independent incomes and neither had any surviving children. In fact Khas Mahal, the first wife, who had suffered much at her husband's hands, had left Garden Reach altogether, and 'has been for sometime living entirely separate from His Majesty outside his premises. Indeed', the report continued, 'she is supposed to be living in adultery with one Hakeem Mahomed Munshee and Peary Sahib, a relation of hers'.[26] This was a tricky one. The 'Special or Exceptional Queen', niece of the former chief minister 'Ali Naqi Khan, the poetess after whom the Alam Bagh in Lucknow had been named and who flew into rages when things went wrong had, like the tigress, escaped the palace. But she was still queen.

Verbal discussions with Wajid 'Ali Shah about her pension are not recorded, only the end result. The king proposed to continue payments 'conditionally' on her 'continuing to be faithful to His Majesty and dismissing those persons from her service who have been proved disloyal to His Majesty'. As we have seen, Khas Mahal had her own household around her, which she maintained until the end of her life. Akhtar Mahal, the second living nikah wife, was also ordered to continue being 'faithful to His Majesty', as were the mut'ah wives. Even the khilawati wives, who did not get an increased pension 'as they are in reality little more than domestic servants', were told that they should remain faithful too.[27] The king had lost control over his household. His spiteful gesture in divorcing twenty-seven mut'ah wives had backfired. The committee agreed with Thomson that Wajid 'Ali Shah had a moral obligation to support them, even if he was no longer married to them. Their treatment had been 'both ungenerous and unjust'.

By May 1879, Thomson reported that 'His Majesty has consented of his own accord to continue their previous allowances and to renew the Motah contract with them.' Most of the mut'ah wives were quietly remarried to the king later that year. But having tasted freedom, three of the divorced women refused to be remarried 'without some guarantee against future ill-treatment and some compensation for the injury to which they have already been subjected'. One begam even divorced the king 'of her own accord' and another left his protection and was subsequently dismissed. The committee could not order the women to be remarried, and it remained non-committal about the condition of faithfulness.

While the committee was in session, the death of Mashuq Mahal, the king's first mut'ah wife, was reported on 19 November 1879. After thirty years of loyal and loving service, she had been divorced when the couple's eldest son, Prince Farid-ud-din Qadr, had asked his father for more money. On her deathbed, Mashuq Mahal had asked her ex-husband 'to pardon all her faults and have her buried in Mecca'. Farid-ud-din then sent a petition to his father asking to be reinstated in his favour. He got no reply. When Thomson re-submitted the prince's petition, Wajid 'Ali Shah falsely claimed he had had nothing to do with Mashuq Mahal during her lifetime (in spite of their four children and grandsons), and that he had nothing to say in answer to her dying wish.

After an agreement on the wives' allowances had been reached, and the remarriages had taken place, attention turned to the king's sons and daughters. On the day the committee started work, there were twenty-five princes and twenty-seven princesses alive. The princesses presented less of a problem, because they would be married with dowries which were subsidised by the British government. But the princes had to be considered separately. Following the death in 1874 of Prince Hamid 'Ali, the heir apparent, the title passed to Farid-ud-din Qadr. He was now the eldest surviving son of Wajid 'Ali Shah, born to Mashuq Mahal in about 1846. He had been first married when he was about six years old, to a daughter of the chief minister, 'Ali Naqi Khan, who seemed to have an inexhaustible supply of female relatives as brides for the Awadh family. These complicated family intermarriages meant that the king's second nikah wife, Akhtar Mahal, was also the sister-in-law of Farid-ud-din Qadr. But once again, Wajid 'Ali Shah had got himself into an impossible situation. He had named Farid-ud-din Qadr as his heir apparent, but at the same time had stopped the boy's meagre monthly allowance of 90 rupees and had divorced his mother. Thomson was not unsympathetic to the young heir's case. Although the British government did not recognise the title of heir apparent, because there was no longer a kingdom to inherit, Thomson said that Farid-ud-in Qadr should get a decent allowance from his father. 'He would undoubtedly succeed to the *guddee* [throne] if the ex-King had one to leave', but in reality he would only get a son's share equally with his twenty-four brothers and half-brothers on their father's death.

Trying once again to wriggle out of his financial obligations, Wajid 'Ali Shah first claimed that Farid-ud-din Qadr had 'no superior rank' and then, because of the number of his children, said he could only afford to pay each son 90 rupees a month. He argued that if he gave the heir more than the others, 'it would only result in upsetting my household arrangements by making my children disobedient and turning them away from their present state of contentment to aspire after higher allowances'. He added that Farid-ud-din Qadr and his mother had been well provided for with valuable jewellery, government bonds and gifts of land (*jagirs*). But not surprisingly, given his inadequate monthly allowance, Farid-ud-din Qadr had fallen into debt and owed money to the manager of his jagir. In order to pay off this debt, he had mortgaged the estate to Hakeem Muhammad Munshi, the same man who was now supposedly in a relationship with the king's first wife, Khas Mahal. Apart from his financial problems, Farid-ud-din Qadr claimed 'there is talk at Garden Reach to set up a younger brother of mine by name of Mirza Khosh Bukht as my rival'. He added that whatever 'His Majesty might be induced by interested parties' to write to the agent, he, the prince, would like to be kept informed 'in order that *I may also have my say* before it goes to the Government for final orders'.[28]

Farid-ud-din Qadr is also likely to have been the author of an anonymous letter sent to Captain Durand, who was Thomson's predecessor as agent with the king. The letter, dated 10 October 1877, came from 'a son of the King (who fears the disclosure of his name before actual enquiry)'. It gave a vivid insider picture of the fear and frustration among Wajid 'Ali Shah's relatives at Garden Reach, who saw their money being squandered away while they themselves lived in poverty.

'His Majesty', the writer began, 'owing to our misfortune, never associates with persons bold enough to hold independent opinions of their own on any subject. He is surrounded by sycophants and courtiers who always mind their own interests and entirely disregard ours.'[29] The late Safdar 'Ali was described as 'impoverishing' the royal treasury and he was blamed for much of the current financial deficit. 'When he entered the King's service he was a poor man—when he died the King owed him Rs 40 lakhs.' It was Safdar 'Ali who had instigated the sale, by auction, of the crown jewels rescued by Sir Henry Lawrence, even though the munshi himself 'had spent 84 lakhs of the King's pension over seven years!'

The present estates manager, Amir 'Ali, was proving to be just as bad, the letter continued. The British government had recently given him an advance of 3 lakhs 'to repair our building [at Garden Reach] but, Kind Sir, our residences and those of our mothers are wretched hovels still and would not bear comparison to even the kitchens of European gentlemen. They are low and ill-ventilated *godowns* [sheds] with no flooring or efficient drainage… Pay our hovels a visit though for once, and see with your own eyes also the accommodation of, and the waste of money that is being lavishly spent for, the tigers, monkeys, beasts and birds. I can assure you Sir, that in comparing these you will see, as it were, heaven and hell side by side.' The king was spending about 10,000 rupees monthly on 'beasts and birds which his officers supply and get cash down for it'. The writer concluded chillingly, 'I warn you, Sir, against the *color-de-rose* reports and the oily words of the Manager, which have hitherto been the cause of blinding people interested in my father's affairs.' Whether this letter was from Farid-ud-din Qadr or not, it led to the governor general ordering that the prince was to receive 2,500 rupees a month, which would be deducted at source from the king's stipend and paid directly to him. It would also be backdated to 1 January 1878.

Although the committee's remit had been primarily to make recommendations to the government of Bengal about the cost of providing for the king's family, other matters were considered too, particularly where there were financial implications. The king's pension of 12 lakhs a year, equivalent to £10,000 every month, was not going to be increased, and it would cease on the king's death. It could be decreased by allowances made directly to his relatives, where the king refused to do so voluntarily, but in the end it was a finite sum. The obvious answer was to persuade the king to cut back on his monthly expenditure, including the huge monthly outgoing on the menagerie. A table of allowances was worked out for the king's descendants, based on their age. Daughters-in-law also had to be considered, particularly where their husbands, the king's sons, had died. The late Prince Hamid 'Ali had left five wives, all ill-provided for. His second wife, Kaukab Mahal, had been forced to sell her jewellery for a meagre sum in order to feed herself and the king's grandson. 'His Majesty cares nothing for us', she complained, 'being entirely engrossed with his affection in his birds and beasts.'[30]

The king seemed remarkably compliant to the committee's recommendations, once he realised that the government could, and would, deduct allowances for his relatives from his stipend. 'So far from appearing to resent the enquiries the Committee thought necessary to make, or to assume an hostile or antagonistic attitude towards them, His Majesty has rendered them all the assistance in his power', which the committee recommended. It seemed almost too good to be true. The king had even agreed to an inspection of the Garden Reach premises by the Sanitary

Commissioner of Bengal, or the local Civil Surgeon, accompanied by Thomson. There was still some quibbling over the allowances to his widowed daughters-in-law. The fifth wife of Prince Hamid 'Ali had moved in to live with her mother-in-law, Khas Mahal, 'who is the possessor of thousands and thousands', claimed the king. He maintained that his daughters-in-law were not close relatives. The ranking, according to him, was firstly children, followed by wives, grandsons, granddaughters, daughters-in-law whose husbands were alive, and lastly daughters-in-law whose husbands were dead. Nevertheless, there was general agreement on future provision for the family of Wajid 'Ali Shah, and this had been the committee's brief.

In its close scrutiny of the king's relatives, the committee had found a number of young princes at Garden Reach who were the sons, and in some cases grandsons, of Wajid 'Ali Shah. Little attention had previously been paid to the younger male members of the vast Awadh family. The heirs apparent, Prince Hamid 'Ali and, after his death, Prince Farid-ud-din Qadr, had, on the whole, been treated sympathetically by the British government, particularly as both princes were articulate, intelligent and, to a certain degree, anglicised. Both had spoken out vigorously against their father's extravagance, and his meanness in not allocating them a decent income. This was a useful stick for the British government to wield over the king's head, but there were other less articulate princes hanging idly around the Garden Reach estate. In allocating a scale of allowances for the children, the committee recommended that as the younger princes reached the age of eight, they should be enrolled as boarders in a new school to be established at Garden Reach. A sum of 100 rupees a month would be deducted from their allowances and paid to the school as fees.

The idea of schools under royal patronage in Awadh was not a new one. The Lucknow Observatory had been set up by nawab Nasir ud-din Haidar not only to scan the heavens, but 'more particularly as a school for the young courtiers in which some knowledge of Astronomy and Physics might be taught'.[31] Long before Wajid 'Ali Shah had the Observatory closed down in 1849, the school had been abandoned because of the lack of interest and application by the 'young courtiers'. The king's own father, nawab Amjad 'Ali Shah, had set up a Shi'a college in the Great Imambarah which, although running at a loss, had over two hundred fee-paying scholars. The college was closed down after annexation on economic and ideological grounds, because the British authorities did not want to be seen supporting 'an educational establishment which teaches and fosters an exclusive creed, and religious tenets to which the Government cannot subscribe'.[32]

But there was nothing to stop Wajid 'Ali Shah from setting up his own school in Garden Reach for his own sons. The first attempt was made in 1869, but failed, apparently because it had too few rules. Two years later a prospectus was sent to the central government entitled 'Rules and Regulations of the Madrissa of the King of Oude at Garden Reach ... issued agreeably to the instructions of His Majesty on 23 January 1871'.[33] (Although a *madrassa* is today usually associated with teaching Islamic theology, the word simply means 'school' in Arabic.) It is clear that Wajid 'Ali Shah, with his usual love of detail, had involved himself closely in formulating the rules.

All princes aged five and above were to attend school from 10.00 a.m. to 5.00 p.m., and they would be picked up by carriage from their various houses in Garden Reach. 'The madrassa is a place of education', explained the king, 'and not for showing their rank or dignity.' The princes should consider themselves as students and not bring with them their attendants or friends, although they were allowed one *khitmatgar* (servant) each 'to attend upon them in case of necessity'. Because many of the young princes were of 'tender age' and would be at school all day, their mothers were allowed to send them 'something in the shape of refreshments' at a given time.

After morning lessons there was to be an hour for recreation, then writing practice 'upon wooden boards and metallic paper'. At 3.00 p.m. English and Bengali were to be studied, and at 4.00 p.m. there were physical activities including 'wrestling with daggers', riding, and what sounds like cricket. Staff would be drawn from the king's own establishment to teach Arabic, Persian, English and Bengali, so there was no need to appoint any 'new hands'. A monthly examination would test the boys' attainments and proficiency, and at the end of three months there would be a special examination by His Majesty himself and staff members. The princes who did well would be entitled to prizes. The examination in English would be carried out by the maulawi Deen Mahummad, assisted by another person proficient in the English language. (Wajid 'Ali Shah could not speak English himself.) Once the boys had a grasp of the Arabic alphabet they would begin studying the Qur'an and Persian grammar. The *Gulistan* and *Bostan* by the thirteenth-century Persian poet Sa'adi were set books, together with an English spelling book. The boys were to be 'well grounded in the principle of the Sheeah sect, and made capable of keeping up the fasting and other ceremonies and prayers as prescribed by their religion'. At the same time they would receive instruction in the 'principles of morality and the art of letter-writing'.

It sounded an ideal education for young princelings, who were not expected to work for a living, no matter how small their allowances. Eighteen boys aged between five and fifteen were enrolled, divided into four classes. So what went wrong? Details of the committee's inspection of the school are unfortunately missing from its long report. What we do know is that the committee found it 'so ill-regulated an establishment' that it hardly deserved the name of school.[34] There were twenty maulawis teaching Persian, Arabic and Urdu, but there was no organisation, no classes, no one to make sure the boys attended, slovenly staff who had no authority over the boys, and poorly selected textbooks, which were in some cases 'positively bad'. Not only was the school obviously useless for its intended purpose, thundered the committee, 'it is worse than useless, it is positively mischievous'. The king offered to double his grant towards the school, but this was rejected.

The committee concluded: 'If these children [the princes] are to be weaned from the depraving influences by which they are surrounded, and to become decent members of society, some radical change in the system under which instruction is now imparted must be effected ... What is wanted, is not only an institution where a good practical education can be obtained, but a place where the pupils will reside, and will be thus separated from those demoralizing influences with which at present their home life is surrounded.' All the king's good intentions and his careful drawing-up of the syllabus had been thwarted by the king's own in-house staff, untrained to teach or to attempt discipline of their royal master's sons.

One of the committee members, the resourceful Amir 'Ali, had already drawn up a scheme for a new Madrassa Sultan-i-Oudh (the King of Oudh's School), to operate at a cost of 3,000 rupees per month per student. There was to be an English principal and two English teachers. The number of maulawis was drastically cut to three. There would be a riding master, a clerk, servants and horses, and it was to be a boarding school, thus removing the pupils from their home surroundings. Sadly, the new school was to be no more successful than its predecessors. A building was hired through the letting agents Mackinnon and Mackenzie, and the school opened in September 1881. It stood in the compound of a cotton mill, so became known as the Jinwali Kothi.[35] A board of management was set up, which included the Commissioner of the Presidency Division and Colonel William Prideaux, the new agent who had replaced Thomson on the latter's retirement. There was also a school inspector, a mujtahid, a magistrate, a maulawi and a barrister, as well as one of the older princes, Prince Jehan Qadr, son of the late Sikandar Hashmat. The king declined to serve on the board, as he objected to his nephew's inclusion.

The madrassa lasted for less than seven years, and was closed down a year after the king's death in 1887. This was particularly bad luck for its principal, Mr Billing, who had been appointed less than two years earlier. He had previously been the headmaster of the well-regarded Mohammedan College of Calcutta, popularly known as the Calcutta Madrasah, which had been founded by Warren Hastings in 1780. The obvious question arises of why the Awadh princes were not sent there, to an old established college specifically set up for Muslim pupils, with a fine library of Arabic and Persian books. But no one on the committee had suggested it, neither had the lieutenant governor, nor the king, nor any of the princes themselves. Garden Reach, after the king's arrival in 1856, was described by some as 'a second Lucknow'. In particular, Sharar said admiringly, after pointing out the supposed delights of the new 'kingdom': 'it didn't even appear to anyone that they were in Bengal'. And this was precisely the problem. Not only was there a refusal to acknowledge that the times had changed, there was a deliberate attempt to ignore geography as well. Calcutta, with all its intellectual richness, society, business and culture might have been five hundred miles away, rather than the five miles that separated it from Garden Reach. The royal family lived in a bubble of the king's making, which may have seemed superficially attractive to young men like Sharar, but which imposed an archaic way of life, attitude and thought on those held captive inside the iridescent circle.

It was inevitable that the Madrassa Sultan-i-Oudh would fail. The board of management had no legal power to make the princes attend and the absentee rate was high. Pressure was put on the students to attend by withholding their allowances, but this did not work either. The main problem was the boys' mothers, who did not see why their sons should be formally educated anyway. 'Their mothers are their principal abettors in their evasion of the rules of the school ... as the ladies exercise scarcely any influence over their sons in a right direction.'[36] Financially the school had been breaking even, because the king put in 1,000 rupees a month, and deductions from the pupils' allowances, the principal source of income, were nearly as much again.

A report of 1886 showed twenty-three pupils in attendance, reading English, Persian, Hindustani and Arabic, 'the highest standard arrived at being that of the Calcutta University entrance examination'. But at the same time, doubts were expressed about whether the curriculum stretched the boys enough. Did it go 'far enough to place the boys, when grown up, on a par with young men trained in the higher institutions of the country? What facilities for special instruction are afforded to an aspiring youth, who exhibits abilities or industry above the average?' It was recommended that the madrassa should be brought 'more into the current of educational progress. The King is, or was, however, jealous of interference, and of attempts to remove the teaching from the old lines.'[37]

In spite of this, and notwithstanding the febrile atmosphere of Garden Reach, two of the princes approached the new lieutenant governor, Sir Auckland Colvin, with a request to go to England for further study. Prince Muhammad Babur, now aged twenty-four with his education complete, wanted to become a doctor. His younger half-brother, Prince Dara Jah, was fifteen when he too applied for permission to travel to England. Their request put Colvin in a difficult position. He wished to encourage the Awadh princes to seek a life for themselves outside Garden Reach, and to become independent. At the same time there were practical difficulties, the chief of which was the king's attitude to foreign travel and the expense it would incur. Learning that Muhammad Babur wanted to study abroad, he vetoed the proposal immediately. 'The King is opposed to the step', wrote Henry Durand to Colvin. 'The lad's present income from his father, though that is now virtually assured to him by our recent orders, would not be sufficient to support him in England', and naturally the king would not increase it, nor could the government force him to do so. The monthly allowance of 150 rupees, which was all he had, would amount to little over £10 in England. Another problem was that the prince's education was 'not sufficient to enable him to embark on the study of medicine with much chance of success'.[38]

'It is painful to refuse such a request, which is in itself rather pathetic, but I do not see what we can do. I do not think the King should be allowed to stop his sons from going to England when they are of age, but unfortunately they have no money, and we can hardly undertake to pay for their expenses.' In Prince Dara Jah's case, because he was underage, 'his father can exercise power over his movements'. Both Auckland and Durand agreed that 'when the King dies, it is to be hoped that something may be done for this unfortunate family. Until then we can really do nothing unless with the approbation [approval].' The matter was discussed at the highest level, showing that Wajid 'Ali Shah and his family were still emotive subjects, to be treated carefully.

If the elder prince did have an aptitude for medicine, Colvin suggested, then could he study at a medical college in India? 'Later on, if he shows he is in earnest and was capable, we might reconsider the question of assisting him to complete his training in England.' He asked Durand to consult the Surgeon General of Bengal, to see if the prince could start at Calcutta's Medical College. Dr John Coates, principal of the College, said that if the prince passed the University entrance examination, he could attend classes and become eligible for a certificate. However, he would have to pass a Latin examination too. The cost for a year's tuition was negligible, at 200 rupees, but Colvin thought that 'probably the King and the young man will not like the idea', and he was right, because the prince's application was postponed in May 1888.[39]

With the king's death, the absentee rate at the school intensified, now that its founder and financial backer was gone. Pupil numbers dropped from twenty-three to fourteen. The school's closure, seven months after the king's death, was an opportunity for the government of Bengal to consider the future of the princes, and indeed how many princes there were at Garden Reach. The lieutenant governor's secretary thought that 'the future education and employment of the late King's descendants are matters of importance both politically and financially. We do not want to find the family by and by growing out of even liberal pensions like the Sind Talpur family.'[40]

In June 1888 twenty-two of the late king's sons were alive and living in Bengal. The eldest prince, Qamar Qadr, was aged about thirty-six, and the youngest was Prince Afsar-ul-Malik, one of two seven-year-old boys who were supposed to be illegitimate. Wajid 'Ali Shah's ability to father children, at the age of sixty, had been called into question by the Bengal government. It was a delicate question too, and one which could not easily be answered. An untraceable rumour, a complaint by a disgruntled wife, a sniggering courtier—something must have triggered it off, but the government's sources were not named. Following the 1880 Committee's report, Ashley Eden recommended that any children born of His Majesty's wives were not to be formally recognised by the government. A note in the margin says, 'His Majesty was understood to be impotent.'[41] A letter was sent to the king at the beginning of 1881 stating: 'The Government will not, according to general practice, look upon every child that may be born of the womb of the supplicants's wives from and after the date of the Committee's report as Your Majesty's child.'[42] Not surprisingly the king complained, 'My humiliation and indignity have been proclaimed to the high and the low', although he did not refute the charge.

But what was the future for those princes whose legitimacy was not in doubt, and who were now, after their father's death, deprived of even the small allowances he had made them from his own pension? 'Male descendants should be encouraged and assisted to employ themselves usefully', wrote William Cunningham, undersecretary to the Foreign Department. He said that English lessons at the madrassa had benefited the princes, resulting in some of them now being 'fit for Government service'. It seemed an extraordinary suggestion at first, but in fact the government of Bengal, since it had taken over responsibility for the Awadh royal family in 1880, had to its credit been careful to separate its attitude towards the king, who was considered beyond redemption, from its behaviour towards his sons. (The government appeared to have no view on the princesses.) It was important to wean the princes away from the idea of a government pension and towards supporting themselves. It was helpfully pointed out that one of the sons of the ex-king of Delhi, Bahadur Shah Zafar, had got a job as a *tehsildar*, a revenue officer, in the North West Provinces.

As if to support this radical idea, Prince Asman Jah, now in his mid-thirties, applied to the governors of several provinces, including Burma, for help in finding employment. The prince had moved out of Garden Reach into Gardner's Lane, central Calcutta, and got his petition to Lord Dufferin, the Governor General, printed and submitted in May 1888. Calling himself 'your Excellency's Humble Petitioner', the prince confessed that he did not know English but hoped there might be a job for him in the subordinate Executive Service of the North West Provinces, Bihar or the Punjab that did not require any knowledge of English. The prince did not ask for any special consideration, or a made-up job, but said his request was 'simply a sincere desire to serve the Government instead of whiling away the time'.[43] The princes were beginning to realise that, with their father's death, the constraints that had kept them captive in the curious time-warp of Garden Reach had fallen away. Escape was not possible for everyone, of course, and for some it was easier to remain imprisoned by the memory of past glories than to make a bid for freedom, as the unfortunate tigress had done all those years earlier. It is impossible to trace the lives of all the king's sons and to see whether or not they prospered. That would require a different kind of history, but we do at least know that the youngest prince, Afsar-ul-Malik, legitimate or not, did grow up to lead a useful and fulfilling life, as we shall see in the Conclusion to this book.

The escape of the tigress from the menagerie led to fear and annoyance in Calcutta. The importance of animals to the king and his royal status have been examined. Attempts to control the animals by government inspections were followed by attempts to control the king's continuing extravagance and challenge his lack of financial provision for his wives and children. The education of the princes at the king's madrassa was unsatisfactory and left the young men unsuited to earn their own living.

7

A MIMIC KINGDOM

Wajid 'Ali Shah is a recluse in his little kingdom, keeping up a way of life that is long out of date, yet one that still binds his subjects to him. He compares his lot bitterly to that of other, more amenable, exiled Indian princes. British officials have long anticipated the king's death. When this happens, the governor general assumes complete authority to dismantle the Garden Reach estate, which is rapidly sold off to shipping and railway companies for development.

In the autumn of 1874, the Calcutta correspondent of the *New York Times* persuaded Mowbray Thomson to get permission for him to visit Garden Reach. The correspondent's name was not given, although he had something of a scoop. His vivid (if sometimes erroneous) description of the estate and its ruler was published in November of that year.[1] American readers were presented with an exotic miniature kingdom on the banks of the Hugli. The British government could not interfere in it, readers were told, except over legal matters, and 'within the four walls of the Ex-King of Oude's mimic kingdom … the King is supreme. His kingdom, though small, is compact. His subjects are in all about 6,000, and devoted to him. His court is perfect in form. His officers of state, several of the chief of whom accompanied us over the grounds, have their titles and gradations as they …

had in Oude.' After describing the menagerie and serpentarium at great length and before listing the numbers of royal women, the ex-king's routine was noted. 'He spends his days in his menagerie, and in drawing, painting, and writing poetry. His songs are said to be excellent, according to native taste...' Wajid 'Ali Shah's evenings were spent among musicians and dancing girls, when the buildings were lit with 'innumerable small lamps of different colours', reflected in glass balls hung from the ceilings. One of the three principal houses would be selected for the next twenty-four hours and here the king would spend a day and night—'Calcutta meanwhile as ignorant of his pleasures and he of its as if he were still in Oude.' All this of course entailed lavish expenditure, and the correspondent was not the first to note that 'the King maintains a little town, providing the elite of it with choice amusement, and the whole town with amusement of some sort, in addition to providing them with the means of living. The little camp is, in its way, royal—as Eastern peoples understand royalty.'

There was, as the correspondent implied, something almost magnificent in the king's refusal to acknowledge changing times. A few miles outside the walls of his small kingdom lay the capital of British India, at that time the largest city in the subcontinent, with an estimated population of over 400,000 people. Then, as now, Calcutta was a place of radical, even revolutionary ideas—a city of poets, musicians, cooks, intellectuals, traders and businessmen. The Bengal Chamber of Commerce had been set up in 1856, municipal government was in place from the 1840s, and the Indian Museum and the Asiatic Society of Bengal had their origins in the late eighteenth and early nineteenth centuries. While it is understandable that the Hindu-led Bengal Renaissance would not be of much interest to a Muslim monarch still intent on keeping up the style of the great Mughals, there were innovations in the fine arts and drama that might have attracted his attention.

A MIMIC KINGDOM

By the 1870s there were a number of theatres in town, both Indian and British. While Britons enjoyed popular Gilbert and Sullivan operas like *The Pirates of Penzance* at the Corinthian Theatre, innovative Parsi theatre companies were providing dramas for an Indian audience. Their repertoire included *Fasana Ajaib* (The Strange Tale), and by the summer of 1875 the Parsi Operatic and Dramatic Company was performing at the Theatre Royal in Chowringhee. Among its productions was a popular medieval romance, *The Fairy Drama of Gul Bakavli*, followed by 'the Splendid Opera of Indur Sabha under the patronage of the Jewish Community'. There was also the dramatisation of a long narrative poem, *Qissai Benazir aur Badremunir* (The Story of Benazir and Badremunir) by Mir Ghulam Hasan, performed by the Parsi Elphinstone Dramatic Club.[2] Its author was a Lucknow poet who had composed the *Qissai* during the reign of nawab Asaf-ud-daulah. No reports have been found to suggest that Wajid 'Ali Shah ever visited the Calcutta theatres, although he is said to have seen seen a Hindu drama, *The Victory of the Pandavas*, at the Basu family home in Bagbazar. He could also summon the theatre to him, and it is likely that Parsi dramatic groups did perform at Garden Reach, providing one of the 'choice amusements' that entertained the courtiers on soft Bengal evenings.

Wajid 'Ali Shah had established his own household entertainers too, according to his last major work, *Musammat Banni*, published in 1875. There were the twenty-four Sultan Khana Players, named after his principal residence; eleven members of the Khas Manzil troupe; and various other groups, including the mimics (*naqi walian*), showmen (*tamasha walian*) and the *marsiyah* troupe, who recited mourning poems during Muharram. The performers numbered 216 and, together with 145 musicians, their salaries came to nearly £1,300 a month.[3] Costumes, scenery and prizes for the best performers were an extra expense. The great days of the Qaisarbagh performances could not be repeated, but there were certainly a number of musical entertainments held in Garden Reach and directed by the king. A revival of the Radha Krishna play was staged, with the actors in elaborate costumes and jewellery. While the fairy chorus wore Indian dresses and embroidered wings, the demon in the play, Ifrit, appeared as an Englishman in formal black jacket and trousers, and wearing gloves.[4] His appearance must have provoked howls of laughter and recognition.

But apart from entertainments, what bound the court-in-exile together? The Calcutta correspondent reported that Wajid 'Ali Shah's 6,000 subjects were devoted to him. 'The people employed are more than feudal retainers; they belong to the ex-King, body and soul.' Was this an oriental exaggeration to titillate American readers, or a practical description of a community that revolved around one man? Certainly there was employment for a good number of people, simply to maintain the estate.[5] There were gardeners and sweepers, menagerie staff, stable-hands, dairymen, water carriers, carriage drivers, engineers, lamp-lighters, 'the boat establishment', guards, police, door-keepers, messengers, carpenters and bearers. To run the estate a general manager was needed, who in turn employed staff in charge of various departments, including the Postal Department and the paymaster's department, dealing with wages and other financial claims. The admirable Amir 'Ali had managed the estate until his death in January 1880. After that no one seems to have been specifically appointed to oversee Garden Reach. The king's many wives needed their own female staff, and the king needed his palace staff including cooks, kitchen-hands, confectioners, sweet-makers, people to prepare paan and the hookah, valets, washermen, tailors, a doctor and personal servants. Spiritual and intellectual needs were catered for by maulawis, munshis, men employed to chant the Qur'an, *ta'ziyah*-makers, poets and artists. A small bazaar was built along Garden Reach Road and rented out by the estate to shopkeepers, who would have included butchers, grain merchants, fishmongers and vegetable sellers, bringing stock in daily from the big Calcutta markets.

All these employees provided necessary services to keep Garden Reach running. But there was something more here that marked it out from the usual run of satellite townships. If Wajid 'Ali Shah saw himself as the last king in India, then his courtiers had to believe this too. They remained loyal, even as it became increasingly clear that the kingdom of Awadh would never be restored and that the majority of them would never see Lucknow again. Although his personal life was less than happy, with his quarrelling, disloyal wives and sons, nevertheless the king possessed sufficient authority and personality to ensure that while he lived, so did his small kingdom. He was not given credit for this by the British; indeed, it would have negated the very act that deposed him in 1856. While government officials continued to anticipate his death, which did not happen until 1887 when he was sixty-six years old, they complained about his behaviour and extravagance without considering his achievements in holding together a sizeable establishment that lasted for thirty years. Clearly money had something to do with it, and a number of people made a lot of money from the king. But where information is available, the wages for his domestic staff were not excessive. Although rent was not charged for accommodation within Garden Reach, living conditions were far from luxurious for many who had come from Lucknow, leaving family houses behind. The usual perks for courtiers could no longer be handed out. There could be no more grants of land (jagirs), no state offices to hold, and thus no opportunities for making money, no more palaces to be built, and no small private armies to command. Yet something intangible held the little kingdom together still, and as long as Wajid 'Ali Shah behaved like a king, then the illusion remained.

If the continued existence of the kingdom was a secular act of faith, then was Wajid 'Ali Shah seen as a religious focus for

Shi'as? Sharar hints that the Muharram processions in Calcutta were even grander than those of Lucknow days, and he claimed that thousands of pilgrims were attracted to them.[6] On the other hand British officials spoke only of 'noisy processions on the high road', without specifying what these processions were. Wajid 'Ali Shah had begun building the Sibtainabad Imambarah, which would house his tomb, in the early 1860s, and it was completed by 1864. This was a public imambarah, second only in importance to the great imambarah upriver at Murshidabad. Although greatly different in style, size and cost, the Calcutta imambarah can stand comparison, in religious terms, with the Great Imambarah at Lucknow, built by the nawab Asaf-ud-daulah in 1784. It was a visible affirmation of Wajid 'Ali Shah's commitment to his faith. It provided a haven, in a foreign and sometimes hostile environment, for Shi'as, and it immediately became the centre of Muharram rituals, in which the king participated. Here the huge and elaborate *ta'ziyah* (replica tomb) was housed during the year, to be taken out in procession on the fourth day of mourning to the Shahi (royal) burial ground, along Garden Reach Road.[7] Two days later, a second procession would accompany the *ta'ziyah* to the burial ground again, before returning to the imambarah. India is a land of constant processions, and the commemoration of Muharram by a Shi'a king in exile does not seem to have evoked any descriptions or any illustrations. Yet we cannot dismiss the attraction that Wajid 'Ali Shah had for Shi'as in Bengal. He spent freely on Muharram, with almsgiving and food for the poor, and he led the recitation of mourning songs with his marsiya troupe. The fact that Muharram is still extravagantly marked by Shi'as in Kolkata today is continuing evidence of Wajid 'Ali Shah's influence.[8]

How did the king see himself in his now diminished role? Apart from his still palatial surroundings (not shared by everyone at Garden Reach), his large family, his courtiers, his pension and his entertainments, what other signs of royalty remained?

A MIMIC KINGDOM

While we have a good number of Wajid 'Ali Shah's own books and his correspondence with British officials, we have virtually no evidence of letters written to his peers.[9] As a prolific writer, he would certainly have corresponded with other royal or quasi-royal households in India. While he was officially barred from contacting people in Awadh, we know there were links with the once-powerful house of Murshidabad, which lay upstream on the same river that flowed past Garden Reach, and there were similar connections with Hyderabad in the south. Unfortunately archives and private collections that may contain material are often poorly catalogued and cannot easily be searched without several years of dedicated work. We have mainly to rely, for the moment, on records in the National Archives of India, Delhi, and the India Office Library, London, which of necessity were formal documents. These do, however, drop a few hints about Wajid 'Ali Shah's reactions to his reduced status.

Wajid 'Ali Shah was to retain the title of 'king' during his lifetime, but it would not pass to his sons. There was nervousness among the British when the title of 'heir apparent' was used for his eldest son, because this might imply that there was a kingdom to inherit. Officials were punctilious in referring to Wajid 'Ali Shah as 'the king', sometimes as 'the ex-king' but always as 'His Majesty', whatever their private feelings may have been. An early example of the delicate protocols surrounding an 'ex-king' came immediately on his arrival in Calcutta. As we have seen, there was initial confusion when the new governor general's staff refused to acknowledge his presence, because they had not been informed of it 'in the proper manner'.[10] However, when the 21-gun salute was eventually fired to mark Wajid 'Ali Shah's arrival in Calcutta, it was to be his last salute. Many years later, in 1869, within days of the appointment of a new governor general, the Earl of Mayo, Wajid 'Ali Shah put in a request for the revival of the 21-gun salute previously fired in his honour. He said it was 'necessary for the preservation of my honor and dignity and the friendship existing between the [two] Governments rendered stable and firm'.[11] This was incendiary language, suggesting that Wajid 'Ali Shah was the head of a government on a par with that of the British government in India. It was an opportunist move too, in the belief that Mayo, without the Indian background of his predecessor, John Lawrence, might grant the king's request from the ignorance of a newcomer. Luckily for Mayo, his advisors were on hand to give him the background to the case, and surprisingly it was revealed that Wajid 'Ali Shah had visited the former governor general at Government House. The date of the meeting and the discussion between the two men is not known. Lawrence spoke Hindustani well enough to make public speeches, so there would have been no need for an interpreter. Moreover, it had been made clear beforehand that the meeting was a private interview, and the king was brought into Government House through a private entrance. The point that Durand, the Secretary to the Foreign Department, wanted to make was that no salute guns had been fired on this occasion, nor would there be on any other occasion involving the king.

Only three Indian rulers were entitled to a 21-gun salute: Hyderabad, Baroda and Mysore. Other rulers got lesser salutes, from 15 to 11 guns, depending on how they had behaved during the Uprising. The loss of the king's salute caused him particular pain because before his downfall he had stood second in the order of precedence only to the king of Delhi. Queen Victoria herself had agreed the 21-gun salute for Wajid 'Ali Shah. On the recommendation of the pre-1858 government of India, he had been placed in front of five other rajas and nizams.[12] Durand explained that the king's salute had not been taken away because of suspicions about his behaviour during the Uprising, but because the British government had dethroned him after his refusal to sign the treaty of February 1856 and 'had assumed to itself the government of Oude exclusively and for ever'. It was 'impolitic to continue to him an honor calculated to nurse vain hopes of restoration'.[13] Although the Awadh mission to England had failed, it was imperative that the government did nothing that could be construed as an admission that the ex-king might indeed have a claim.

It was purely an act of grace on the government's part, continued Durand, that Wajid 'Ali Shah could continue to hold the title 'King of Oude', and 'it is pure pretension on his part to talk of the friendship existing between the Governments being rendered stable and firm'. The 21-gun salute that had been extracted on the king's arrival in Calcutta was not an acknowledgment for him as head of the Awadh government, but 'a consideration of the personal dignity of the King', and definitely not a proof of friendship between two governments. Durand argued well, if speciously. He warned darkly that 'there is a class who make political capital out of every slip of the British Government of this kind and it is an imperative duty on the Government of India to guard against the endorsement of covert pretensions of this description, for no-one can predict how soon they may be turned against the Government and blossom into very unexpected results'. Exactly which class of troublemakers Durand had in mind is not clear, and whether they were in Britain, which had just elected a Liberal government headed by Gladstone, or on the borders of Afghanistan, as Russia punched its way south, devouring the old Central Asian kingdoms. At all events, Wajid 'Ali Shah's request was refused as being pretentious, 'as if he were still an independent or allied Sovereign, exercising authority and wielding substantial power'.[14]

Perhaps in order to show that he bore no personal ill feeling towards the king, the Earl of Mayo did accept an invitation from him to visit Garden Reach. This took place within a few months of the governor general's arrival in India, probably during April 1869, and it was a formal, present-giving meeting. We do not know what Wajid 'Ali Shah gave Mayo, but in return he got '1 silver-gilt inkstand, 1 gilt and glass flower vase, 2 hand mirrors,

1 enamelled tea cup with saucer and spoon, 1 enamelled jewel box and 1 enamelled *paan* box', which the agent of the time, Captain Randall had been sent out to buy.[15] The king's letter of thanks for the gifts, even when translated from Persian to English, was almost unintelligible in its effusiveness: 'the inkstand of the choicest workmanship, which is the box for the production of the pearl of the essence of friendship ... the coffee cup with spoon and saucer, which is the means of removing idleness from the brain for the preservation of amity ...[may] the gurgling sounds of the goblet of supremacy of your Lordship, firmament-like high in dignity, caused by the wine of justice and the protection of subjects, remain for ever unceasing and that through the instrumentality of the Agent Sahib Bahadur [Captain Randall], all my desires, aspirations, and requirements be represented to the mind of your Lordship, exalted as the Heavens'.[16] Captain Randall joked that this was a 'truly Oriental epistle' and sent a spare copy for Mayo.

Although in British eyes Wajid 'Ali Shah was no longer head of his government, this did not stop him from writing similarly flowery letters to British royalty and to the governors general. The Earl of Elgin, on his short-lived appointment, got a letter of congratulation 'as writing is ever the means of shewing what is in the heart, this letter of congratulation is submitted to your Lordship that it may call to mind the obedient friend and represent that which is in the heart of his [Elgin's] sincere well-wisher'.[17] On the death of Lady Canning from malaria in 1861, the grief-stricken Governor General received a *taziatnamah*, a letter of condolence. 'The world is a dream of which death is the interpretation. Young and old are alike a prey to the appointed time ... Ah! As death, the destroyer of pleasures, is in fear of no-one and as the arrow shot from the bow of the archer Death can be stopped by no shield, what can be done? At the time of the approach of so intense a grief what can the wisest man do further than sew up the lacerations of the heart with the needle of resignation and submission, and if a friend does not anoint the wounds of the afflicted heart with the salve of patience, what can he do?'[18] On Prince Albert's death in 1862, Queen Victoria also received a *taziatnamah* that began: 'On hearing the mournful intelligence of the departure of His Royal Highness Prince Albert, the exalted in rank, to the wide realms of death, the lament of pain and grief has pierced the artery of the five senses, and the gasp of boundless grief and sorrow has rent the skirt of the garment of tranquility and repose as has never before happened.'[19]

There were happier occasions, too, for penning a letter, a habit that the king kept up throughout his life. On 2 March 1882 there was an unsuccessful assassination attempt on Queen Victoria at Windsor railway station, the sixth such assault during her long reign. The queen was unhurt, and the attack brought an outpouring of sympathy. 'It is worth being shot at—to see how much one is loved', Victoria is reputed to have told her daughter. The news brought another letter from Wajid 'Ali Shah, this time a *mohubutnamah* (a friendly letter). It arrived in a bag with his seal attached, and was presented in a silver roll wrapped in a *kincob* of silk and gold thread. 'Her Most brilliant luminous Majesty, whose towers resemble the sky and whose stirrups the new moon…' it began, and went on to refer to her as 'the proprietress of the Kingdom of England and the Empress of Hindustan'.[20] Her eldest son, the Duke of Connaught, received a letter of congratulation on being awarded a new title; and Lord Ripon, appointed governor general in August 1880, was welcomed with a congratulatory letter, and then a letter of sympathy when he fell ill a year later. Although the king's letters were written expressing his own views and feelings, underneath all the elaborate Persian similes and archaic forms of address remains the impression of a man writing to his peers, and expecting his letters to be read, if not necessarily answered.

Wajid 'Ali Shah was only one of a number of rulers who had been deposed by the East India Company, but he was the one who made the most strenuous efforts to retain his court around him. In 1799 Tipu Sultan, the ruler of Mysore, had been killed in the last of four wars launched against him by the British. His wives and sons were allowed to remain at Vellore Fort, as pensioners of the East India Company. Seven years after Tipu Sultan's death, there was a short, brutal uprising by sepoys against Company soldiers at the Fort, and a son of the late ruler was put forward as a successor to his father. The revolt was immediately put down in an equally brutal manner by the Company's army, and the surviving relatives were deported to Calcutta in 1806. It was policy to move rebellious rulers and their heirs far away from their power-bases and into Company territory. This was a clever ploy, because it meant firstly that the lines of support for men who opposed the Company were severed; secondly that the heirs and relatives, who could have become a focus for renewed unrest, could be closely monitored; and lastly it produced an intangible but demoralising feeling of loss on being removed from familiar surroundings.

There had been a number of such shifts. The Maratha *peshwa* Baji Rao II was exiled from Poona to Bithur, a small village on the banks of the Ganges, just north of the British cantonment at Cawnpore. The exile took place in 1818, after the peshwa's defeat in the third Anglo-Maratha War. His establishment of relatives and followers was considerably larger than that of Wajid 'Ali Shah, being estimated at some 15,000 people who were spread out in an area of some six square miles. Although this exile had happened almost forty years before the deposition in Awadh, and in very different circumstances, there was a curious parallel which, because the Company was so bound up with precedence, may have influenced its treatment of Wajid 'Ali Shah. The peshwa was awarded a very large pension of 8 lakhs a year (£80,000). This hitherto unprecedented sum was defended by Major General Sir John Malcolm, who had led the British to victory over the peshwa. Malcolm thought the pension was justified because of 'our own dignity, considerations for the feelings of Badjee Rao's adherents, and for the prejudices of the natives of India. We exist on impressions; and on occasions like this, where all are anxious spectators, we must play our part well or we should be hissed.'[21] The governor general of the time, the Marquess of Hastings, allowed the pension to the peshwa to be offered because he thought Baji Rao, then in his forties and having 'dissolute habits', did not have very much longer to live.[22]

This could almost be a blueprint for justifying the pension offered to Wajid 'Ali Shah on the surrender of Awadh and the British notion, repeated down the years that Wajid 'Ali Shah's days were numbered too because of his 'dissolute' lifestyle. Because it had not been made clear to the peshwa that the annual 8 lakhs pension and his title would cease on his death, his adopted son, Nana Sahib, demanded that both be continued to him. This was refused, in spite of a well-publicised journey to England by the Nana's advisor, Azimullah Khan, and it was the chief cause of the Nana's violent revolt at Cawnpore in 1857. It also explains why the government frequently reiterated that the title of 'king' would cease on Wajid 'Ali Shah's death, together with his pension.

Other deposed rulers, or rulers who had opposed the Company, generally suffered the same fate. The amirs of Sindh, who were treated even more shabbily than most after Sindh was annexed by the Company in 1843, were exiled first to Poona, then to Calcutta, where they arrived the following summer and settled down at Dum Dum. There was severe criticism in Britain of the Company's treatment of the amirs and their families. Their state wealth was seized from the treasury, as well as their personal possessions. To mollify public opinion, a generous pension was settled on them and, unusually, those who survived were allowed to return to Hyderabad (in Sindh), arriving home in the summer of 1855.[23] Others were not so lucky. The Maharaja Duleep Singh, heir to the Sikh kingdom, was deposed by the Company when he was a young lad of eleven years old. He was exiled from Lahore to Fatehgarh, a small town on the Ganges, above Cawnpore, and put under the guardianship of Dr John Login and his wife before choosing to settle in England.[24] The last Mughal emperor Bahadur Shah Zafar, was exiled to Burma accompanied by a few relatives after the failure of the revolt at Delhi in 1857. Conversely, the Burmese royal family arrived at Ratnagiri in the Bombay Presidency after their defeat in the Third Anglo-Burmese War of 1885–6. It all seemed like a gigantic chessboard, with real kings and queens being moved around by British players.

Wajid 'Ali Shah's case was unusual, in that he had not been forced out of Awadh on its annexation. He chose to go to Calcutta, but having got there was not allowed to return to Lucknow.[25] Because the Mysore princes, Tipu Sultan's descendants, were also in exile in Calcutta, comparisons were inevitably made between the head of their family, Prince Ghulam Muhammad, and the newly arrived king of Awadh. The fact that the British agents to the king also acted as agents to the Mysore princes made this easier. Ghulam Muhammad had the advantage of having settled in Calcutta exactly half a century before Wajid 'Ali Shah arrived. He had built two handsome mosques there in memory of his father. Both still stand today: one in central Calcutta, completed about 1832 and named the Tipu Sultan Shahi mosque, the other on the road to Tollygunge and the Russapuglah suburb where the Mysore princes had settled on their arrival. Here, too, there had been garden houses built for the British, including the present-day Tollygunge Club, originally home to a British indigo planter. The Mysore princes and their families were poorly lodged at first in bungalows, and it was almost entirely due to Ghulam Muhammad that their position improved. He visited England at least twice to plead for increased pensions, bringing gifts for Queen Victoria and her children. He was finally successful in 1860 when the Secretary of State for India, Sir Charles Wood, agreed a one-off settlement of over £500,000, to be invested, with the interest to be a 'perpetual endowment' for Tipu's descendants.

The size of the sum caused protests both in Britain and Calcutta, but Wood justified it to the House of Commons, pointing out it would solve the family's financial problems once and for all, and adding that the British government had a 'moral obligation … to provide in a fair and liberal manner for these persons'.[26] During the 1860s the Mysore family thrived, living in Tollygunge and owning land where the Royal Calcutta Golf Club stands today. In addition they bought houses in other parts of Calcutta, including six houses at Alipore which were rented out. A sociable life with the cream of British society was enjoyed too. 'Prince Gholam Mahomed's Ball comes off on the 15th and is sure to be most enjoyable', gossiped *The Pioneer* in January 1867.[27] The Ball was given in honour of the governor general, Sir John Lawrence, and his wife Lady Lawrence, who were greeted at the door by the prince and his son, Feroze Shah. The following month another huge ball took place for the departing lieutenant governor of Bengal, Sir Cecil Beadon, and his wife, when five hundred guests were present. Shortly before his death in 1872, Prince Ghulam Muhammed was awarded the title of Knight Commander of the Order of the Star of India by Queen Victoria, an order created after the Uprising to honour Indian chiefs and princes, as well as British administrators.

None of this went down very well with Wajid 'Ali Shah. In a prolonged outpouring to the Governor General, the Marquess of Ripon, he bitterly compared his lot with that of the Mysore princes: 'these pension holders are no other than persons who rose in arms against the British Government and stained their hands with blood, as its avowed enemies. But in my case, it may be truly said that I was created in this world of trial and probation only to obey and carry out the orders of the British Government and I have, to the best of my knowledge, never given it any cause of offence. I surrendered my territories without fighting and bloodshed, and never murmured at the indignity of being placed in confinement in Fort William without any reason. Further, in consideration of the pecuniary assistance which my forefathers rendered to the British Government at times of need, not a farthing was added to my pension. Again ever since the surrender of my Kingdom of Oudh, I have not received a single pice in the shape of interest, on the debts due by the East India Company for which I hold in [my] hands bonds under the signature of preceding Governors General. For these reasons, there is, and shall be, none in all India so much entitled to the kind indulgence of the government in this country, and to the favourable consideration of her Imperial Majesty in England.

If I had not been made homeless, I should not have come to my present pitiable and distressed condition. Just and impartial historians perhaps have written that I have made a *nazar* or present of my Kingdom, wealth and all, to Government, in [a] true spirit of allegiance.'[28]

No-one reading this today could deny the king's right. No one reading this today could deny the king's right to feel angry and cheated. Everything he said was true. But why was he treated so differently from the Mysore princes, with whom he chose to compare himself? The answer is complex and bound up with the attitudes and beliefs of officials at the head of the British government in India, attempting to justify the actions of its predecessor, the East India Company. Prince Ghulam Muhammad's father, Tipu Sultan, had died a hero's death, fighting to the last, and was struck down defending his palace at Seringapatam. Although his earlier treatment of captured British soldiers was deplorable, nevertheless there was a recognition at home and in India that his death marked a watershed in the history of Mysore.

A number of intensely dramatic paintings of the event were exhibited by British artists in the early 1800s, including 'The

A MIMIC KINGDOM

Last Effort and Fall of Tippoo Sultan' by Henry Singleton and 'Finding the Body of Tippoo Sultan' by Samuel Reynolds. There was something almost noble, almost classical, in the depiction of the sultan's death. His palace was comprehensively looted by Company soldiers and sepoys, and relics of the sultan, including clothes, weapons and his throne, were brought to Britain. Perversely, the odd British trait of expressing sympathy for a defeated enemy led to a grudging respect for the manner in which Tipu Sultan met his death. In contrast, Wajid 'Ali Shah surrendered his kingdom in 1856 without a shot being fired, or indeed any pictorial representations at all, until the Indian director Satyajit Ray filmed the scene for *The Chess Players* in 1977, a fictionalised account of the annexation of Awadh.[29]

Although this timid surrender was highly convenient for the East India Company, who had threatened and plotted it for two decades, it was hardly the stuff of legend. This was compounded by the impression that the king had ducked out of going to England in person to plead his cause, and instead had sent his elderly and ailing mother. Although this was not entirely true, as we have seen, it was another black mark against him. By contrast, the urbane Ghulam Muhammad had persuaded the Secretary of State for India to take up his case. The Mysore prince spoke English and was well integrated into Calcutta society. He had no band of exiled courtiers around him. Wajid 'Ali Shah chose not to compete, but contented himself by sending flowery Persian letters to English royalty and governors.

Another British trait, not entirely extinguished even today, was a dislike of anything too 'arty' or culturally pretentious. This went hand in hand with a robust distrust of intellectuals. Although the king could not claim to be among the latter, he was certainly among the former. The musical events at Garden Reach were not accessible to the British, either physically, because they were not invited, or culturally, because Indian drama and music were not at that time widely appreciated by foreigners. The days when a British Resident could be entertained by a nautch in a rich man's house were long gone. Wajid 'Ali Shah had been labelled as a weak and dissolute ruler before he came to the throne. Thus all these feelings—wrong impressions, irrational prejudices, non-comprehension—were added up against him. The very thing that Wajid 'Ali Shah perceived as a virtue, his obedience to the British government, seemed to count for little. There was also the irritant of his frequently reminding that same government of the huge financial loans made to it by him and his forefathers. No one likes to be reminded that they owe money, not even governments, particularly when the sums cannot easily be paid back.

Very little sympathy was shown by British officials to Wajid 'Ali Shah in his declining years. He had become 'a querulous old man not altogether responsible for the working of his representations', the governor general was informed in 1886.[30] Colonel V. E. Law, acting agent, agreed: 'The King is not in good health, and at best, looking to the kind of life he has left, cannot have many years of this world left to him ... he is very obstinate and very obstructive and very troublesome. But his position was not always what it is now, and whatever liberality may now be shown to him will hardly be a charge in the revenues for many years.'[31] The assistant secretary to government at Fort William conceded that 'The King has been unfortunate in his life and he is a soured and discontented man.' He was also, by July 1886, 'very infirm for his age, and, in the last hot season especially, suffered very much from ill-health'.[32] Colonel Prideaux, as permanent agent, told Dufferin that 'instead of being surrounded in his old age by his children and their families, the King lives in the midst of a band of parasites and harpies who on receiving the first symptom of his approaching dissolution, would make it each his business to appropriate what spoil he could'.

From a photograph of Wajid 'Ali Shah taken in old age it seems he had never lost any of the weight acquired as a young man. In later life he took no exercise at all and was carried everywhere in a sedan chair, while remaining committed to his hookah and paan. He is reported to have suffered from an anal fistula, causing him to spend many painful hours on the commode. There is not enough written evidence to show the cause of Wajid 'Ali Shah's death, but a suggestion that he had been poisoned by one of his ministers can be dismissed. Everyone at Garden Reach knew that with the king's death their lives, too, would be irrevocably altered.

Wajid 'Ali Shah died at 2.00 a.m. on 21 September 1887 in a room on the ground floor of the Sultan Khana, opening into a small court which was full of monkeys and pigeons.[33] It was the beginning of Muhurram, the month of mourning. A messenger was immediately sent with the news from Garden Reach to Colonel Prideaux's home in Alipore Lane. Shortly before 7.00 a.m. the telegraph office in Park Street was opened and the news transmitted to the Viceroy, the Earl of Dufferin, at Viceregal Lodge, Shimla. The first telegram, number 06893 and marked 'Urgent', was sent at 6.55 a.m. and read simply, 'King of Oude died this morning. All quiet.'[34] This was followed a minute later by telegram 06894 from the commissioner of police to the Foreign Secretary, Durand, advising him that the 'King of Oude died last night. Police down there sharp all quiet.'

The police presence was more to prevent the king's relatives and servants from looting their late master's property than to put down any disturbances that might flare up at Garden Reach. Indeed, a newspaper editorial in *The Statesman* a week before Wajid 'Ali Shah's death reported that 'while he lies abed his attendants seem to be helping themselves to his effects. It is even hinted that his goods are being removed by the cart-load.'[35] But there was always the possibility, in the minds of British officials, that trouble could break out now that the head of the little kingdom was no more. The king had been scrupulously monitored during his thirty-year exile. His actual potential for causing trouble was considerably over-rated by the British, but old habits died hard and the fact that the king was now dead too did not diminish, in British eyes, his capability for causing unrest in India.

Although it had been made quite clear to Wajid 'Ali Shah that the title of 'king' ceased with him, there was the possibility that his eldest surviving son, Prince Qamar Qadr, might take it into his head to declare himself the new king. It was, after all, a short step from being a prince to becoming a king on the death of one's father. The government had a fear, fuelled by suspicion, that a court-in-exile might be formed at Garden Reach, which already contained hundreds of armed followers. It would have been a huge embarrassment if a focus for malcontents became established no more than five miles from Government House, particularly while its occupant was enjoying the summer in Shimla. The lieutenant governor of Bengal was also absent, having moved to the hill station of Darjeeling for the hot weather. Alerted by Colonel Prideaux, the lieutenant governor also sent a telegram to Shimla, timed at 9.15 a.m. Three-quarters of an hour later, Dufferin received his third telegram of the morning, from Khas Mahal, first wife of the king and now his widow. This was not only to inform the Viceroy of her husband's death, but to throw herself on his mercy. 'Now I have no protection but God and Your Excellency and her most gracious Majesty [Queen Victoria] whom God preserve ... I trust that my widowed condition will meet with your warm sympathy. Reply prepaid two rupees.'[36]

Dufferin did not rise to the bait of the pre-paid reply, but instead telegraphed Colonel Prideaux asking him to convey his sincere condolences to the wives and family of the late king. He also asked Durand to telegraph the news to the Secretary of State for India in London. (A punctilious clerk enquired if the 2 rupees sent by Khas Mahal for the pre-paid reply should be returned to her, and was told not to be silly.) Colonel Prideaux was at Garden Reach by midday, and having assessed the situation, which was indeed 'all quiet', telegraphed Durand about arrangements for the funeral, which was to be held that same evening. Prideaux, careful not to waste money on superfluous words, suggested 'propriety of military escort at funeral of King Oude this evening'. His telegram, 07001, sent from the Garden Reach post office at 12.18 p.m. was marked 'Very urgent—any precedent?' Durand telegraphed back that there was no precedent. Indeed, how could there be? There had only been one king in India with a British-bestowed title, and now he was gone.

Time was too short to consult the Military Department, so Durand advised that there was 'no political objection to escort if local military authorities agree'. And if they did, then the authorities at Fort William were to act without waiting for further orders. So the king's body was escorted from Garden Reach along the road towards Calcutta, with all the British pomp that could be mustered at short notice. His corpse had been washed and wrapped in several sheets of fine linen, inscribed in red with verses from the Qur'an. The funeral procession, lit by flaming torches, started at about 10.00 p.m. as a large crowd gathered outside the gates of the estate. The promised escort of native soldiers was provided by the Loyal Poorbeah Regiment, their weapons reversed in mourning, following the bier which was carried aloft under a green canopy, supported at the four corners by spears. A military band played the solemn 'Dead March' from *Saul*, an oratorio by Handel, and this was accompanied by loud wailing and lamentations from the crowd—particularly from the king's retainers, dressed for the last time in their blue uniforms. The principal mourner leading the procession was the king's heir, Prince Qamar Qadr. It took the best part of an hour to reach the Sibtainabad Imambarah on Garden Reach Road. A Muslim correspondent for *The Statesman* described the mood of the crowd watching the funeral cortège pass by: 'The wailing cries were heard incessantly. The feeling was universal, and it has scarcely ever been my lot to witness so impressive and so mournful a scene. The entire Mahomedan community seemed to have felt a sense of personal calamity in the death of the King of Oudh.'[37]

On 22 September, the day following the king's death and funeral, a council meeting was held at Viceregal Lodge in Shimla. Its purpose was to ratify the final Act relating to Wajid 'Ali Shah, Act XIX, which was 'to provide for the Administration of the Estate of His late Majesty the King of Oudh'.[38] The Act was to have significant consequences for the late king's family and the Garden Reach estate. Its terms had been proposed more than a year earlier, in July 1886, when Colonel Prideaux had the foresight to write a long, detailed memorandum, anticipating the king's death and suggesting what should be done when it occurred. The government, he urged, needed to consider the 'proper devolution of the King's property on his death' in order to reduce the financial allowances to the numerous members of the family. When Prideaux drew up the memorandum there were twenty-one sons and twenty-six daughters surviving. Of the daughters, twenty were already married, which meant that the need for further dowries and marriage expenses, part-funded by the government, was reduced. But there were numerous grandchildren, the two nikah wives, Khas Mahal and Akhtar Mahal, and of course all the mut'ah wives.

Under Muslim law the two official wives and the forty-seven children were entitled to a share in the proceeds of the king's property, which included both moveable goods and the houses themselves. Very little in the way of jewels or valuables belonging to the king remained, as far as Prideaux knew. He thought that jewellery brought from Lucknow more than thirty years earlier had been 'probably distributed among [the king's] favourite wives', although this turned out subsequently not to be entirely true. In spite of his possessions and his numerous children, Wajid 'Ali Shah died intestate. He had not made a will up to the time of Prideaux's 1886 report, because of a 'superstitious dread of the consequence of such an act', and the agent thought it unlikely he would make one in the future. So government needed to act to avoid 'various interested parties' from losing out if there was a free-for-all, as well as to sidestep 'a goodly crop of litigation'.[39] Even if a Will *had* been made, there was no guarantee that litigation would not take place, so numerous and vociferous were the claimants.

The terms of Act XIX were uncompromising. They gave the governor general exclusive authority to act in the administration of property 'of whatever nature' left by the king. Dufferin was to settle all claims on the estate and to distribute the remaining property or proceeds among the king's family and dependants as he saw fit. Whatever the governor general decided could not be challenged in any Court of Law. In addition, Prideaux, as agent, could not be held liable for any actions he may have carried out since the day preceding the king's death, and no legal action could be brought against him. Anyone attempting to collect debts owed to them by the late king had to justify their actions to Prideaux first. The Act also specified 'that the winding up of the estate will include the closing of the large establishment at Garden Reach', and in view of the late king's 'peculiar legal position' steps were to be taken immediately to 'secure his property and to provide for its distribution without exposing it to the risk of robbery or the delays and costs of litigation'.[40] This is why Prideaux had rushed down to Garden Reach by midday on 21 September, in order to try to prevent any further looting of the palaces by servants and dependants.

There were an estimated four to five thousand people at Garden Reach, the majority of whom had been dependent on the king in one form or another, and who would now lose their livelihoods and living quarters. His wives, children and their servants accounted for nearly another thousand souls. A few weeks before the king's death his seals of office had been stolen from the palace, and it was suspected by Council members that these had already been used to 'authenticate' a number of false documents and to make fraudulent claims.[41] The 'enormous household' of the late king still had to be provided for. The more that was pilfered in the hours immediately after his death, the less there would be for his relatives, many of whom had no independent income at all.

This pre-emptive move by the governor general could be seen as the final act of spite against the king and all that he had represented. Certainly the Garden Reach estate was parcelled up and sold off fairly promptly, as we shall see. But harsh as it may seem, it did avoid the years and expense of claims that would have been made on the estate and the pathetic scenario of the king's widows living and dying penniless in the crumbling palaces. Sir Andrew Scoble, the legal representative on the Governor General's Council, helpfully pointed out that because the late king had benefited from previous Acts which had secured him special immunities and privileges, 'exceptional legislation' was now justified on his demise.[42]

Less than a month after the king's death a confidential letter was passed to Colonel Prideaux, who had been deputed to wind up the estate. 'In the event of the property at Garden Reach being sold', it began, it was possible that Messrs Gillanders, Arbuthnot & Company 'may be in a position to make an offer for a portion of it, and requesting that the matter be kept secret'.[43] Gillanders, Arbuthnot & Co., still a flourishing firm in Kolkata today, was established in the 1830s as an import and export business. Some of its exports at this period were Indian labourers, shipped overseas to work on plantations in British Guiana under a scheme which stopped just short of slavery. Robert Mitchell, the 'Emigration Agent for British Guiana', followed up the secret offer six months later. Mitchell was anxious to get his hands on the Badami Kothi at 24 Garden Reach Road, because he had heard from another trading company that the government's Agricultural Department had their eye on it.[44]

In winding up the Garden Reach estate, there were a huge number of things that Prideaux had to organise, and it all had to be done quickly, but also tactfully. The Secretary of State for

India, Viscount Cross, wrote to him personally on behalf of the British government. 'We wished the late King's premises and establishment at Garden Reach to be broken up as soon as possible. We were particularly anxious that any attempt to maintain the semblance of a court under the King's sons should be firmly repressed. At the same time it was our object to avoid as far as possible hurting the susceptibility of either the King's family or the Mohammedan community.'[45] The Colonel was advised to take the Shi'a Muhammedan law as a general guide.

There was a delicate balance to be struck in selling the late king's possessions and houses while his family were still in residence. Prideaux was adamant that the way forward was by auction sales held in the Garden Reach houses themselves, and he reported at the beginning of January 1888 that the auctions 'have so far caused no discontent'. All those things on which Wajid 'Ali Shah had lavished money—the silver-plated beds, the glassware, the chandeliers, the rich furnishings and much more—were knocked down to eager buyers. Everything went except those books, pictures and effects that Prideaux considered 'may possess historical interest'. He put these to one side as he prepared a 'special report' which was ready in May that year, when the auction sales of moveable property had been completed. The late king's library was transferred to the office of the Board of Examiners, a quasi-academic body whose duties including vetting candidates in Indian languages and approving suitable textbooks. Colonel Jarratt, secretary to the Board and a Persian scholar, offered to examine the collection, with the assistance of Maulawi Kabir-ud-din Ahmad. 'The more curious and valuable manuscripts will be priced at a fair and reasonable rate', reported Prideaux, who suggested they should be offered to the Lucknow Museum and similar institutions 'before they are thrown on the market'.[46] How many manuscripts there were we do not know, but the bulk of the collection formed works of a 'polemical character' which Prideaux suggested could go to the

Sibtainabad Imambarah 'after due precautions have been taken that they should not fall into the hands of the Sunnis'.

'The King possessed no pictures of historical interest', continued Prideaux, 'but I have reserved a few portraits of himself and his family, of which one, an oil painting taken by a native artist shortly after his accession to the throne of Oudh, might be presented to the Lucknow Museum, if the authorities of that institution desire to have it.[47] The others, which are of no value whatever might be distributed among the senior members of the family.' Having disposed of a lifetime's collection, Prideaux went on to examine the *tosha-khanah*, or wardrobe of Wajid 'Ali Shah. Not surprisingly, it was 'of large extent' and the agent gave it his close personal attention. Clothes which had actually been worn by the king were handed over to his eldest son, Prince Qamar Qadr, for distribution among old and deserving servants, as had been the custom at Lucknow on the ruler's death. A large quantity of Kashmir shawls were found, all perfectly new and never used, so these were auctioned. Six 'swords of State' and a few articles of jewellery went off to Messrs Hamilton & Co., also for auction. The only personal belongings that went to the prince were an illuminated Qur'an, to be retained as an heirloom in the family, one sword, and a ring, as suggested in the book *Mohammedan Law* by Sir William Macnaughton. Prideaux had conscientiously consulted this, on the advice of the Secretary of State for India; and just to make sure, he recorded the page number of the book, and the edition.

What Prideaux did not concern himself with were the papers in the *daftar*, the king's office, which held correspondence going back over thirty years. No archive of Wajid 'Ali Shah's personal papers has ever been discovered, nor even a rumour of one. Unless clerks took away the ledgers and files for sentimental reasons when the offices were being cleared, the most likely scenario is that they were sold as waste paper. Before the plastic bag appeared in India there was always a market for good quality used paper, which was folded and glued into sturdy bags for sweets, fruit and small items. Paper from printed books was usually too soft, or too small, to recycle as bags, but large documents on good paper, as these would have been, were in demand. The royal daftar clearly had an efficient copying and filing system, because the king would sometimes quote from letters he had sent, or received, years earlier. But all the office copies of the mohubutnamahs, the *purcha pyams*, the *taziatnamahs* and the petitions have disappeared. Their Persian originals are occasionally found, beautifully written, gold-flecked with painted borders, but carelessly folded and bound into British government records. Because the title of king, and by implication his Garden Reach kingdom, died with Wajid 'Ali Shah, there must have seemed little point in retaining papers from his office. His heir, Prince Qamar Qadr, would never have the authority to write to the governor general and the Queen Empress, Victoria, as his father had done. The British government had demanded that everything was to be cleared out in a rush. Clerks, messengers, calligraphers and gold-leaf specialists all lost their jobs on the king's death. What was simpler than calling in the *kabariwala*, the scrap dealer, to cart away so much useless paper and to receive a few rupees in return?

A problem that could not be so easily disposed of was the menagerie. Even though Wajid 'Ali Shah was devoted to his animals, he had made no provision for them after his death. Prideaux was informed in October 1887 that the animals and birds were rapidly dying off because none of their erstwhile keepers were looking after them or feeding them. Before the king's death, the agent had estimated that the most valuable items of his personal property were probably the menagerie and 'the machinery belonging to his water and gas works'. Now the first of these assets was in danger and William Rutledge, Calcutta's leading animal dealer, was called in. This was the same man who had been paid by the king to provide beasts and birds for the menagerie some years earlier, and who had a reputation as 'a keen practical naturalist' and a specialist in wild animals.

Auction sales were arranged for the inhabitants of the menagerie, the serpentarium and the aviary, and these took place in the winter of 1887–8. Rutledge was to receive 10 per cent of the sale price, and Prideaux said this was well deserved and that Rutledge had done a great deal of work in preparation for the auctions. He first had to catalogue the menagerie, then catch the large number of birds, many of which were 'loose about the premises'. About 18,000 pigeons were brought down from the terraces of the houses in Garden Reach, sorted and caged in pairs, or by the dozen. It was thought that the birds would achieve better prices caged than sold by the flock. The deer in the park were rounded up, and about a hundred peacocks that were 'flying about wild from the houses' were caught.[48] The animals and birds had to be fed while they were waiting to be sold off, and because Rutledge and his assistants had to remain on the premises to supervise this, Prideaux soon found extra tasks for the naturalist. He was put in charge of the late king's stable, his carriages and the cattle, as well as looking after the gas lights. Rutledge was also asked to keep an eye on the 4,000 servants still left at Garden Reach and make sure they did not tamper with articles in the houses while sales were taking place and inventories being made by Messrs Mackenzie Lyall & Co.'s men. It may have seemed an unlikely alliance between the colonel and the naturalist, but Prideaux was clearly hard-pressed and needed all the help he could get.

A few private sales were made before the animal auctions took place. The nawab of Bhawalpore bought some animals and birds, as did the 'Envoy of Cabul', the Afghan ambassador. Ram Brahma Sanyal, the king's old friend and director of the Alipore Zoological Gardens, bought two rhinoceros at 1,000 rupees each and a giant rat for 60 rupees. By February 1888 everything was gone—the cows, buffalo, sheep, goats and dogs, as well as the more exotic animals. Milton & Co. were the auctioneers, and Prideaux thought they had 'done rather well in the business'. The total sum raised was nearly £3,000, a respectable amount, but of course only a fraction of what Wajid 'Ali Shah had lavished on his lifelong hobby.[49]

The king's family, who by his own admission had taken second place in his heart to the menagerie, would have been left entirely unprovided for if the governor general had not assumed control of the estate through Act XIX. It was well known that relations between the king and his wives and children were very strained before his death. 'If the King had his own way, not one of them probably would benefit by any testamentary disposition of his estate', reported the Bengal government.[50] But under Shi'a law, which was being strictly applied by Prideaux, the two nikah widows, Khas Mahal and Akhtar Mahal, were the chief beneficiaries, followed by the sons and daughters, the latter receiving half that given to their brothers. The mut'ah wives were not entitled to anything.

The final count of close dependants who had relied solely on pensions from the king was made in December 1887, as follows:

- 2 nikah wives
- 33 mahals
- 176 begams
- 14 khilawatis
- 27 new begams (married since the date of the Committee's report in 1880)
- 22 sons
- 17 daughters
- 10 grandsons and nephews
- 7 granddaughters
- 6 daughters-in-law

Pensions for a single month totalled about £1,310.[51] The value of the silver rupee had fallen in real terms in the 1870s after the adoption by European countries of the gold standard. Although this did not affect the king's pension, and the amounts he paid to his dependants, it did mean that in relative terms pensions bought less than they had in the 1860s and imported goods became more expensive, leading to frequent royal complaints about not having enough money. Prideaux's immediate concern during the autumn of 1887 was how to fund the dependants before the estate and its contents had been sold and the final settlements made. There was the worry of the servants too, and their wages of £1,000 per month. This was partially solved by dismissing two-thirds of them at the end of October, including the menagerie staff. Former employees received a month's pay in lieu of notice, and Prideaux noted that 'the majority are taking advantages of the liberality of the Government to return to their own country', which sounds as if most of the staff did not come from British India. At any rate, the month's pay was useful, because it meant that they did not spend time hanging about in Calcutta and possibly causing trouble.[52]

By the end of January 1888, four months after the king's death, the establishment had been reduced to the following numbers:

- 1 general manager
- 6 departmental officers
- 7 clerks and mohurirs
- 7 men in the wages department
- 42 at the Sibtainabad Imambarah
- 26 police establishment
- 95 guards and pyadas
- 5 orderly sowars
- 3 boat establishment
- 9 chapprassis and hurkurras
- 2 engineers
- 15 stable establishment
- 150 bearers and other indoor servants
- 17 water carriers
- 159 gardeners
- 54 sweepers

Only sufficient staff would be retained 'to prevent the buildings and gardens from falling into disrepair and a defective sanitary state' before they were sold off.⁵³

Prideaux's most difficult task, however, came when he tried to separate the king's ladies from their jewellery, in order to add it to the estate. The system of loaning jewellery to the wives for special occasions has already been mentioned, and when Bhikan Khan, keeper of the royal jewels, was called on to surrender what he had, he replied he had nothing in his possession. Prideaux said that he did not believe him, but because the register of loans in the *peshkari* office had not been kept up to date, he had really no evidence to challenge Bhikan Khan.⁵⁴ Jewellery to the value of about £1,500 had gone missing among the mut'ah wives, and a list was circulated among them detailing what they had borrowed and requesting the return of the jewels. Not surprisingly no notice at all was taken of the list. On the contrary, some of the wives said they considered the jewellery to be their personal property, while others, rather bolder, said that they had sold their jewels and that the peshkari register was wrong. 'Not one has shown any inclination to return the jewellery', noted Prideaux dryly. He also learned that when Wajid 'Ali Shah gave favoured women large presents of jewellery which he intended them to keep as gifts, it was always confirmed by a firman or written order. By May 1888 it was clear that there was no point in pursuing the matter further, particularly because government officials thought 'it might have some appearance of harshness if we insisted on its [the jewellery's] restoration or the deduction of its estimated value from the ladies' shares and allowances'. It was agreed to give the mut'ah wives the benefit of the doubt.

There was, though, 'a matter of some delicacy' over the king's eldest, unmarried, daughter, Padshah Ara Kaniz ul-Hadi, known as Shahzadi Sahibah, who was about eighteen years old and had 'enjoyed a more than common share of her father's affections'.⁵⁵ As a result the princess had apartments in one of the newest and most richly furnished houses, as well as an additional allowance of 480 rupees a month, and she was also put in charge of many 'very valuable articles of jewellery'. When the princess was asked by Prideaux's assistant to produce her jewellery so that it could be properly assessed and catalogued, there were sulks and refusals. Eventually, after some disinclination, a succession of jewels were handed through the purdah screen, one by one, to be catalogued, but they had to be handed back to the young woman. In subsequent interviews, the independent-minded princess said that not only was she going to keep the jewels, but that she was entitled to choose her own residence and her own husband too—in that order. Shahzadi Sahibah wanted to marry one of her father's *darogas*, or superintendents, who had risen from a very humble background to a position of great influence. Henry Durand dealt personally with the situation. 'A most unsuitable marriage', he minuted, that would involve 'a flagrant violation of the feelings of the family and of Muhammadan susceptibilities in general'.[56] The couple were told that they would not get the usual marriage grant of 10,000 rupees if they defied Durand, and the princess was packed off to stay with her brother and sister-in-law, taking with her the jewellery and two of the gifts presented to her late father by Lord Mayo.

Lady Dufferin took her husband, the governor general, for a drive around the estate at the end of 1887 and noted in her diary how Prideaux was dealing with king's widows:

'His ladies were nearly as numerous as his animals, and they are now being despatched to their own homes as quickly as possible. They go at the rate of seven or eight a day, but there are still a great number left; and when [Dufferin] approached their habitation they collected behind some venetian shutters, and set to work to howl and weep with all their might. The effect was most extraordinary, but did not excite the pity it was intended to evoke. I am sure they will be much happier with their own little income, guaranteed by the British Government than they ever would have been shut up together, the slaves of an hard-hearted old man who cared more for his cobras and his wild beasts than he did for them.'[57]

As the houses were emptied, they were put up for sale. There was resistance from tenants and squatters living in huts at Bechali Ghat, one of the riverside jetties of Garden Reach, who refused to leave or to take on the monthly tenancy offered them by the government. In the end a suit had to be filed for possession of the site so that it could be put up to auction. The king's sons and heirs were consulted on the reserve prices for the houses, and the auctions were due to begin on 18 March 1888 when Prince Jehan Qadr asked that the Sultan Khana and the Goshai Sultani houses be excluded from the sale because they contained small mosques and imambarahs within their premises. The prince had already put potential buyers off purchasing Bengali Bazar, saying it contained a mosque and burial places. The superintendent of the twenty-four Parganas, Mr Upton, thought that the prince's request was 'frivolous' and merely an attempt to retain the palaces as a residence for himself and his brothers. Nevertheless, the government was still hypersensitive to Muslim opinion, particularly when a petition was presented from the community reiterating the prince's request. It would be 'a pity to rush a matter in which feelings run pretty high and damage may be done'.[58] There was also the worry that if two important lots were withdrawn from the auction, offers for the other properties would be lower.

The matter could have escalated into an unpleasant dispute. Senior Muslim clerics were consulted, who maintained that the Sultan Khana mosque continued to be a place of worship and was considered as *waqf* property—that is, land which could not be sold. Reluctantly, the government agreed to postpone the auction, but made it clear that the postponement was not because 'holy places' had been discovered, but because the questions raised by their alleged existence could not be settled before 18 March. Interesting arguments were employed by the government to resolve the case. An inspection had shown that the mosque in question had a flat roof, with no domes or minarets, and it was described as an imitation of the tomb of Imam Hussain at Karbala. It was found that there had been a similar dispute at Bhagalpore, where Muslims had required access to a mosque in a property which had been sold. In the end it was decided to 'fence off' the small, free-standing mosque. 'We can leave that alone, and sell the remainder', advised the government solicitor. 'Once the Sultan Khana is gone, I fancy the opposition will cease.'[59] The auction went ahead on 4 June, with a total reserve price on the properties of 9 lakhs, equivalent to some £60,000. Most of the existing properties bought by the king had appreciated in value over the years, and only in a few cases, like the Tafrih Bakhsh house at No. 26 Garden Reach Road, was the reserve price lower than that paid by Wajid 'Ali Shah on its initial purchase.

Much of the Garden Reach estate was bought by Messrs James Robinson and Morrison, two separate agents acting on behalf of a syndicate, whose main interests lay in shipping. The Port Commissioners were allocated part of the riverside from the Matiya Burj jetty to the Sultan Khana premises, and by the mid-1890s the headquarters of the Bengal Nagpur Railway (BNR) was established in the former garden houses. The Peninsular and Oriental Steam Navigation Company (today's P&O) bought property here, and houses No. 12 and 13 became the immigration offices for Fiji and Trinidad respectively. Railway lines and tidal docks have carved up the area, although the Sultan Khana itself survives, minus its southern portico, as the private residence of the railway's general manager. A little mosque also remains, thanks to the princes' insistence that it should not be sold, as well as two small imambarahs. The Shahi burial ground has not been so lucky and is a miserable, disputed area surrounded by factories, with only a few remaining tombs. The most visible reminder of Garden Reach is the Sibtainabad Imambarah, the king's burial place, on the newly renamed

Nawab Wajid Ali Shah Road. His tomb lies to the left of the main hall, in a small room enclosed by a glass and metal grill. Within the room are a red velvet throne-like chair with gilt arms and lion mask legs and a number of china jardinières which give an informal, almost homely, air. The tomb itself is marked by a *ta'ziyah*, and above it stand a silver dome or umbrella and fly whisks, the ancient symbols of royalty. Matiya Burj is classed today as a poor urban area, predominantly Muslim, with a substantial number of tailors, sweet-makers and small shopkeepers, many of whom claim descent from those who served the Garden Reach court.

As for the king's own descendants, not surprisingly there are a substantial number, including descendants of Birjis Qadr, the boy prince who was briefly the nominal head of Awadh during the Uprising. Understandably there are rifts between different branches of the family, just as there were during Wajid 'Ali Shah's time. Some are to do with property, or lawsuits, but others concern *'izzat*, that subtle word for honour and status, which is jealously guarded. Interviews with a few of the descendants uncovered charming, upper-class Indians engaged in business enterprises, education, medicine and good government jobs. Disappointingly they have virtually no family stories to tell about their revered ancestor. If the king seemed a distant figure to his many children, then he is even further removed from his descendants, although his memory remains a matter of pride: a king born out of his time.

Wajid 'Ali Shah remained aloof from entertainments in Calcutta, preferring to arrange his own musical performances at Garden Reach to entertain his courtiers and staff. The 'little kingdom' he built around him, although satisfying, prevented him from integrating into British India as other exiled princes had done. He continued to seek recognition of his royal status and wrote to Queen Victoria on friendly terms. On his death the government was anxious to dispose of Garden Reach and its inhabitants, both human and animal, as quickly as possible. All the king's possessions, including the palace archives, are dispersed or lost.

CONCLUSION

'There was a time when showers of pearls were trodden underfoot. Now I feel the cruel sun above and pebbles underfoot.'

                                Attributed to Wajid 'Ali Shah

As the Bengal Legislative Council gathered to meet early in December 1940 for the day's business, they were requested to stand for a minute to honour the memory of 'Prince Akram Hossain', who had died nearly two months earlier on 15 October. The Council had much on its mind. Although the outbreak of war in Europe was not to affect Calcutta directly, for the moment, there were unsettling events afoot.[1] The British would, eventually, leave India, and had been making arrangements to do so by devolving power from the centre to the provinces. This was to be welcomed, although there would be no move until the war was over, and in 1940 its outcome was far from certain, even with the support of Indian troops. The idea of India divided along religious lines, at first unthinkable, was slowly becoming a possibility. The Muslim League, founded at the start of the twentieth century, had started to speak of a new country to be called Pakistan. Nearer home, the trauma of Calcutta's loss of status when the capital was transferred to New Delhi had subsided, although the Bengal Chamber of Commerce was unforgiving.[2] Calcutta never regained its political nor its commercial former pre-eminence.

Who was the prince who had caused the honourable members to pause 'as a mark of respect to the memory of the illustrious deceased', as the Extract from Proceedings described him? He was in fact Prince Afsar-ul Mulk Mirza Mohamed Akram Hossain Bahadur, the only surviving son of Wajid 'Ali Shah, who had been a pupil in the king's madrassa (see Chapter Six). 'The Prince was a bachelor', continued the extract, 'and so his death has removed the last direct link of this province with the ancient Ruling dynasty of Oudh.' The prince had been born at Garden Reach in 1881, his mother being Mumtaz Mahal Sahibah, whom the king had married about 1873. As we have seen, the government of India, at the time of the prince's birth, had recommended that the king's children were no longer to be formally recognised, because the king was understood to be impotent. But this recommendation was tactfully ignored by the Legislative Council now. Prince Afsar-ul Mulk had been a model prince, exactly the kind of person that the British might have wished his father to become.

'He was a well-known social figure and took to public life at an early age, serving as the Sheriff of Calcutta,[3] Commissioner of the Calcutta Corporation, member of the Central Assembly and of the Council of State. In 1931 the prince acted for a time as a Member of the Executive Council of the Governor of Bengal. He was also connected with various associations, being a member of the Royal Asiatic Society of Bengal and the Bengal Flying Club.

'He was popular with both the Hindu and Muslim communities because of his sincere efforts at establishing communal harmony. In 1936, he was elected President of the All-India Shia Political Conference held at Lucknow, the capital of his forefathers. He had been in poor health for some time... May his soul rest in peace!'[4]

Afsar-ul Mulk would only have been a child at the time of his father's death, and given Wajid 'Ali Shah's declared aversion to

CONCLUSION

most of his family as he grew older, it is unlikely that there was much rapport between son and father. The young prince would have seen the king as a fat old man, almost unable to walk, lumbering around his menagerie and being rude to his wives. But perhaps something intangible had passed between the two that inspired the prince to strive for communal harmony, as his father had done in very different circumstances, almost a century earlier.

Wajid 'Ali Shah was the victim of a complicated set of British interests, but also a victim of poor timing, about which he could do nothing. He was damned from the start simply by his ancestors, whom the British considered dissolute and extravagant (with some justification, it has to be said). Geographically, the kingdom of Awadh was at first a useful buffer state in the lawless days of the late eighteenth century. By the mid-nineteenth century it had became an irritant as the East India Company remorselessly extended its territorial remit and saw Awadh as a large and inconvenient obstruction between Bengal and Delhi. It was 'ripe' for annexation at the peak of Company expansion in the 1850s, just as the king inherited the throne. Politically, public and official opinion at home in Britain, fuelled by lurid reports on rural Awadh and its sophisticated capital, demanded that something be done. The days when a rich Indian monarch in his own kingdom was an object of wonder and admiration to visitors from the West were long gone, although Wajid 'Ali Shah was slow to recognise this, and perhaps having done so, never admitted it to himself. The king's efforts at land reform and civil administration, which the Company appeared to demand in return for lifting the threat of annexation, were negated and sabotaged by Company officials themselves.

If the king failed to appreciate that times were changing, then the British were equally culpable of misreading the situation in Awadh. They sneered at the rich cultural life in the capital, unlike their predecessors in the 1770s and 1780s who had participated in *musha'iras*, musical concerts, feasting and festivals.⁵ They completely ignored the religious importance of the king to his Shi'a followers and the wider community, as well as his support for pilgrims to Mecca and his links with Iraq. They believed that the fertile kingdom of Awadh would flourish under British administration, but failed to realise that its inhabitants preferred to be ruled by their own king, whatever his faults, than by exemplary foreigners. The fashionable idea among Company officials that Britain had a duty to 'rescue' Awadh, for its own good, was simply unacceptable to the kingdom's inhabitants, both rural and urban.

Thus having failed to anticipate both the consequences of annexation in 1856 and the Uprising the following year, the Company, and subsequently the British government, wildly over-reacted in their treatment of the king. He was to be punished by incarceration in Fort William, for no discernable crime, but at the same time deferred to with exquisite politeness. As a political prisoner, his jailers were scrupulous in monitoring his health. Had he died in prison, it would have given impetus to the disaffected sepoys in the Bengal Army, many of whom came from Awadh. Although the king had made it clear that he did not support the rebels, even offering to lead his own men against them, he had become, unwittingly, a figurehead of the revolt. On his release, he was settled outside Calcutta with a gift of houses and a very large pension. For the rest of his life, British officials vacillated between trying to protect the king from unscrupulous tricksters and threatening to leave him to the consequences of his own extravagance. Their approach was that of an inconsistent parent faced with a wilful child ('a spoilt child', as he was actually called), who finds that neither promises nor threats can alter its behaviour.

In the matter of the king's treatment of his wives and children, British officials were to take a sterner line. There was surprisingly little criticism of the number of wives (about 375) whom the king married, and it was not until the appointment of Mowbray Thomson as agent to the king in 1874 that the implications of so many mut'ah marriages and divorces began to trouble the authorities. To their credit, government officials seemed genuinely concerned with the plight of the discarded wives, particularly those who had been with the king from youth and who had grown old in his service. Officials were prepared to over-ride the king's religious objections in providing for the divorced women and their children, and they deducted money from his pension for his dependants. There was sympathy too for some of the adult princes who wanted to make a life for themselves away from their father's *ancien régime*.

What can we conclude from the king's lifelong struggles against British officialdom? What often seemed like perverse behaviour on Wajid 'Ali Shah's part can also be interpreted as the actions of a man who is resigned to his fate but is not going to go down quietly. The more he was criticised for his extravagance, the more he spent. The humiliation of becoming financially dependent on the British undoubtedly drove many of his actions, particularly when threats that he would not be bailed out over his debts were never implemented. Government censure of the way he treated his wives and children led to him severing almost all relations with them. Stripping him of his Awadh kingdom resulted in the creation of a new, smaller kingdom at Garden Reach.

As for his sons, clearly many of them realised that they would have to make their own way in the world. Not only would there be no more government stipends, but their father's extravagance meant that there was nothing to inherit either. There was no landed property left, not even their childhood homes. Prince Afsar-ul Mulk had made the best of an unpromising start and had been rewarded with the appointment as Sheriff of Calcutta, followed by executive posts in which he could influence, however slightly, political events. He preferred to work within the system of British India rather than remaining stubbornly outside it, as his father had done.

Because Awadh was the last kingdom to be annexed by the British, the question of deposing further Indian rulers did not arise again, at least not in such dramatic circumstances. After 1858 an estimated 600 states ruled by hereditary princes existed in British India, including Hyderabad, which had broken away from the Mughal Empire around the same time as Awadh. While the Rajput states were allowed to coast along with minimal interference from the central government, others were closely monitored by British political agents or Residents. In some cases these government officials even acted as marriage brokers, or at least suggested suitable brides for the young princes. An English education was considered desirable for future rulers, an opinion that had been voiced after the failures of the king's madrassas. When some of these princes outgrew their English governesses, there were princely establishments like Mayo College and Rajkumar College to attend.[6] It was too late for the Awadh princes, of course, since there was no kingdom left for them to rule. But we can fruitfully speculate that the distinct post-Uprising move to 'Westernise' potential leaders in those states that had escaped direct rule must draw some lessons from what had happened in Awadh. There would be no further direct confrontations between government and ruling princes or their heirs. The welfare of their subjects was encouraged, and the advantages of a contented population under the broad British umbrella of Empire were pointed out. The new inclusive policy would see no more little kingdoms established in British India after the demise of Garden Reach.[7]

The remaining ninety years of British rule saw successive overtures to India's princes, beginning with a new system of honours awarded to them by Queen Victoria. This was followed by three excessively splendid assemblies and durbars of 1877, 1903 and 1911, in which they pledged their loyalty to the British crown.

CONCLUSION

By 1919 the princes were invited as 'imperial allies' to attend the Versailles peace conference and later to meetings of the League of Nations in Geneva. Clearly it was better to work with Indian rulers than against them. It was the leaders of the Independence movement who were now seen as troublemakers, and who had to be curbed and imprisoned. Whether Wajid 'Ali Shah, had he been born a century later, would have taken his place with his peers around the negotiating table, or whether he would have diverted his undoubted talents into the creative arts, we cannot say. But what we are left with is the portrait of a man who lived through eventful times and whose name, despite his undoubted failings, is still synonymous in India today with *tehzib*—the grace and courtesy of kings.

NOTES

INTRODUCTION

1. Alternative spellings, more common in the nineteenth century, were Oudh or Oude. Present-day spelling varies between Awadh and Avadh, although the former is generally preferred.
2. See Mir's complaint in Ralph Russell and Khurshidul Islam, *Three Mughal Poets* (1969). 'The ruins of Jahanabad [Delhi] were ten times better than Lucknow; Oh, that I had stayed there to die—not come to live distracted here.' Note: publication details of all books quoted are given in the Bibiliography.
3. See the author's *A Fatal Friendship: The Nawabs, the British and the City of Lucknow* (1985), p.81.
4. See the exhibition catalogue by Stephen Markel et al., *India's Fabled City: The Art of Courtly Lucknow* (2010).
5. See the author's *A Fatal Friendship*, pp.88–9.
6. The full text of this letter is given in the author's *The Great Uprising in India 1857–58: Untold Stories, Indian and British* (2007), pp.115–16.
7. The Bengali author Sudipta Mitra is writing a book provisionally entitled *Banished: Nawab Wajid Ali Shah's Kingdom of Metiyaburj*, and the scholar Richard Williams is researching the king's musicians at Garden Reach.
8. See Mirza Kaukab Qadr Sajjad 'Ali, *Vajid 'Ali Shah ki adabi aur saqafati khidmat* (Taraqqi-yi-Biyuro, New Delhi 1995) for a comprehensive listing and critique of the king's books.

1. 'THAT ENERGETIC OLD LADY'

1. *The Times* 1 September 1856.
2. *Punch, or the London Charivari* 30 August 1856.
3. *Punch* 23 August 1856.
4. The story is told in William Knighton, *The Private Life of an Eastern*

Queen (1865). Long regarded as a fictional account of Janab-i 'Aliyyah's life, as told by a fictional maid-servant, Elihu Jan, this is in fact a fairly accurate and useful source of reference. Elihu Jan appears in a government of India list of former royal servants in receipt of a pension in 1860.

5. Knighton, op. cit., p.12.
6. Private Papers, Eur Mss F231, 22 March 1856, IOR.
7. Known today as Kanpur, the name was changed after Independence in 1947.
8. Private Papers, Eur Mss F231, 23 March 1856, IOR.
9. Ibid., 3 May 1856, IOR.
10. Foreign Political Consultations, 20 June 1856, No. 438, NAND.
11. Ibid., 20 June 1856, No. 453, NAND.
12. Ibid., 20 June 1856, No. 455, NAND.
13. Private Papers, Eur Mss F231, 15 June 1856, IOR.
14. Ibid., 23 April 1856, IOR.
15. Michael Fisher, 'The Multiple Meanings of 1857 for Indians in Britain', *Economic and Political Weekly* 12–18 May 2007 vol. 42 no. 19, pp.1703–9.
16. Private Papers, Eur Mss F231, 3 June 1856, IOR.
17. *The Englishman and Military Chronicle* 25 June 1856, National Library, Kolkata.
18. Private Papers, Eur Mss F231, 30 June 1856, IOR.
19. Ibid., 26 June 1857, IOR. Increased activity by Christian missionaries, particularly Evangelicals, was held to be one cause of the Uprising of 1857. Vernon-Smith was not alone in trying to reduce their influence in India, after an earlier charter of 1813 had allowed them to proselytise there for the first time.
20. Ibid.
21. However, he was always referred to as 'Mr Brandon' by British officials.
22. See the author's *Engaging Scoundrels—True Tales of Old Lucknow* (2000) for a chapter on the Barber of Lucknow, pp.65–85.
23. *The Englishman and Military Chronicle* 7 June 1856, National Library, Kolkata.
24. Private Papers, Eur Mss F231, 30 June 1856, IOR.
25. Outram to Edmonstone, 7 February 1856, Enclosure 13 in *Oude Blue Book or Parliamentary Papers: Papers relating to Oude presented to both Houses of Parliament by command of Her Majesty, 1856*.
26. Private Papers, Mss Eur F231/13, 8 August 1856, IOR.
27. Ibid. f.48, 23 August 1856, IOR.
28. Ibid f.53, 10 November 1856, IOR.
29. Ibid. f.51, 10 September 1856, IOR.
30. *The Times* 30 August 1856.

31. *The Times* 28 August 1856.
32. Ibid.
33. *The Times* 2 September 1856.
34. Foreign Political Consultations, 28 March 1856, No. 165, NAND.
35. Private Papers, Eur Mss F231 f.73, 25 December 1856, IOR.
36. The two men wore ankle-length loose robes with embroidered borders and long sleeves.
37. Sadly we do not have the menu, so cannot know if the lunch met the dietary requirements of the guests. Halal or vegetarian food was always a problem for visitors from abroad, which is why many brought their own cooks with them.
38. Parliamentary Blue Books are official reports on various subjects, containing statistics and information.
39. *Illustrated London News* 14 March 1857.
40. Queen Victoria gave birth to her ninth and last child, Princess Beatrice, on 14 April 1857.
41. Private Papers, Eur Mss F231 f.101, 26 March 1857, IOR.
42. The king's imprisonment seems to have been unknown to his family in London at this point, although the Court of Directors had been informed by telegraph.
43. Queen Victoria's Journals, the Royal Archives, Windsor. The gracious permission of Her Majesty The Queen to quote material from the Royal Archives is most gratefully acknowledged.
44. Kamal ud-Din Haider, *Qaisar-al Tawarikh*, vol. I, pp.413–15.
45. Photograph in the Royal Photograph Collection, Windsor Castle, RCIN 2906233.
46. Hansard vol. 147 cc.1119–21.
47. Warwick Road West later became part of Warwick Avenue.
48. Foreign Department Secret Consultations, 30 November to 6 December 1857, No. 622, NAND.
49. Foreign Department Secret Consultations, 22 January 1858, No. 638, NAND. Colonel (later General) Sir Orfeur Cavenagh was the Town Major of Calcutta and responsible for its security, including Fort William.
50. Ibid.
51. Foreign Department Secret Consultations, 24 October 1857, No. 615, NAND.
52. Queen Victoria's Journals, 22 October 1857, online at www.queenvictoriasjournals.org.
53. It was reported that a toast had been drunk 'To the King of Delhi' at a dinner in Germany, and Irish immigrants in New York expressed 'sympathy with the sepoy mutiny'. See the author's *The Great Uprising in India 1857–58. Untold Stories, Indian and British* (2007), p.20.

54. *Le Journal des Débats* 25 January 1858. Bibliothèque Nationale de France online digital library Gallica. The baby was either Kaniz-i Husain, an adopted daughter of Janab-i 'Aliyyah, or princess Rif'at-ara Begam Sahibah, daughter of Sikandar Hashmat and one of his two Rajput wives.
55. *Le Journal des Débats* 26 January 1858.
56. Ibid. The sketches were subsequently reproduced in *The Narrative of the Indian Revolt from its Outbreak to the Capture of Lucknow* (1858), pp. 315–24, published by George Vickers.
57. Foreign Political Consultations, 15 October 1858, Nos. 363–4, NAND. Following the statement in the House of Lords by the Earl of Derby that Wajid 'Ali Shah was to be 'investigated', the prince wrote to Lord Canning that any such investigation or trial should be conducted with 'fairness and impartiality'. No trial did in fact take place.
58. Information from Richard Morgan, author of *The Diary of an Indian Cavalry Officer 1843–1863: John Hatfield Brooks* (2003).
59. Foreign Consultations Internal A, June 1885, Nos. 43–52, NAND.

2. PAGEANTS AND PANTOMIMES

1. Even so, the painting has probably been slightly cut down, because the lower corners of the square are missing and there is an unexplained white tent (?) in the foreground.
2. Quoted at length in M. Aslam Qureshi, *Wajid 'Ali Shah's Theatrical Genius* (1987).
3. *The Asiatic Annual Register for the Year 1804*, vol. vi, pp.9–10.
4. Qureshi, op. cit., p.18.
5. These tunes were to drive the defenders of the Lucknow Residency mad during the siege in 1857, as they were tauntingly played by rebel musicians beyond the makeshift barricades.
6. Qureshi, op. cit., pp.9–11. This event took place in the Falak Sair, the monsoon palace.
7. See Chapter Four, 'The House of Fairies', for a description of this book.
8. The gist is that Janab-i 'Aliyyah was told by an astrologer at the time of Wajid 'Ali Shah's birth that her son would become a yogi and that this could only be warded off if he dressed as a Hindu holy man on his birthday. However, there are no contemporary references to this story.
9. Qureshi, op. cit., pp.24–5.
10. The second lady may be Sleeman's niece, Elizabeth Briggs, who visited her aunt and uncle in Lucknow frequently. Information from two of Sir William's descendants.
11. The author's 1985 book *A Fatal Friendship: The Nawabs, the British and*

the City of Lucknow (1985) was the first to examine critically the nawabi architecture of Lucknow.
12. Ibid., p.234.
13. John Terry, *The Charm of Indo-Islamic Architecture* (1955), p.60.
14. Edward Hilton, *Guide to Lucknow and the Residency* (1934), p.70.
15. The author's edited *Lucknow: City of Illusion, photographs from the Alkazi Collection of Photography* (2006) reproduced Felice Beato's great panorama of Qaisarbagh and other images from 1858.
16. Dr Neeta Das, *Kaiserbagh: The Garden Palace of Lucknow*, UP Tourism Board, (1999).
17. One of the small marble kiosks was dismantled and brought to England as a gift for Queen Victoria to mark the end of the Uprising in 1858. It stands in Home Park at Windsor.
18. The king intended that 'his tomb will form part of the buildings' of Qaisarbagh, and wished the Resident to supervise an endowment fund for the palace's upkeep after his death. This was not agreed to by the British government. The Safed Barahdari, with its prominent central position, may have been the intended site for the tomb. Ref. Political Consultations, 29 July 1853, No. 53, IOR.
19. Satyajit Ray's 1977 film *Shatranj ke Khilari* (*The Chess Players*) is the best example.
20. Quoted by Mirza Ali Azhar in *King Wajid 'Ali Shah of Awadh* (1982), p.194 ftn. Imdad Husain Khan had had his own small state of Farrukhabad taken away by the East India Company in 1802, in return for a substantial pension.
21. Foreign Political Consultations, 29 November 1845, No. 186, NAND.
22. This figure was provided by a local historian, Roshan Taqui, using 1856 census details published in an Urdu newspaper, *Tilism-i-Laknau*, and calculating eight persons to a houshold.
23. There are two lists of departments published in English, one by Ranbir Sinh in *Wajid Ali Shah: The Tragic King* (2002) and one by G. D. Bhatnagar in *Awadh under Wajid Ali Shah* (1968). The lists, which are fairly consistent, come from two published Urdu histories, by Ram Sahai Tamanny and Amjad Ali Khan.
24. Bhatnagar, op. cit., p.9.
25. Foreign Political Consultations, 14 August 1847, Nos. 128–9, NAND. A 'perpetual loan' got round the problem of the king benefiting from the interest, which is strictly forbidden in Islam. Richmond would have invested the money in Company bonds and arranged payment direct to the imambarah staff.
26. Foreign Political Consultations, 24 March 1847, No. 94, NAND.

27. The jewellers are likely to have been Jains, the most pious of whom wear face-masks so they will not unwittingly breathe in any small insects.
28. Political and Foreign Consultations, 17 April 1847, No. 94, IOR.
29. Political and Foreign Consultations, 11 December 1847, No. 132, IOR.
30. Ibid. The story is also related at length by William Sleeman in *A Journey through the Kingdom of Oude* (1858), vol. I, pp.3–10.
31. Political and Foreign Consultations, 11 December 1847, No. 122, IOR.
32. Ibid., No. 156.
33. Ibid., No. 202.
34. Ibid, No. 159. The treaty referred to was signed in November 1801 between nawab Sa'adat Ali Khan and the Company, when the nawab was forced to cede half of Awadh to the British, a move for which Lord Wellesley, the governor general of the day, was heavily criticised. A further agreement between the nawab and Wellesley was signed in February 1802. Copies of treaties and agreements were kept in the Residency archives for ready reference.
35. Political and Foreign Consultations, 11 December 1847, No. 162, IOR.
36. Ibid., Nos. 164–9.
37. Ibid., No. 191.
38. Ibid., Nos. 161 and 102.
39. Ibid., No. 199.
40. Ibid.
41. Political and Foreign Consultations, 3 April 1847, No. 35, IOR.
42. Political and Foreign Consultations, 11 December 1847, Nos. 185–8, IOR.
43. States after 1858 which were not under the direct rule of the British government.
44. Ibid.
45. Ibid., No. 192.
46. Mirza Ali Azhar, *King Wajid Ali Shah of Awadh* (1982), pp.205–7.
47. Add. Or. 742, India Office Library.
48. Political and Foreign Consultations, 11 December 1847, No. 102, IOR.
49. Ibid., No. 201.

3. THE SORROWS OF AKHTAR

1. Foreign Consultations Political A, August 1870, Nos. 22–4, NAND.
2. This dichotomy has been well explored by Michael Fisher in his article 'The Imperial Coronation of 1819', *Modern Asian Studies* 1985 vol. 19, issue 2, pp.239–77.
3. Almost certainly it was made by Ede & Ravenscroft, English robe-makers since the end of the seventeenth century, although the firm today has no documentation for this specific order.

4. Captain Godfrey Mundy, *Pen and Pencil Sketches, being the Journal of a Tour in India* (1832), vol. I, p.13.
5. Present-day Iraq, formerly Mesopotamia, was known at this period as Turkish or Ottoman Arabia and formed part of the Ottoman Empire. The political agent at Baghdad was Major (later Major General) Sir Henry Rawlinson, who became a noted Assyrian scholar and chairman of the Court of Directors. It was he who welcomed the king's brother and son to lunch at Leadenhall Street in January 1857.
6. This was the nawab Iqbal-ud-daulah, a grandson of the fifth ruler of Awadh. See the author's *Engaging Scoundrels: True Tales of Old Lucknow* (2000), pp.108–11.
7. *Nazm-i Namvar*, printed at the Matba'e Sultani, the royal press, Calcutta in 1870.
8. See for example G. D. Bhatnagar, *Awadh under Wajid Ali Shah* (1968), p.40.
9. Palton is the Urdu pronounciation of platoon. For a list of the royal regiments, platoons and arsenals see Roshan Taqui, *Lucknow 1857: The Two Wars of Lucknow: the Dusk of an Era* (2001), pp.15–16.
10. India Political Consultations, 15 May 1857, No. 136, IOR. Other foreigners in the king's army were Jacob Johannes (an Armenian who had joined up in 1814), A. C. Dubois, Joseph Delmerick, Captain Felix Rotton, Lieutenant Sinclair, Lieutenant Graham, Lieutenant Joseph Johannes, Lieutenant Jacob Leblond, Lieutenant James Rotton and Captain John Rotton.
11. See the author's article 'Africans in the Indian Mutiny', *History Today* December 2009, pp.40–7.
12. William Forbes-Mitchell, *Reminiscences of the Great Mutiny 1857–59* (1910), p.58.
13. Political and Foreign Consultations, 3 April 1847, No. 56, IOR.
14. Political and Foreign Consultations, 9 April 1847, No.13, IOR.
15. Muster rolls compiled in March 1856 India Political Consultations, 4 March 1856, No. 173, IOR.
16. The story of the abortive reforms is told in Samuel Lucas, *Dacoitee in Excelsis: or The Spoliation of Oude* (1857), pp.102–8.
17. Dr Aloys Sprenger, *A Catalogue of the Arabic, Persian and Hindustany Manuscripts of the Libraries of the King of Oudh* (1854), preface, pp. iii-iv.
18. Milo Cleveland Beach and Ebba Koch, *King of the World* (1997), p.13.
19. Elliot's best known work, *The History of India as told by its own Historians*, was edited and published posthumously in eight volumes, 1867–77.
20. Foreign Consultations, 8 November 1850, No. 147, NAND.

21. Sprenger, op. cit., p.v.
22. Foreign Consultations 8, November 1850, No. 146, NAND.
23. Kamal-ud-Din Haider, *Qaisar-ut-Tawarikh*, vol. 2, p.222.
24. India Political Consultations, 2 September 1848, No. 77, IOR.
25. Lucas, Dacoitee in Excelsis, p.109.
26. William Sleeman, *A Journey through the Kingdom of Oude 1849–1850* (1858), p.xviii.
27. Minute from Dalhousie, 18 June 1853, quoted in Foreign Consultations, 28 December 1855, No. 319, NAND.
28. Sir William Lee-Warner, *Life of the Marquess of Dalhousie* (1904), vol. 2, p.317.
29. Sleeman, op. cit., vol. I, p.xlvi.
30. See Chapter Four, The House of Fairies.
31. *Wazirnama*, a book compiled by Amir 'Ali Khan Bahadur, the king's agent at Garden Reach.
32. Sleeman, op. cit., vol. 1, p.lx.
33. The regulations are reproduced in Mirza Ali Azhar, *King Wajid 'Ali Shah of Awadh* (1982), pp.252–62.
34. Sleeman, op. cit., vol. 1, p.xlvii.
35. Ibid., vol. 1, pp.l-li.
36. Ibid., vol. 1, p.lii.
37. Foreign Political Consultations, 23 June 1849, No. 68, NAND.
38. Sleeman, op. cit., vol. 1, pp.liii-iv.
39. Ibid., vol. 1, p.lxxv.
40. John Pemble, *The Raj, the Indian Mutiny, and the Kingdom of Oudh 1801–1859* (1977), pp.97–103.
41. J. G. A. Baird, ed., *Private Letters of the Marquess of Dalhousie* (1910), p.169.
42. Sleeman, op. cit., vol. 2, p.369.
43. Ibid., vol. 1, p.lx.
44. Ibid., vol. 1, p.lxxix.
45. India Political Consultations, 6 October 1849, No. 130, IOR.
46. Ibid.
47. Sleeman, op. cit., vol. 2, p.356.
48. Ibid., vol. 2, p.369.
49. Ibid., vol. 2, p.377.
50. Ibid., vol. 2, p.382.
51. See the author's *The Great Uprising in India 1857–58* (2007), pp.5–7.
52. Foreign Political Consultations, 12 August 1853, Nos. 105–6, NAND.
53. Foreign Political Consultations, 19 January 1855, Nos. 107–8, NAND.
54. Sleeman, op. cit., vol. 2, p.355.
55. Foreign Consultations, 2 January 1852, Nos. 90–4, NAND.

56. India Political Consultations, 29 August 1851, No. 123, IOR.
57. India Political Consultations, 19 September 1851, Nos. 156–7, IOR.
58. Foreign Political Consultations, 5 January 1855 No. 113, NAND.
59. Foreign Political Consultations, 28 December 1855, No. 319, NAND.
60. Azhar, op. cit., vol. 1, p.363.
61. Ibid., p.389.
62. Foreign Political Consultations, 28 December 1855, Nos. 339–46, NAND.
63. Charles Allen, *Ashoka, the Search for India's Lost Emperor* (2012), p.xiii.
64. Foreign Consultations, op. cit. Nos. 339–42. Notes on a meeting on 1 August 1855. NAND.
65. The conflict is explored in greater depth in two books: J. R. I. Cole, *Roots of North Indian Shi'ism in Iran and Iraq* (1988), pp.244–9; and Michael Fisher, *A Clash of Cultures, Awadh, the British and the Mughals* (1987), pp.227–34.
66. Foreign Political Consultations, 28 December 1855, No. 349, NAND.
67. Foreign Political Consultations, 14 December 1855, No. 51/2, NAND.
68. Foreign Political Consultations, 6 June 1856, Nos. 186–219, NAND.
69. Dalhousie's minute of instructions to Outram, the proposed treaty and draft proclamations all appear in the *Oude Blue Book*, and are also given in full in Mirza Ali Azhar, *King Wajid Ali Shah of Awadh* (1982), pp.529–43.
70. *Oude Blue Book*, Part 4, pp.287–9.
71. Enclosures to Secret Letters from India, 1857, f.461, IOR.
72. Ibid.
73. Private Papers, Eur Mss F231/5, p.171, IOR.
74. Foreign Department Secret Consultations, 18 December 1857, No. 577, NAND.
75. Bishop Reginald Heber, *Narrative of a Journey through the Upper Provinces of India from Calcutta to Bombay 1824–1825* (1849), vol. 1, pp.19–20.
76. Foreign Department Secret Consultations, 29 January 1858, No. 613, NAND.
77. Op. cit., 25 June 1858, Nos. 419–20. Letter dated 25 January 1858, NAND.
78. Amjad Ali Khan, ed., *Masnavi Huzn-i-Akhtar* (1981).
79. Zulfiqar ud-Daulah's sister was Afsar un-nisa, nawab Nishat Mahal Sahibah, who was married to the king in 1830. Zulfiqar ud-Daulah was later implicated in cheating the king by overcharging him for goods and services provided at Garden Reach.
80. Foreign Department Secret Consultations, 26 March 1858, Nos. 233–5, NAND.
81. Foreign Political Consultations, 24 December 1858, Nos. 80–1, NAND.

82. Prince Hamid 'Ali eventually returned to Calcutta in September 1859.
83. The terms viceroy and governor general are not interchangeable. A viceroy is the representative of the king (or queen), while a governor general is an administrative post.
84. See the author's *The Great Uprising*, pp.118–25, for Begam Hazrat Mahal's part in the Uprising and the installation of Birjis Qadr on the Awadh throne.
85. Foreign Political Consultations, 15 July 1859, Nos. 380–94, NAND.
86. Once he was released from prison, the king wrote to Canning using venomous tones to describe his former wife, Begam Hazrat Mahal, calling her an 'ill-disposed enemy', an evil-doer, an 'imbecile' and much else. Foreign Political Consultations, 9 September 1859, Nos. 204–8, NAND.
87. Foreign Political Consultations, 15 July 1959, Nos. 380–94, NAND.

4. THE HOUSE OF FAIRIES

1. Foreign Consultations, 26 June 1865, No. 48, NAND.
2. This photograph has a curious history. It appears in William Low, *Lieutenant-Colonel Gould Hunter-Weston of Hunterston ... one of the defenders of Lucknow ... 1857–8. A biographical Sketch* (1914); in this book, Colonel Hunter-Weston relates how he looted two boxes of glass negatives from the house of Ahmad 'Ali Khan during the recapture of Lucknow in 1858, and took them home with him to Ayrshire. In spite of intensive enquiries by the author, the whereabouts of the remaining priceless negatives are still unknown.
3. This might be the book subsequently described as 'most disgusting and obscene' by British officers, when it was printed on the king's antique press in 1879 in Calcutta. It would have circulated in manuscript form before being lithographed for the press.
4. Tahsin Sarvani, *Pari khana: rangile piya, jan-i 'alam Vajid Ali Shah Akhtar ke khudnavisht dastan-i mu'ashqah* (1965), p.19.
5. See the author's biography *A Very Ingenious Man: Claude Martin in Early Colonial India* (1992).
6. Dr Joseph Fayrer, whose summarised reports from the palace described how during a typical day 'His Majesty recited to Khas Mahal his new poem on the loves of the bulbuls [songbirds]'. *Recollections of my Life* (1900), p.92.
7. Christians and Jews are considered by Muslims to be *ahl-i-kitab*, 'people of the book', that is, the Bible and the Torah.
8. *Pari Khana*, p.96.
9. Ibid.
10. Ibid., p.97.

11. Ibid., p.171. Nawab Jalal-ud-daulah, son of an earlier ruler, had died in 1848. His house was on the Sitapur Road, north of the Gomti.
12. Although a few contemporary paintings of Wajid 'Ali Shah are known, and there is an album of fragile pencil drawings of the king with some of his wives, now in the State Museum, Banarsi Bagh, Lucknow.
13. William Sleeman relates the story in *A Journey through the Kingdom of Oude 1849–1850* (1858) vol. 1, pp.46–7. The 'other person' was Razi-ud-daulah, one of the singers at Court, but Safaraz Mahal was found to be cohabiting with another singer too, Ghulam Raza.
14. Pronounced Ambar, the word means ambergris, but is also a complimentary term for dark-skinned people, particularly African male slaves, e.g. Malik Anbar of Ahmadnagar. Claude Martin owned an African slave called Amber. See Nusrat Naheed, *Jane Alam aur Mehakpari* (2005), p.63.
15. *Hijras* are normally males who adopt a feminine identity and would be invited to dance at special events, e.g. childbirth celebrations.
16. Emily Eden, *Up the Country: Letters from India* (1983 edition), p.233.
17. Foreign Consultations, 26 June 1865, No. 48, NAND.
18. Foreign Consultations Internal A, May 1888, Nos. 177–82, NAND.
19. Foreign Consultations Political A, January 1862, No. 194, NAND.
20. *Pari Khana*, p.170.
21. Abdul Halim 'Sharar', *Lucknow: the Last Phase of an Oriental Culture* (1975).
22. A courtesy title, not necessarily denoting the holder of any particular office. Noblemen would be addressed as 'nawab sahib'.
23. Foreign Political Consultations, 7 July 1849, Nos. 82–6, NAND.
24. Foreign Department Secret Consultations, 30 July 1858, No. 236, NAND.
25. Foreign Political Consultations, 2 September 1859, No. 172, NAND.
26. Foreign Consultations, 16 March 1860, Nos. 120–34, Major Herbert's letter of 26 December 1859, NAND.
27. Ibid., Major Herbert's letter of 5 January 1860, NAND.
28. See the author's *The Great Uprising in India 1857–58* (2007), p.152.
29. Foreign Consultations, 16 March 1860, No.125, NAND.
30. Reported in the newspaper *The Friend of India* 2 August 1860 and 20 September 1860.
31. Foreign Consultations Political A, 16 April 1860, No. 295, NAND.
32. Ibid. This long account comes in a report from Major Herbert to the Secretary to the Foreign Department. Herbert was told it was not his business to interfere in the king's private affairs.
33. Foreign Consultations Political A, October 1861, Nos. 82–4, NAND.
34. Foreign Consultations, 21 October 1859, No. 79, NAND.
35. Ibid.
36. Foreign Consultations, 26 June 1865, No. 48, NAND.

37. Ibid.
38. John Kaye and George Malleson, *History of the Indian Mutiny of 1857* (1864), vol. 1, pp.95–6. There are many editions of this work: John Kaye died in 1876 after producing the first two volumes, which were published under the title *The History of the Sepoy War in India 1858–58*; Malleson added a further four volumes and edited the whole publication.
39. P. J. O. Taylor, *A Companion to the 'Indian Mutiny' of 1857* (1996), p.329.
40. Foreign Consultations Internal A, July 1886, Nos. 51–67, mohubutnamah dated 5 July 1884, NAND.
41. Ibid., mohubutnamah dated 31 December 1884.
42. Proceedings of the Lieutenant Governor of Bengal, Political Department, Calcutta, May 1879, File 98, pp.137–258, IOR.
43. Prince Hamid 'Ali, who had been so reluctant to return home to India, had died of cholera in July 1874.
44. Ibid., pp.197–9.
45. Ibid.
46. Foreign Consultations Internal A, July 1886, Nos. 51–67, mohubutnamah dated 5 July 1884, NAND.
47. Proceedings of the Lieutenant Governor of Bengal, Political Department, Calcutta, May 1879, File 98, p.212, IOR.
48. Proceedings of the Lieutenant Governor of Bengal, File 98, 1 August 1878, p.212, IOR.
49. Ibid., p.194.
50. Proceedings of the Lieutenant Governor of Bengal, File 98, 1 August 1878, p.231, IOR.

5. AT GARDEN REACH

1. Alfred Spencer, ed., *Memoirs of William Hickey* (*c*.1925), vol. 4, pp.26–7.
2. Saibal Bose, *Garden Reach: A Railway Story* (2007).
3. Private Papers, Eur Mss F231, Lord Canning to Robert Vernon-Smith, 3 June 1856, IOR.
4. Foreign Consultations Internal B, June 1890, NAND.
5. Foreign Consultations Internal B, April 1888, Nos. 390–5, NAND.
6. Foreign Political Consultations, 5 August 1859, Nos. 212–13, NAND.
7. Foreign Political Consultations, November 1861, Nos. 57–68, NAND.
8. Ibid., 19 December 1859.
9. Foreign Consultations, 16 March 1860, Nos. 120/134, Letter from Lord Canning, 5 January 1860, commenting on Major Herbert's diary entry of 17 December 1859, NAND.
10. Foreign Consultations Internal A, 5 July 1884, NAND.

11. Foreign Department Secret Consultations, 29 January 1858, Nos. 619–36, NAND.
12. Foreign Political Consultations, November 1861, Nos. 57–68, NAND.
13. Foreign Consultations Political A, January 1862, No. 194, NAND.
14. Foreign Consultations Political A, September 1864, Nos. 166-8, NAND.
15. Foreign Political Consultations A, September 1864, Nos. 166-8, NAND.
16. Ibid., No. 167.
17. Ibid., No. 167.
18. Ibid., No. 166, Major Herbert's Diary, 24 August 1864.
19. Foreign Political Consultations, 8 October 1868, No. 44, NAND.
20. Foreign Consultations General A, January 1866, No. 3, NAND.
21. Ibid., No. 13.
22. Quoted in *The Friend of India* 24 (1867) as an article from 'the Native Press'. National Library Kolkata.
23. Foreign Consultations General B, 13 October 1868, 'Claims against the King of Oude', NAND.
24. P. J. O. Taylor, *A Companion to the 'Indian Mutiny' of 1857* (1996), p.264.
25. *Allen's Indian Mail & Oriental Gazette* 30 September 1867, p.767.
26. India Political Department Collections, 28 February 1867, Coll. 119/1, IOR.
27. India Political Department Collections, 23 March 1867, Coll. 119/2, IOR.
28. Ibid.
29. India Political Department Collections, 26 August 1867, Coll. 95, IOR.
30. Ibid., 9 November 1867, Coll. 95, IOR.
31. Captain Hayes was cut down by a rebellious sepoy officer in May 1857 on the Grand Trunk Road.
32. Foreign Consultations Political A, July 1867, Nos. 44–6, NAND.
33. Foreign Consultations Political A, 8 October 1868, No. 43, NAND.
34. Foreign Consultations Political A, 8 October 1868, No. 52, NAND.
35. Foreign Consultations Political A, 8 October 1868, Nos. 236–47, NAND.
36. Ibid.
37. Foreign Political Consultations, 9 September 1859, Nos. 100–1, NAND.
38. Ibid.
39. Foreign Consultations Political A, February 1862, Nos. 71–6, NAND.
40. 'Alsatia' was an area in North London that preserved the right to sanctuary to the end of the seventeenth century. As a result it attracted criminals and became a synonymous term for a rowdy area where the law could not be applied.
41. Foreign Consultations Political A, February 1862, Nos. 71–6, NAND.
42. Foreign Consultations Political I, May 1883, Nos. 61–70, NAND.
43. Foreign Consultations Political I, April 1884, Nos. 108–12, NAND.

44. Foreign Consultations Political I, 23 October 1883, NAND.
45. Foreign Consultations Political I, April 1884, Nos. 108–12, NAND.
46. Foreign Consultations General A, March 1870, Nos. 43–5, NAND.
47. Foreign Consultations General A, June 1870, No. 6, NAND.
48. Abdul Halim Sharar, *Lucknow: The Last Phase of an Oriental Culture* (1975), pp.65–76.
49. Foreign Consultations Internal B, February 1888, Nos. 504–5, NAND.
50. Foreign Consultations Political A, March 1875, Nos. 365–75, NAND.
51. Ibid.
52. Bengal Political Proceedings, 1881. Committee Report dated 7 February 1880, pp.17–90, IOR.

6. A TIGRESS ESCAPES FROM THE MENAGERIE

1. The title 'Royal' was awarded in the 1860s, and unlike Kew, its name was always in the singular. Today it is the Acharya Jagadish Chandra Bose Indian Botanic Garden, named after Sir Jagadish Chandra Bose, botanist and archaeologist.
2. Bengal Proceedings, Judicial, March 1879, Nos. 35–36. IOR. All of the information on the tigress's escape and subsequent actions comes from this long report, which covers the period from 11 January 1879 to 8 December of the same year.
3. Bengal Proceedings, Judicial, March 1879, Nos. 35–6, p.108, IOR.
4. Ibid., p.109.
5. Plate XVI of *Oriental Field Sports* by Thomas Williamson and Samuel Howitt (1807) is captioned 'Chasing a tiger across a river'.
6. Bengal Proceedings, Judicial, March 1879, Nos. 35–6, p.111, IOR.
7. Ibid., p.114.
8. Bengal Proceedings, Judicial, March 1879, Nos. 35–6, p.116, IOR.
9. See Malcolm Brown, 'A "Complimentary Mission" from Nawab Nasir-ud-din Haider to King William IV', *Journal of the Royal Society for Asian Affairs*, November 2001 vol. 32 No. 3 pp.279–86.
10. William Knighton, *The Private Life of an Eastern King* (1856), pp.123–41.
11. Abdul Halim Sharar, *Lucknow: The Last Phase of an Oriental Culture* (1975), p.121.
12. Revd William Tennant, *Indian Recreations* (1803), vol. 2, p.415.
13. See the author's *Engaging Scoundrels: True Tales of Old Lucknow* (2000), pp.137–8.
14. A. C. Bose, *Hazrat Wajid Ali Shah King of Oudh* (1962), p.61.
15. William Howard Russell, *The Prince of Wales Tour: A Diary in India*

(1877). In spite of a number of stories in India about the Prince of Wales having met Wajid 'Ali Shah in Calcutta, and being presented with a jewelled sword, I have found no mention of this in any of the official diaries of the tour, nor is it listed among gifts presented to the Prince of Wales.
16. Today's A3 highway.
17. Thompson's report, dated 17 June 1879, is contained as a separate item within the Bengal Proceedings Judicial for 1879, IOR.
18. Abdul Halim Sharar, *Lucknow: The Last Phase of an Oriental Culture* (1975), pp.72–3.
19. Proceedings of the Lieutenant Governor of Bengal, Political Department, 1879, IOR Report from Thomson dated 2 June 1878, p.190.
20. Bengal Political Proceedings for 1881, Report of the Committee, dated 7 February, p.28, IOR.
21. Sharar, op. cit., p.73.
22. Proceedings of the Lieutenant Governor of Bengal Political Department, 1879, IOR. A 'purcha payam' (message) from the king dated 28 April 1878, with Thomson's comments in the margin, p.181.
23. H. E. A. Cotton, *Calcutta Old and New* (revised edition 1980), p.336.
24. Proceedings for the Government of Bengal, Political Department Nos. 5–6, p.63, 7 March 1879, Alfred Lyall, secretary to [central] government to the government of Bengal, IOR.
25. Bengal Proceedings for March 1881, pp.17–90, IOR. The committee does not seem to have been given a specific name.
26. Ibid., p.18.
27. Ibid.
28. Proceedings of the Lieutenant Governor of Bengal Political Department, 1879. Letter from Farid-ud-din Qadr to Colonel Arthur Elderton, 11 September 1877, IOR.
29. Ibid., p.151.
30. Proceedings of the Lieutenant Governor of Bengal Political Department, 1879, p.206, IOR.
31. D. B. Diskalker, 'Foundation of an Observatory at Lucknow', *Journal of the United Provinces Historical Society* July 1937 vol. 10, Part 1, pp.10–11.
32. India Political Consultations, 31 October 1856, No. 109, IOR.
33. Foreign Department Political A, May 1871, Nos. 114–17, NAND.
34. Bengal Political Proceedings, March 1881, pp.17–90, IOR.
35. A cotton 'gin' (short for 'engine') processed raw cotton, thus *jinwali kothi* is the place where the engine was housed.
36. Foreign Consultations Internal A, June 1888, No. 7, NAND.
37. Foreign Consultations Internal B, August 1886, Nos. 134–6, NAND.

38. Ibid.
38. Foreign Consultations Internal B, July 1886, NAND.
40. The Talpurs were the rulers of Sindh before the state was annexed by the Company in 1843.
41. Foreign Consultations Internal A, July 1886, Nos 51–67. Report from Henry Durand dated 23 July 1885, NAND.
42. Ibid., quoted by the king in his letter of 31 December 1884 to the Governor General, NAND.
43. Foreign Consultations Internal B, June 1888, Nos. 102–3, NAND.

7. A MIMIC KINGDOM

1. *New York Times* 11 November 1874, 'A Retired King. The ex-King of Oude at Calcutta. A Royal Pensioner of the British Government—his Mimic Court and State'.
2. Advertisements in *The Statesman* newspaper from the 1870s.
3. M. Aslam Qureshi, *Wajid Ali Shah's Theatrical Genius* (1987), pp.37–8.
4. Ibid., p.32.
5. Foreign Consultations Internal A, May 1888, Nos. 114–22, NAND. The extent and number of staff was not realised until after the king's death, when they had to be paid off and discharged.
6. Abdul Halim Sharar, *Lucknow: The Last Phase of an Oriental Culture* (1975), p.74.
7. Information from Shahinshah Mirza, one of the king's descendants.
8. The Muharram ceremonies conducted today at Mahmudabad, Uttar Pradesh, not only still use *marsiyas* composed by Wajid 'Ali Shah, but continue with much of the ritual from nawabi days.
9. The king's letters to his wives, written from prison, await translation.
10. Foreign Political Consultations, 20 June 1856, No. 455, IOR.
11. Foreign Consultations Political A, March 1869, Nos. 144–6, NAND.
12. India Political Consultations, 21 August 1857, Tables of Salutes; Salutes for Anniversaries and Native Sovereigns and Chiefs, IOR.
13. Op. cit. ref. 10.
14. Ibid. The king's official correspondence was written in Persian, transmitted through the British agent and a translation made before the original was forwarded. In a letter to a religious official in Bombay, Wajid 'Ali Shah referred to himself as 'the centre of wealth' (*sirkar daulat madar*), which the governor general noted with 'surprise and regret' as being inconsistent with the king's present position and circumstances. Foreign Consultations Political A, October 1869, Nos. 67–9, NAND.
15. Foreign Consultations General B, May 1869, Nos. 155–6, NAND.

16. Foreign Consultations General B, July 1869, Nos. 220–1, NAND.
17. Foreign Consultations General B, May 1862, Nos. 183–4, NAND.
18. Foreign Consultations Political B, 23 November 1861, Nos. 6–7, NAND.
19. March 1862 Private Papers L/PS/6/520 Coll. 62/3 IOR.
20. Foreign Consultations General A, July 1882, Nos. 93–9, NAND.
21. Rodney Pasley, *'Send Malcolm!' The Life of Major-General Sir John Malcolm* (1982), p.103.
22. P. J. O. Taylor, *A Companion to the 'Indian Mutiny' of 1857* (1996), p.34.
23. See the chapter by Rosemary Raza, 'Picturing Sindh: British representations' in Pratapaditiya Pal, ed., *Sindh: Past Glory, Present Nostalgia*, Marg vol. 60, no. 1, pp.120–33.
24. It was John Login's wife (later Lady Login) who befriended Janab-i 'Aliyyah while Dr Login was stationed in Lucknow. The two ladies were later to meet again for the last time in London in 1857.
25. In 1882 the king had to get government permission to make a short railway journey, which was agreed, providing he was accompanied by the agent. The governor general added, 'He must not go to Oude for obvious reasons.'
26. Hansard 8 February 1861, vol. 161, cc208.16.
27. *The Pioneer* 18 January 1867, under 'Outstation Gossip'. The newspaper was published from Allahabad, hence the delay in announcing an event after it had taken place.
28. Foreign Consultations Internal A, 5 July 1884, NAND.
29. Ray's film was based on a short story by the writer Munshi Premchand called 'Shatranj Ke Khilari', published in 1924.
30. Foreign Consultations Internal A, July 1886, Nos. 51–67, NAND.
31. Ibid.
32. Foreign Consultations Secret I, July 1886, Nos. 175–7, NAND.
33. The Marchioness of Dufferin and Ava, *Our Viceregal Life in India—Selections from my Journal 1884–1888* (1889), p.241.
34. Foreign Consultations Internal B, October 1887, Nos. 47–56, NAND.
35. *The Statesman* 15 September 1887.
36. Foreign Consultations Internal B, October 1887, Nos. 47–56, NAND.
37. *The Statesman* 23 September 1887.
38. Foreign Consultations Internal A, May 1888, No. 44, NAND.
39. Foreign Consultations Secret I, July 1886, Nos. 175–7, NAND.
40. Foreign Consultations Internal A, May 1888, No. 44, NAND.
41. Ibid.
42. Ibid.
43. Foreign Consultations Internal B, November 1887, Nos. 89–91, NAND.
44. Foreign Consultations Internal B, June 1888, Nos. 136–40, NAND.

45. Foreign Consultations Internal A, May 1888, No. 44, letter dated 22 March 1888, NAND.
46. Foreign Consultations Internal B, 8 May 1888, Nos. 398–9, NAND. A substantial number of items eventually found their way to libraries in Aligarh and Patna.
47. The Lucknow Museum was at this date housed in the Lal Barahdari, where the kings' coronations had taken place.
48. Foreign Consultations Internal B, February 1889, Nos. 112–20, NAND.
49. Ibid.
50. Foreign Consultations Secret I, July 1886, Nos. 175–7, NAND.
51. Foreign Consultations Internal B, December 1887, Nos. 200–3, NAND.
52. Ibid.
53. Foreign Consultations Internal A, May 1888, Nos. 114–22, NAND.
54. Foreign Consultations Internal A, May 1888, Nos. 114–22, NAND.
55. Ibid.
56. Ibid.
57. Marchioness of Dufferin and Ava, *Our Viceregal Life in India—Selections from my Journal 1884–1888* (1889), p.241.
58. Foreign Consultations Internal B, June 1890, Nos. 73/121, NAND.
59. Ibid.

CONCLUSION

1. Calcutta did not suffer bombing by the Japanese until 1942, when central parts of the city were hit, and the docks at Kidderpore, towards Garden Reach, were targeted.
2. See the author's article 'Delhi: Short-lived Capital of the Raj', *History Today* December 2011 vol. 61 issue 12.
3. Described as a non-political titular position of authority.
4. I am indebted to Dr S. A. Sadiq, a direct descendant of the king, for this information.
5. See the author's chapter 'Lucknow and European Society' in *India's Fabled City: The Art of Courtly Lucknow* by Stephen Markel et al.
6. See the recent book by Caroline Keen, *Princely India and the British: Political Development and the Operation of Empire* (2012), for a detailed analysis of post-1858 relationships between government and the princes.
7. A footnote, literally, to history came on 15 August 1947, the day of India's independence from Britain, when Prince Yusuf Mirza Bahadur, a direct descendant of the king through Prince Hamid 'Ali, was chosen by members of the former royal family to become 'King of Oudh'; he was symbolically crowned at Lucknow.

BIBLIOGRAPHY

Records consulted

Manuscripts

Wajid 'Ali Shah, *Ishqnama*. Windsor Castle Library c.1848.

National Archives, New Delhi (NAND)

Before 1858: Foreign Political Consultations.
1859–60: Foreign Consultations.
1861 onwards: Foreign Consultations Political A and B, Proceedings A and B, etc.
Foreign Department Consultations.
(Awadh was treated as a 'foreign' country, that is, not part of British India).

National Library, Kolkata (Newspaper Department, Esplanade)

The Englishman and Military Chronicle.
The Friend of India.
The Pioneer.
The Statesman.

India Office Records, London (IOR)

Bengal Judicial Proceedings.
Bengal Political Proceedings.
India Political Consultations.
Political and Foreign Consultations.
Private Papers European Manuscripts.
Secret Letters from India.

Online (some only in part)

Allen's India Mail and Oriental Gazette.

BIBLIOGRAPHY

Hansard.
Illustrated London News.
Le Journal des Débats Bibliothèque Nationale de France online digital library Gallica.
New York Times.
Punch, or the London Charivari.
Queen Victoria's Journals.

Books

'Ali, Mirza Kaukab Qadr Sajjad, *Vajid 'Ali Shah ki adabi aur saqafati khidmat.* Taraqqi-y-Biyuro, New Delhi 1995.
Ali, Mrs Meer Hassan, *Observations on the Mussulmauns of India.* 2 vols. Parbury Allen, London 1832.
Allen, Charles, *Ashoka, the Search for India's Lost Emperor.* Little Brown, London 2012.
Asiatic Annual Register for the Year 1804. London 1805.
Azhar, Mirza, Ali *King Wajid Ali Shah of Awadh.* 2 vols. Royal Book Company, Karachi 1982.
Baird, J. G. A. ed., *Private Letters of the Marquess of Dalhousie.* William Blackwood, Edinburgh 1910.
Beach, Milo Cleveland and, Ebba Koch, *King of the World.* Azimuth Editions, London 1997.
Bhatnagar, G. D., *Awadh under Wajid Ali Shah.* 1968.
Blackwood, Harriot Georgina, Marchioness of Dufferin and Ava, *Our Viceregal Life in India—Selections from my Journal 1884–1888.* John Murray, London 1889.
Bose, A. C., *Hazrat Wajid Ali Shah King of Oudh.* Shukla Printing Press, Lucknow 1962.
Bose, Saibal, *Garden Reach a Railway Story.* South Eastern Railway, Kolkata 2007.
Brown, Malcolm, 'A "Complimentary Mission" from Nawab Nasir-ud-din Haider to King William IV'. *Journal of the Royal Society for Asian Affairs* November 2001 vol. 32 no. 3.
Cole, J. R. I., *Roots of North Indian Shi'ism in Iran and Iraq: Religion and State in Awadh 1722–1859.* University of California, Berkeley 1988.
Cotton, H. E. A., *Calcutta Old and New.* First published 1909, revised edition edited by N. R. Ray, pub. Surajit C. Das, Calcutta 1980.
Das, Neeta, *Kaiserbagh the Garden Place of Lucknow.* UP Tourism Board 1999.
Diskalker, D. B., 'Foundation of an Observatory at Lucknow'. *Journal of the United Provinces Historical Society* July 1937 vol. 10 Part 1.

BIBLIOGRAPHY

Eden, Emily, *Up the Country: Letters from India*. First published 1866, reprinted Virago Press, London 1983.

Fayrer, Dr Joseph, *Recollections of my Life*. W. Blackwood & Sons, Edinburgh 1890.

Fisher, Michael, 'The Imperial Coronation of 1819'. *Modern Asian Studies* Cambridge 1985.

Fisher, Michael, *A Clash of Cultures: Awadh, The British, and the Mughals*. Manohar, Delhi 1987.

Fisher, Michael, 'The Multiple Meanings of 1857 for Indians in Britain'. *Economic and Political Weekly* 2007 vol. 42 no. 19. Sameeksha Trust Publications, Mumbai.

Forbes-Mitchell, William, *Reminscences of the Great Mutiny 1857–59*. Macmillan, London 1910.

Haider, Kamal-ud-Din, *Qaisar-ut-Tawarikh*. 2 vols. Newal Kishore Press, Lucknow 1879.

Heber, Bishop Reginald, *Narrative of a Journey through the Upper Provinces of India from Calcutta to Bombay 1824–1825*. 2 vols. John Murray, London 1849.

Hickey, William, ed. Alfred Spencer, *Memoirs of William Hickey*. 4 vols. Hurst and Blackett, London 1913–25.

Hilton, Edward, *Hilton's Guide to Lucknow and the Residency*. Lucknow Publishing House, Lucknow 1934.

Keen, Caroline, *Princely India and the British: Political Development and the Operation of Empire*. I. B. Tauris 2012.

Knighton, William, *The Private Life of an Eastern King*. G. Routledge & Co., London 1856.

Knighton, William, *The Private Life of an Eastern Queen*. Longman, Roberts & Green, London 1865.

Lee-Warner, Sir William, *The Life of the Marquess of Dalhousie*. 2 vols. Macmillan, London 1904.

Llewellyn-Jones, Rosie, *A Fatal Friendship: the Nawabs, the British and the City of Lucknow*. OUP, Delhi 1985.

Llewellyn-Jones, Rosie, *A Very Ingenious Man: Claude Martin in Early Colonial India*. OUP, Delhi 1992.

Llewellyn-Jones, Rosie, *Engaging Scoundrels: True Tales of Old Lucknow*. OUP, Delhi 2000.

Llewellyn-Jones, Rosie, *The Great Uprising in India 1857–58. Untold Stories, Indian and British*. Boydell Press, Woodbridge 2007.

Llewellyn-Jones Rosie, 'Africans in the Indian Mutiny'. *History Today* December 2009, London.

Llewellyn-Jones, Rosie, ed., *Lucknow: City of Illusion*. Prestel, Munich 2006

BIBLIOGRAPHY

Lucas, Samuel, *Dacoitee in Excelsis: or The Spoliation of Oude by the East India Company*. J. R. Taylor, London 1857.

Markel, Stephen et al., *India's Fabled City: The Art of Courtly Lucknow*. Los Angeles County Museum of Art, 2010.

Morgan, Richard, *The Diary of an Indian Cavalry Officer 1843–1863: John Hatfield Brooks*. Pagoda Tree Press, Bath 2003.

Mundy, Captain Godfrey, *Pen and Pencil Sketches, being the Journal of a Tour in India*. John Murray, London 1832.

Naheed, Nusrat, English translation by Dr Bhatti, *Jane Alam aur Mehakpari*. Amin-ud-Daula Public Library, Lucknow 2005.

Oude Blue Book or Parliamentary Papers: Papers relating to Oude presented to both Houses of Parliament by command of Her Majesty, 1856.

Pasley, Rodney, *'Send Malcolm!' The Life of Major-General Sir John Malcolm 1769–1833*. BACSA, London 1982.

Pemble, John, *The Raj, the Indian Mutiny and the Kingdom of Oudh 1801–1859*. Harvester Press, Hassocks 1997.

Qureshi, M. Aslam, *Wajid Ali Shah's Theatrical Genius*. Vanguard Books Ltd, Lahore 1987.

Russell, Ralph and Khurshidul Islam, *Three Mughal Poets: Mir, Sauda, Mir Hasan*. George Allen & Unwin Ltd, London 1969.

Russell, William Howard, *The Prince of Wales Tour: A Diary in India 1877*. H. B. Bigney, Montreal 1877.

Sarwani, Tahsin, *Pari khana: rangile piya, jan-i'alam Vajid Ai Shah Akhtar ke khudnavisht dastan-i mu'ashqah*. Karachi 1958.

Sharar, Abdul Halim, *Lucknow: The Last Phase of an Oriental Culture*. Paul Elek, London 1975.

Sinh, Ranbir, *Wajid Ali Shah: The Tragic King*. Publication Scheme, Jaipur 2002.

Sleeman, Major General Sir William, *A Journey through the Kingdom of Oude, in 1849–1850*. 2 vols. Richard Bentley, London 1858.

Sprenger, Aloys, *A Catalogue of the Arabic, Persian and Hindustany Manuscripts of the Libraries of the King of Oudh*. Calcutta 1854.

Taqi, Roshan, *Lucknow 1857: The Two Wars of Lucknow: The Dusk of an Era*. New Royal Book Company, Lucknow 2001.

Taylor, P. J. O., *A Companion to the 'Indian Mutiny' of 1857*. OUP, Delhi 1996.

Tennant, Revd William, *Indian Recreations consisting chiefly of strictures on the domestic and rural economy of the Mahommedans and Hindoos*. 2 vols. Edinburgh 1803

Terry, John, *The Charm of Indo-Islamic Architecture*. Alec Tiranti, London 1955.

Wajid 'Ali Shah, ed. Amjad Ali Khan, *Masnavi Huzn-i-Akhtar*. Calcutta 1981

BIBLIOGRAPHY

Wajid 'Ali Shah, *Reply to the Charges against the King of Oude*. J. F. Bellamy, Calcutta 1856.
Williamson, Thomas and Samuel Howitt, *Oriental Field Sports*. London 1807.

INDEX

Abdul Subhan, escapes jail, 116–117
African slaves, servants and soldiers 12, 15, 76, 90, 134, 137, 141, 171; female soldiers 90; (see also Diyanat ud-Daulah)
Afsar-ul-Malik, prince, 235, 237, 276–277, 279
Ahmad 'Ali Khan, (Chhote Miyan) architect, photographer, 57, 128; looted negatives, 292 n2
Akhtar Mahal, official wife of king, 128, 143, 222–223, 224, 260; refuses to sign affadavit, 157
'Ali Naqi Khan, 103, 106, 108, 113, 114, 223, 224; acts as king's deputy, 99; appointed chief minister 74–75, 76, 79, 80; arrested in Lucknow 23–24; commands regiments, 90; illness in jail 119; Lucknow house looted, 171; of Mughal descent, 131
'Ali Riza Khan, Police superintendent, Lucknow, 69
Allen's Indian Mail, newspaper, 184
Amin-ud-daulah (see Imdad Husain Khan)
Amir 'Ali, sunni maulawi, 111–112
Amir 'Ali Khan Bahadur, king's manager, 159, 181, 182, 185–186, 197–198, 216, 222; criticism of, 226–227; death of, 242; member of menagerie committee, 217, 219; negotiates loan for rebuilding 201; scheme for new school, 231
Amjad 'Ali Shah, king, 14, 15, 60, 133, 229; death of, 66, 67, 73; last marriage 142–3
Anglo-Burmese wars, 82, 98, 104, 252
Anglo-Sikh wars 68, 81, 82
Asaf-ud-daulah, nawab, 56, 59, 212, 242
Asman Jah, prince, 236
Awadh (see also Oude); annexation of, 16, 30, 114–115, 255, 277–278; army of, 89–91, 110; crown jewels, of, 146–147; description of, 62–63; government departments before annexation 63–66; land revenue, 63, 64, 90, 91–92; treaties, see under East India Company
Ayodhya, 110, 111

Babu Dwarkanath Mitter, lawyer, 182

INDEX

Babu Ramprasad Roy, official, 169
Baghdad, 67, 87
Baji Rao II, Maratha *peshwa*, 250–251
Baqar Ali, munshi, 19
Basant, Spring festival, 55–56
Bengal Legislative Council, 275
Bengal Nagpur Railway, 272
Biermann, Adolph, curator, 206–207
Bird, Captain Robert Wilberforce, king's agent, 20–21, 23, 25, 35, 71, 79; acting Resident 96; advice to king, 106; author *Dacoitee in Excelsis*, 37; friendship with Brandon, 28; joins royal party 31–32; public speeches, 32, 47; sent to Agra, 92
Birjis Qadr, king's son by Hazrat Mahal, 5, 123, 124; birth 133; descendants 273
Brandon, John Rose, king's agent, 27–28, 31, 35, 43, 47, 101, 112; Canning's comments on, 28; holds press conference 33
Brandon, Mary Rose, attendant to queen-mother, 27, 39

Calcutta; description of, 240; Fort William, 116–117; High Court, 182; Hugli river, 205, 208, 239; Municipal improvements in, 198; Royal Botanic Garden, 205–208, 210; tiger exhibition, 213; theatres in, 241; Zoological Gardens, 214, 215, 217
Canning, Lord, governor general 17, 24, 192, 248; appointed Viceroy, 123; arrests the king, 116–117; comments on queen-mother, 29; correspondence with Vernon-Smith 24; orders 21 gun salute for king 20; refusal to recognise king's agent, 18, 29; retires to England, 193; warns king about debts, 170; warns king again 173; writes to king, 121
Cavenagh, Colonel Orfeur, town major at Calcutta, 116; visits king in jail 118, 120, 122
Cawnpore, 17, 79, 250, 251
Chand Mehtab Bahadur, Maharajah of Burdwan, 20, 167
Chess Players, The (*Shatranj ke Khilari*), film 255
Clarendon, Lord, 44
Clark, Sir George, governor of Bombay, 35, 40
Colvin, Sir Auckland, 233, 234
Crimean War, 11, 106
Currie, Sir Frederick, chairman East India Company, 21, 98

Dalhousie, Marquess, governor general, 14, 16, 26; annexation 'a parting coup' 109; comments on king 101–102; refuses to meet king, 106; takes up office, 82; views on Awadh, 97–98
Dara Jah, prince, 233–234
Delhi, king's property in, 172; National Archives, 9, 245
Derusett, George Harris ('Barber of Lucknow'), 27
Digest of Mohummudan Law, 132, 155
Diyanat ud-Daulah, eunuch, 76, 90, 120; buys goods for king, 188; death of, 189
Dufferin, Lord Frederick, governor general 159, 256, 257, 261, 270
Duke of Wellington Fund, 105–6
Duleep Singh, deposed maharajah, 11, 39, 251

INDEX

Durand, Major General Sir Henry Marion, 174
Durand, Captain Henry Mortimer, agent to king, 197, 225, 233, 246, 257, 270

East India Company; annexation policy, 68; charter renewed 1853, 25; Court of Directors, 17, 36, 82, 113, 166; loans from Awadh rulers, 67, 84, 254, 256; 1801 treaty, 62, 81, 288 n34; 1837 treaty, 72, 104; 1856 treaty, 114, 115
Eden, Sir Ashley, lieutenant governor Bengal, 209–210, 221, 235
Eden, Emily, 139
Edmonstone, George, secretary Foreign Department, 18, 19
Elgin, Earl of, governor general 173, 174, 248
Elliot, Sir Henry, secretary Foreign Department, 78, 80, 92, 93–95
The Englishman and Military Chronicle newspaper 23, 26, 213

Faizabad, 62, 110, 112
Falak Qadr, prince, heir apparent, 77–78, 79; death of, 100
fall of the rupee, 268–9
Farid-ud-Din Qadr, heir apparent, 156, 224–227, 228
Farzand 'Ali, Police deputy superintendent, Lucknow, 69, 72, 75
Fateh-ud-daula, paymaster general 118; death in prison, 120
Fayrer, Dr (later Sir) Joseph, 107, 108, 214

Gajadhar Lal, accountant, 178–179
Garden Reach, (Matiya Burj) Calcutta; auctions at, 263; archives, 9, 264; *daru'l hakumat*, 88; 'debauchery and rioting' in, 194; dependants left at, 267; description of, 165–167, 239–240; entertainers at, 241; fire at, 147; furnishings for, 178; gas lights at, 202; hired houses at, 20; jurisdiction in, 191; menagerie at, (see separate heading, menagerie); palace accounts, 179; policing in, 193, 196; poor construction of, 201; population of, 144; sanitary conditions poor, 196–197, 226; schools at, 228–233; 'second Lucknow' 232; servants left at, 268; 'Sharar's' description of, 199–200, 201–202; Sibtainabad Imambarah, 244, 259, 264, 272; staff employed at, 242–243; Sultan Khana house, 167–168, 169, 173, 218, 241, 257, 271–272; supposed decline of, 198; 1864 cyclone, 200
Garden Reach Road, (now Nawab Wajid Ali Shah Road), 167–8, 242, 244 259, 272–273
Ghazi ud-Din Haider, king, 84–86
Gomti river, 55

Hakeem Mahomed Munshee (Muhammad Munshi), 223, 225
Hamid 'Ali, prince, heir apparent, 12, 34, 35, 36, 41, 47, 224, 227, 228; meets James Outram, 108; delays return to Calcutta, 122
Hamilton & Co, jewellers, 147, 264
Hanuman Dubey, sentry, 116
Hardinge, Lord, (Viscount after 1846), 70, 91; farewell tour, 75; meets king at Cawnpore, 79; meets king in Lucknow, 80
Harley House, Marylebone, 31, 33, 42

INDEX

Hayes, Captain Fletcher, 186, 295 n31
Hazrat Mahal, begam, (Mahak Pari), 5–6, 16; birth of son, 133, 142; flees to Nepal 123; left in Lucknow 143; parents, 137
Hazrat Maryam Makani, king's grandmother, 137
Herbert, Major Charles, government agent to king, 8, 146, 169, 179, 184, 189–190, 191, 193; accompanies king from jail, 124; advice on tradesmen, 175–176; denies being 'in charge of king', 192; introduces Amir 'Ali to king, 180; visits Garden Reach after fire, 147–149; visits jail, 118, 122
Hickey, William, author 166
Hodges, William, artist, 165
Home, Robert, court artist 85
Hur Pari, king's wife, 54

Ilbert Bill, 195
Imdad Husain Khan (Amin-ud-daula), chief minister Awadh, 59, 70; dismissed 73–74; kidnapped 71–72; receives pension 77
India Office Library, London, 245
Indian delegations to London, 22
Iqbal-ud-daulah, claimant to Awadh throne, 59, 87
Iqtidar-ud-daulah, eyewitness at Qaisarbagh performance, 52–53
Ishqnamah, (also known as *Pari Khana*), king's autobiography, 54, 129–130; description of, 135–138
Isle of Wight, 11, 165

Janab-i 'Aliyyah, queen-mother, 100, 283 n4, 286 n8; arrival in Paris 44–45; arrival in London 30; arrival in Southampton 11–17, 22; audience with Queen Victoria 40–41; death and funeral in Paris 45–46, 121; lack of funds, 35; leaves Calcutta 23; leaves Southampton by train, 33; meets James Outram 114; pantomime visit 38–39; petitions to Parliament rejected 41–42; receives visitors, 31
Jarratt, Colonel, Persian scholar, 263
Jehan Qadr, prince, nephew of king, 232, 271
Julus-ud-daulah, ADC to king, 34, 41

Kamal-ud-Din Haider, author, 103
Khanum Begam, king's wife, 152
Khas Mahal, official wife of king, 131–132, 133, 142, 143, 258, 260; claims crown jewels, 147; demands separate pension, 146; leaves Garden Reach 222–223, 228; moves to new house 150; refuses to sign affidavit, 151; *takhallus* 'Alam' 132
King, Dr George, superintendent Royal Botanic Garden, 206, 208, 214

Lawrence, Sir Henry, chief commissioner Awadh, 146, 226
Lawrence, Sir John, governor general, 135, 174, 178, 182, 186, 246, 253; comments on High Court case, 183; verdict on king's debtors, 188
Legislative Acts, 1857, Act XIV, 116; 1862, Act VIII, 173, 177, 181; 1868, Act XIII, 186; 1887, Act XIX, 280

INDEX

Login, Dr John, 71, 252
Login, Lady, 30, 139
Lucas, Samuel, radical writer, 37
Lucknow; Akhtarnagar, 64; Alam Bagh, 132, 223; British Residency 60, 71, 146; Chattar Manzil, 80, 130; Daulat Khana Palace, 52; exodus from, 145, 168, 171; Farhat Bakhsh Palace, 60, 66; Hussainabad Picture Gallery, 55, 90, 128; *karbala* Diyanat ud-Daulah, 189; Lal Barahdari, 60, 66–67, 85; menagerie, 212–213; Rashk-e-Iram, 141; royal libraries, 93–95; Qaisarbagh Palace (see separate entry, Qaisarbagh); Sibtainabad Imambarah, 67; Taronwali Kothi (Observatory) 102–103, 228–229; temples destroyed 68–69
Lyall, Alfred, secretary to government, 157

Mackenzie Lyall & Co, valuers, 266
Mackinnon & Mackenzie, letting agents, 231
Mahak Pari (see Hazrat Mahal)
Maine, Henry, lawyer, 175
Malcolm, Sir John, 250
Malleson, Major George, agent to king, 139, 152, 153
Manchester, 25–26; Art Treasures Exhibition 41
Manohar Das, moneylender, 173
Martin, Major General Claude, 131, 293 n14
Mashuq Mahal, king's wife, 143, 161; death of, 224; divorced 156–157; enhanced pension, 159
Masih-ud-Din Khan Bahadur, maulawi, king's agent in England, 34–35, 41, 43, 46, 47, 122; publishes *Oude: Its Princes and Its Government Vindicated*, 38
Mayo, Earl of, governor general, 245–246, 247
Meer Hassan Ali, Mrs, 140
menageries, origins of, 210–212
menagerie at Garden Reach, 207, 209, 210, 213; animals starving, 265; animal fights at 211; auctioned off, 266; costs of, 219–220; criticism of, 207, 209; description of, 218–219; inspection party visit 216; menagerie committee set up, 217, 222; tigers' escape from 206–209
Menzies, Thomas, king's agent, 18, 20
Mir Mahdi, king's companion in Lucknow, 69, 70, 75
Mir Qasim, nawab of Bengal, 83
Muhammad 'Ali Shah, king, 104, 137
Muhammad Babur, prince, 233
Muharram, 67, 86, 88, 102, 111, 241, 244, 257
Munawwar-ud-daula, nawab, chief minister Awadh, 19
Murshidabad, 4, 245
Musharraf ud-daulah (Haji Sharif) i/c king's bodyguard, 75
Mustafa Khan, half-brother to the king, 60
mut'ah marriages, 133; categories of, 139–140; wives at Garden Reach, 269–271
Mysore princes, 222; Ghulam Muhammad, prince, 252–253, 254, 255

Nasir ud-Din Haider, king, 112, 189, 211, 228; employs Brandon, 27

INDEX

New York Times, The, 239
Nosherwan Qadr, prince, king's first son 5, 60, 77

Otway, Sir Arthur, MP, 25, 39
Oude Blue Book, 37–38
Ouseley, Colonel Richard, king's agent, 43–44
Outram, Colonel (later General Sir) James, British Resident 16, 28; arrival in Lucknow 108–109; briefed on annexation 113–114

Paddington Old Cemetery, 46
Pari Khana (see *Ishqnamah*)
paris (fairies) 141–142
Peacock, Captain Henry, agent to king, 186–188, 194, 222
Peel, Sir Lawrence, chief justice, 165, 167
Peninsular & Oriental Company, 272
Père Lachaise cemetery, Paris, 45, 47–48
Pioneer, The, newspaper, 182, 253
Prideaux, Colonel William agent to king, 193–194, 196, 256, 257, 258, 260; winds up Garden Reach estate, 261 et seq
Prince of Wales, 215–216; visit to Calcutta, 217
Private Life of an Eastern King (William Knighton, author) 112–113
Private Life of an Eastern Queen (William Knighton, author) 283 n4
Punch, magazine, 13–14

Qaisar Begam, wife of King, 98, 134
Qaisarbagh Palace; cost of 57; criticism of, 56; description of, 57–58; painting of, 49–50; sack of, 135; Safed Baradari, 6, 50, 58; theatrical performances in, 51; treasury, 146; Yogi Mela, 54–55
Qamar Qadr, prince, heir apparent, 235, 258, 259, 264, 265

Raja Balkrishan, *diwan*, 65, 66, 115
Ram Brahma Sanyal, superintendent Zoological Gardens, 214–215, 266
Randall, Captain, agent to king, 248
Rawlinson, Major Henry, chairman Court of Directors, 36, 289 n5; agent in Baghdad, 67
Rayhan-ud-daulah, garden superintendent, 216, 219
Richmond, Colonel Archibald, British Resident in Awadh, 67, 69, 88; rebuked by governor general, 70, 72; negotiations with kidnappers, 71; vetoes Court appointments, 75–76, 80–81
Ripon, Marquess of, governor general, 249, 253
Roebuck, Rt. Hon. John, MP 25
Russell, William Howard, *The Times* correspondent, 215
Rutledge, William, animal dealer, 219–220, 265–266

Safaraz Pari (later Mahal), wife of king, 134, 136–137
Safdar 'Ali, munshi, king's agent 148, 176, 177, 179–180, 187; creditor to king 157; gets deeds of Sultan Khana, 173; 'Heirs of Safdar 'Ali' 182, 186
Sally Begam, 131–132

INDEX

Sayyid Dildar 'Ali Naqvi, cleric, 87
Sayyid Muhammad Nasirabandi, cleric, 86, 111
Shah Alam II, Mughal emperor, 131, 132
Shah Ghulam Husain, religious activist, 110–111
Shahzadi Sahibah, princess, 269–270
Shakespear, John, British Resident, 61
'Sharar', Abdul Halim, author, 57, 141
Shi'a, faith of the nawabs, 86, 244
Shuja-ud-daulah, nawab 77, 83
Sikandar Hashmat, prince, younger brother to king, 34, 35, 36, 41, 54, 79, 101, 115, 130; death of 46, 122
Sindh, amirs of, 235, 251
Sleeman, Major General Sir William, British Resident, 21, 37, 55, 61, 88; appointed Resident, 96–98; expels Brandon 28; negative reports on king 107; paranoid behaviour, 101; plans to retire, 108; suggests new treaty, 100; winter tour of Awadh 103–104
Southampton, 12
Soutter, Mr, Police commissioner, Calcutta, 206, 208, 209, 216–217
Sprenger, Dr Aloys 93–95
Statesman, The, newspaper, 257–259

ta'luqdars, 62
tawa'if, 3, 141
temporary structures, 52
Theatre Royal, Drury Lane 38
Times, The newspaper 13, 31, 32, 36, 37

Thomson, Colonel Mowbray, agent to king, 153, 201, 216, 219, 221, 222, 225, 239,.279; comments on tiger escape, 208–209; criticises king, 156–160; 'hero of the mutiny' 154; views on king's divorces 155, 223
Tipu Sultan of Mysore, 250, 252, 254–255

Uprising (mutiny) of 1857/58, 40, 116

vaccination in India, 197
Vernon-Smith, Robert, president, Board of Control; comments on royal delegation 25–26, 29–30; visits queen-mother 39
Victoria, queen; agrees gun salute for king, 246; assassination attempt, 249; attitude to king, 36; attitude to queen-mother 39; meets queen-mother, 40–41; patronises 'deposed despots' 29; presented with *Ishqnamah*, 135; privy purse, 181; receives *taziatnamah* from king, 249; 1858 proclamation, 6, 16, 123

Wajid Ali Shah; anticipated death by British officials, 78, 100, 175, 183–184, 251, 256; appointed heir apparent, 60; arrival of wives in Calcutta 145; assaulted by prison guard, 120; blames Safdar 'Ali, 185, 187; borrows money from Company 42; character of 10, 61, 256, 279; claims by creditors, 185–186; complaints boxes, 89; confronts Major Thomson, 162; Cophetua syndrome, 142; coronation of, 66–67; *Dastur-i-Wajidi*, manual of government,

313

99–100; deafness, 59, 80; death of, 257; defends his menagerie, 217–218, 220; describes his journey to Calcutta 19–20; description of, 50, 59, 128, 256; dies intestate, 260; divorces *mut'ah* wives, 154–156, 159–160; education of, 59; education of his sons, 229, 235; funeral of, 2, 259; gullibility of, 177, 183, 187; hypochondriac behaviour, 100–101; illness complaints, 118–119; impotence of, 235; leaves Lucknow for Calcutta 17; describes his journey 19–20; Fort William imprisonment 40, 278; identifies with Lord Krishna, 54; meeting with governor-general, 78–80; narrative poems (*masnavi*) 51, 119; pension from British government 36, 114, 146, 193, 227; pension deductions, 156–161; pleads illness, 23; religious attitude, 88; reply to *Oude Blue Book*, 38; reviews Awadh regiments, 90; 'singing and dancing men,'73; 'sunk in debauchery' 153; support for British 124, 253; theatrical director, 53–54; venereal illness, 98–99, 134; views on 1857 Uprising; visits Zoological Gardens 214–215; *takhallus* (Akhtar) 51; 1847 visit to Cawnpore, 79; 21-gun salutes, 6, 20, 245–246

Wajid Mahal, wife of king; divorced 156, 157–158

wasiqahdars, pensioners of the king, 77

Wauchope, Samuel, Police commissioner, Calcutta, 191–192

Wilcox, Colonel Richard, astronomer, 79, 102–3

Wood, Sir Charles, secretary of State for India, 253

Yasmin Pari, (later Mahal) wife of king, 54, 134, 137

'Zafar', Bahadur Shah, king of Delhi, 86, 252

Zulfiqar ud-daulah, king's brother in law, 120, 176; gets deeds of Sultan Khana, 173